GREAT STAUGHTON AND ITS PEOPLE

HOW A HUNTINGDONSHIRE VILLAGE MADE ITS MARK ON ENGLAND'S HISTORY

Anthony Withers

Published by: Kym Valley Publishing

Copyright © 2023 Anthony Withers

The moral right of Anthony Withers to be identified as the Author of this work has been asserted by him in accordance with the Copyright, Designs and Patents Act 1988

No part of this book may be reproduced, stored in a retrieval system, or transmitted, in any form or by any means, without the prior permission, in writing, of the publishers, or as expressly permitted by law, or under terms agreed with the appropriate reprographics rights organisation, in accordance with the terms of licences issued by the Copyright Licensing Agency.

Every effort has been made to fulfil requirements with regard to reproducing copyright material. Anyone claiming copyright of the Anson Map or Indian Mutiny Map should get in touch with the author so that due acknowledgement may be made at the earliest opportunity.

British Library Cataloguing in Publication Data
A CIP catalogue record for this book is available from the British Library

ISBN: 978-1-7394274-0-5 (paperback)
ISBN: 978-1-7394274-1-2 (hardback)

List of Cover Illustrations (photographs by the author unless otherwise stated)

Sundial inscription.
Hundred Rolls 1279 (courtesy of Huntingdon Records Office)
Will of Ælfhelm Polga (courtesy of The British Library, London)
Death warrant of Charles I [facsimile] (courtesy of the Cromwell Museum, Huntingdon)
John Gaule: *Select Cases of Conscience* (courtesy of the Norris Musuem, St Ives)
Battle of Balaklava (map courtesy of John MacKenzie www.britishbattles.com)

To my partner, Jill Benenson

CONTENTS

Preface

1.	A Little Village in Huntingdonshire	1
2.	The Church of St Andrew	13
3.	A Roman *Mansio*?	21
4.	Peoples From Across the Sea	31
5.	The Will of Ælfhelm Polga	37
6.	Tochestone, Huntedunscire	47
7.	Sir Adam de Creting, Knight of Edward I	57
8.	From Waweton to Walton: Birth of a Staughton Dynasty	71
9.	'Pray For the Good Astate of Olyver Leder'	81
10.	'… that famous and most reverend judge …'	91
11.	George Wauton's 'trayned band' and the Armada	101
12.	Valentine Walton: Curriculum Vitae of a Regicide	111
13.	John Gaule: 'Preacher of the Word at Great Staughton'	125
14.	'Our Ideal Possession of the Peruvian Treasures'	137
15.	The Handasyds, Father and Son	161
16.	Mr Duberly Acquires an Estate in Great Staughton	167
17.	Unravelled: a 200-Year-Old Village Mystery	187
18.	The Unsung Heroine of the Crimea	205
19.	The Rajpootana Column	227
20.	Rev. Wilson and John Henry Newman: the Church Divided	247
21.	The South African Campaign 1899–1902	255
22.	Rev. Watson's Talented Sons	263
23.	Staughton Manor Railway Station	269
24.	The Sacrifice	279
25.	An Uneasy Calm	293
26.	Great Staughton in the Second World War	295
	Epilogue	303

Select Bibliography
Acknowledgements
Biography

LIST OF ILLUSTRATIONS (All photographs by the author unless otherwise stated)

1 Map of the parish of Great Staughton
2 Sundial inscription   i
3 The Town   7
4 Tranchet Axe Head (public domain)   8
5 Greenstone Axe (public domain)   9
6 Church of St Andrew   14
7 Church interior   15
8 Roman Winged Corridor Villa, and   22
9 Roman Villa Bath House (Excavation of a Roman Villa at Great Staughton, E Greenfield et.al 1959)   23
10 *Will of Ælfhelm Polga* (courtesy of the British Library, London)   39
11 *Domesday Book* (Anna Powell-Smith et al. Open Domesday)   54
12 Cretingsbury Moat   59
13 de Creting Coat of Arms (public domain)   60
14 Engaine Coat of Arms (public domain)   60
15 *Hundred Rolls 1279* (courtesy of Huntingdon Records Office)   61
16 Caerlaverock Castle (stocksolutions/Shutterstock.com)   68
17 *Henry VI* (Unknown artist, late 16th or early 17th century © National Portrait Gallery, London)   76
18 *Thomas Cromwell, Earl of Essex* (after Hans Holbein the Younger, early 17th century, based on a work of 1532-1533 © National Portrait Gallery, London)   84
19 Place House   85
20 *Mary I* (Hans Eworth, 1554 © National Portrait Gallery, London)   89
21 Oliver Leder inscription   90
22 The Dyer Monument   92
23 *Edward VI* (Workshop associated with 'Master John,' c. 1547 © National Portrait Gallery, London)   93
24 *Sir James Dyer* (Unknown artist c. 1575 © National Portrait Gallery, London)   97
25 *Elizabeth I* (Unknown English artist, c. 1588 © National Portrait Gallery, London)   104
26 Tomb of Sir George Wauton   109
27 *Oliver Cromwell* (Robert Walker c. 1649 © National Portrait Gallery, London)   116
28 *Death warrant of Charles I* [facsimile] (courtesy of the Cromwell Museum, Huntingdon)   120
29 *Matthew Hopkins* (Unknown artist, woodcut, published 1647 © National Portrait Gallery, London)   128
30 John Gaule: *Select Cases of Conscience* (courtesy of the Norris Museum, St Ives)   132
31 *George Anson, 1st Baron Anson* (James Macardell, 1755 © National Portrait Gallery, London)   139
32 Map of Anson's voyage   141

33 *Capture of the Covadonga* (Samuel Scott c. 1743 © National Maritime Museum, Greenwich, London)	157
34 Handasyd Memorial	165
35 Sir James Duberly (Unknown artist, late 18th century)	168
36 Rebecca Duberly (Unknown artist, late 18th century)	170
37 Commonplace Book (courtesy of Huntingdon Records Office)	189
38 *Johann Georg Zimmermann. Lithograph by P. R. Vignéron* (courtesy of the Wellcome Collection, London)	191
39 The Pope Memorial	203
40 Battle of Balaklava (map courtesy of John Mackenzie www.britishbattles.com)	214
41 Balaklava (svetlana_apo/Shutterstock.com)	215
42 Battle of Inkerman (map courtesy of John MacKenzie www.britishbattles.com)	216
43 Fanny and Henry Duberly in the Crimea (Roger Fenton Royal Collection Trust)	221
44 Siege of Sebastopol (map courtesy of John MacKenzie www.britishbattles.com)	224
45 Indian Mutiny Map (public domain)	227
46 Nana Sahib (public domain)	231
47 Tatya Tope (public domain)	232
48 Rani of Jhansi (public domain)	234
49 Gwalior (Rishabhjain/Shutterstock.com)	239
50 Battle of Belmont (map courtesy of John MacKenzie www.britishbattles.com)	256
51 Battle of Modder River (map courtesy of John MacKenzie www.britishbattles.com)	259
52 Lt Grey William Duberly at Modder River (courtesy of Sir Hugh Duberly)	261
53 Rev. H.G. Watson with son Herbert and daughters c. 1901 (courtesy Watson family archive)	263
54 Sir Charles Gordon Gordon-Watson (public domain)	266
55 John Howey and Staughton Manor Railway Station (courtesy of Romney Hythe and Dymchurch Railway)	271
56 Howey and 'John Anthony' (courtesy of Romney Hythe and Dymchurch Railway)	272
57 Lt John Pickersgill-Cunliffe (courtesy of Imperial War Museum, London)	282
58 Herbert Coleridge Watson (public domain)	284
59 Major Grey William Duberly (courtesy of Imperial War Museum, London)	291
60 Gaynes Hall, Station 61	295

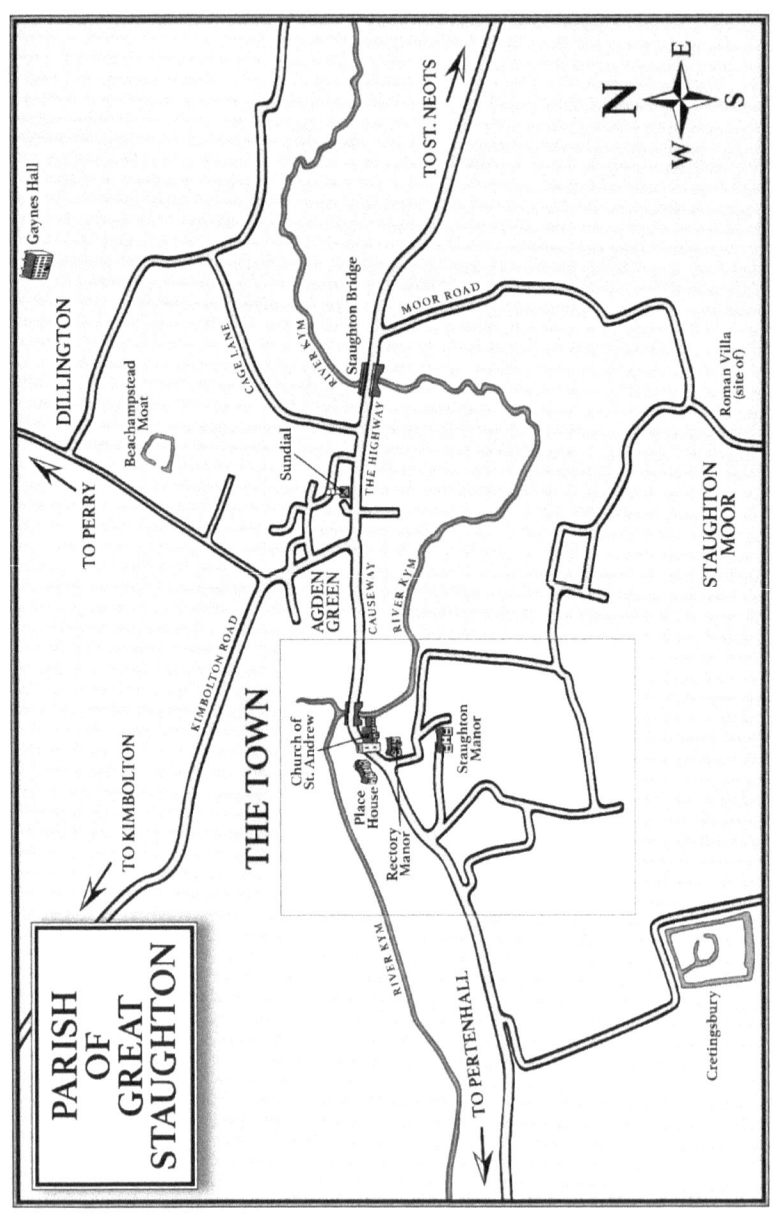

1 Map of the parish of Great Staughton

PREFACE

The sundial has stood on Staughton Highway for nearly four centuries and when I moved into the village over forty years ago, what caught my attention and interest was the inscription on its rear face: 1637 E.I. The usually authoritative *Victorian County History* failed to shed any light on the matter but fortunately the Huntingdon Records Office quickly came to the rescue. The Churchwardens' Accounts for 1640 revealed that one Edmund Ibbutt, churchwarden, landowner, benefactor of the church had taken it upon himself, presumably as an act of social philanthropy, to transform what had been the medieval village cross into a sundial. To this day, Staughton residents pay their silent respects to Ibbutt's legacy as they walk along the Highway.

2   *Sundial inscription*

This was the beginning of the historical journey that led to the writing of *Great Staughton and its People*. This is not the first history of the village: that honour belongs to Rev. Henry George Watson, vicar of St Andrew's Church 1895 to 1909, whose *History of the Parish of Great Staughton* was published in 1916 with a second updated edition appearing in 1919.

Since Watson's time, much research has been done and many new documents have come to light, enriching our knowledge and understanding of the lives of the notable men (and one extraordinary woman) of Great Staughton who were witnesses to and often active participants in some of the great events of England's history. The aim of *Great Staughton and its People* is to set their achievements in a proper historical context using contemporary documents and other records. I have made use of some of Watson's research, particularly his translations of now indecipherable inscriptions on memorial stones. **For the history detective, no less than for the amateur sleuth, it is reassuring to have a Watson at one's shoulder.**

For a modest village tucked away in England's second smallest county, Great Staughton has an astonishingly rich history. Watson could not have known this but the first archaeological evidence for the village came from the excavation of an impressive winged corridor villa built seventeen centuries ago by a high official in the Roman administration. Using the original archaeological report of the excavation, *Great Staughton and its People* examines who might have built the villa and what purpose it might have served in this distant outpost of the Roman Empire.

Watson speculates on the likely origin of Great Staughton in the Anglo-Saxon period. A decade after Watson's death a rare Anglo-Saxon will dated 989 came to light. It was drawn up by a nobleman, a loyal minister of King Edgar 'the Peaceful' and his successors and it gives a fascinating picture of a man whose life revolved around service to his king and the two powerful Abbeys at Ely and Ramsey of which he was a benefactor. More importantly, the will contains the first written evidence of the village, then called *Stoctune*.

A century later the king's Commissioners dutifully recorded details of the population and the tax they owed for the Domesday

Book. One of the longstanding mysteries surrounding village history is how the Norman scribes managed to mangle the name of *Stoctune* in the Domesday Book. This new history offers a solution.

Throughout the medieval period, from the thirteenth to the seventeenth century, people either born in Staughton itself or whose powerbase was centred on the village have made a significant contribution to England's history. In the *Hundred Rolls* of 1279, Sir Adam de Creting is recorded as the largest landowner in Magna Stouton. A knight of Edward I, sheriff of Cork and Marshal of the Army in Gascony, his lasting physical legacy is the moated manor house he built just outside the village and known for the past six centuries as Cretingsbury. The book traces Adam de Creting's eventful career in the service of his king from the Welsh campaigns to his death in Gascony in 1295.

One of the glories of the church of St Andrew is the double monument to Sir James Dyer and his wife, commemorating the man who introduced the concept of legal precedents into English Common Law, which is still used to this day. His career embraced some of the most turbulent years of English history, fully explored in the book. His near contemporary Oliver Leder, one of Henry VIII's backroom boys, a protégé of Thomas Cromwell, was intricately involved in the king's two divorces, from Katherine of Aragon and the Catholic church.

The greatest peril faced by England since the Norman Conquest occurred in 1588 and a chapter of the book examines the preparations made in Huntingdon to combat the threat of the Armada. George Wauton, whose elaborate tomb is one of the glories of the church, marched his 'trayned band' to Tilbury to counter the Spanish threat.

Great Staughton's most notorious son was undoubtedly Valentine Walton, zealous Parliamentarian, brother-in-law of Oliver Cromwell, and one of the killers of the king. *Great Staughton and its People* explores his life in and out of parliament, his attendance at the trial of Charles I, his money-making schemes and finally his eventual demise in Holland.

Who would have imagined that the 'ranting priest' of St Andrew's Church, Great Staughton, would be the man to bring down Matthew Hopkins, architect of the witch trials that brought terror to East Anglia in the 1640s? John Gaule's life, from the meekest of lambs to roaring lion receives full treatment in the book.

A modest plaque to Richard Walter conceals the gripping account, worthy of Patrick O'Brian, of his epic voyage round Cape Horn with Commodore Anson. The fleet faced tempestuous seas, horrific disease, shipwreck and mutiny, all masterfully recorded in Walter's diary.

The Crimean War was fully recorded by William Howard Russell of *The Times* and the photographer Roger Fenton but one of the unacknowledged heroines of the Campaign was Fanny Duberly, a respectable country lady whose *Journals* helped bring the bloody reality of the conflict before the British public. She was present at the Battles of the Alma and Sebastopol, recording the horrific slaughter on both sides and had a grandstand view of the Charge of the Light Brigade.

During the early Victorian era, John Henry Newman was one of the most celebrated and controversial clergymen of his time. He famously left the Church of England to embrace the Catholic faith and one of the reasons for his decision was Rev. Henry Bristow Wilson's devastating riposte to Newman's *Tract 90*, which made Newman's position in the Church of England untenable.

Great Staughton can take some praise for the Romney Hythe and Dymchurch Railway, the brainchild of John Howey who, in 1911, established a 15-inch gauge railway in the grounds of his manor in the village. *Great Staughton and its People* also tells the story of Howey's astonishing escape from his damaged fighter plane, shot down above the trenches in 1915.

In 1915, a 600-page manuscript was rescued from the damp obscurity of the church vestry by the then vicar, who confessed that he had no notion as to its origin or purpose. This new history gives a detailed analysis of the manuscript and discloses the surprising identity of its author.

Great Staughton and its People inevitably focuses on the prominent and the powerful since only they have the good fortune to be officially memorialised by history. The others, the farmers and farm labourers, their wives and children, the merchants, craftsmen and artisans 'which have no memorial, who are perished as though they had never been' are the backdrop to the story but these forgotten figures, who never made it into the history books, have also contributed to the rich history of this village and deserve to be remembered.

Anthony Withers
Great Staughton, February 2023

Note: In this book, I have preserved the original spellings of people and places, inserting the modern equivalent only for purposes of clarification.

1

A Little Village in Huntingdonshire

In its 1,200-year documented history, Great Staughton has undergone numerous iterations of its Anglo-Saxon name of Stoctune. Thus, across the centuries we have Stocton, Stoctune (tenth century), Stotton, Scotton, Stokton, Magna Stouton (thirteenth cent.), Stowghton (fifteenth century), Moche Stoughton (sixteenth century.), plus several other idiosyncratic variants we shall meet with in the course of the book. In 1086, one of William's Norman legati offered his own imaginative interpretation of the original name; it is as Tochestone that Great Staughton appears in the Domesday Book.

Great Staughton is tucked away in the south-west corner of what was formerly the second smallest county in England, Huntingdonshire, and lies on the borders of three counties: Bedfordshire, Northamptonshire and Cambridgeshire. The nearest town is St Neots, on the river Great Ouse, five miles to the south-east; three miles to the north-west is the historic town of Kimbolton. The former county town, Huntingdon, is located twelve miles to the north-east of Great Staughton; Cambridge is twenty miles to the east; Bedford fifteen miles to the south-west and Northampton is thirty miles to the west.

Geology
Geologically the area that comprises what is now Huntingdonshire was formed by a combination of glacial erosion and water deposition and sits mainly on Oxford Clay; below the clay lie other more ancient beds of Cornbrash, Great Oolite Clay and Great Oolite Limestone. An ammonite discovered in the

parish was identified as *Parapatoceras Ancycloceras*, which, according to palaeontologists, is more typically found much further to the west in Wiltshire. The soil is a mixture of clay and gravel, which is fertile for agriculture but relatively hard to work and this factor accounts for the few traces of settlement here in prehistoric times.

In *Britannia* (1586), a geographical and historical survey of the islands of Great Britain and Ireland, William Camden (1551–1623), the English antiquarian and historian, described the central part of Huntingdonshire as 'fenny, verie rich and plentifull for the feeding of cataille', whereas in the south of the county, the gently undulating landscape was 'right pleasant by reason of rising hils and shady groves', and it is between two of these 'rising hils' that the village of Great Staughton is located, in the broad valley of the river Kym.

Leland's *Itinerary*

A generation before Camden, about the year 1540, John Leland (1503–1553), scholar, antiquarian, poet and acknowledged father of local history, provided an attractive guide to Great Staughton in his grandly titled *Itinerary*, his 'laboriouse journey and serche of Johan Leylande for Englandes antiquitees'. The first part of his 'laboriouse' journey brought him to 'Stoughtoun' and we can join him on his delightful introduction to some of the features of a village whose topography has remained remarkably unchanged since his day.

Leland began his 'serche' in Cambridge, proceeding westward to St Neots and thence, by way of Great Staughton, onward to Melchbourne and Kimbolton. He noted 'the rivar there [the river Great Ouse] harde by the towne stondinge on the este syde of it devidithe Huntyndunshire from Bedfordeshire and yet a lytle lower bothe the ripes [banks] be in Huntendunshir'. The river divides the counties of Huntingdonshire and Bedfordshire to this day.

A Little Village in Huntingdonshire

Leland continued his journey along what is now the B645, from 'S. Neotes' to Stoughton village 'by sum enclosid ground a 3. miles, it is in Huntenduneshir'. Crossing the river Kym over Staughton bridge (described as 'Wrong' bridge in numerous bequests for its repair in the early sixteenth century), Leland was now on Staughton Highway, lined with farm labourers' cottages, small allotments and tradesmen's workplaces. Even at that time the Highway was the commercial heart of the village. There would have been little except the bustle of shops and activities of craftsmen to detain Leland as he made his way along the Highway. He could have continued to follow the Highway through the little hamlet of Agden Green and on to Kimbolton. Instead, he turned left into the Causeway down to the Town, the historic centre of the village. Crossing the river Kym over Town bridge, he would have seen to his right the splendid new Place (or Palace) House built by Sir Oliver Leder in 1539, his lodging for the night. 'There hard by the church is a pretty house of Olyver Leders, and pratie commodites about it.'

In Leland's time Place House was a much more imposing mansion than now exists; it was built on the site of a moated manor house belonging to the Charterhouse of London. Place House was ravaged by a fire in the seventeenth century, leaving only the south wing. It still has an extensive moat, one of four in Great Staughton. Two barns, probably dating from 1539, stand in the grounds. Leland did not trouble to investigate the church of St Andrew, directly opposite Place House, but he may have noted the parlous condition of the crumbling west tower, which would within a decade require a considerable injection of funds to repair. Apart from some tenements (dwellings with land attached), the Town would have consisted of open fields and pastureland.

From Staughton, Leland proceeded west to Meilchbourn (Melchbourne) village, seven miles distant, which has an important connection with Great Staughton as Leland duly noted: 'About the quarters of Milchburn, but not hard by it, ryse to [two] armes of brokes [brooks] of divers springs, whereof one cummith owt of Higheham Parke. These 2 … go by How village [How End], whereof the broke is caullid [called] How-water … How water after cummith to Stoughtoun village, and thens about a mile lower … to Use ryver [the river Great Ouse].' Leland was describing the source of the little river Kym (known in Leland's time as the Hayle) that meanders through Great Staughton before meeting the river Great Ouse at St Neots.

The Manors of Staughton

As a historian, Leland would have been well aware of the manors of Staughton. Indeed, his host at Place House, Oliver Leder, may well have boasted that he was the lord of the Manor of Beachampstead. Leland may also have pondered on the origin of the name of the village.

The manor of Staughton does not appear in documents until the Domesday Book of 1086 when William granted large tracts of land, including the lands around Great Staughton, to his loyal lieutenants. For almost two centuries these lands changed hands in a complex series of dealings by descendants of William's followers. It was not until 1275 or thereabouts that Sir Adam de Creting built his motte and bailey castle (some consider it to be a moated manor house) on the ridge a mile south-west of the church and this became known as the Manor of Staughton, shown in old maps as Cretingsbury. The Manor has an outer and inner moat and is one of the four such moated manors in the parish.

The second of the manors of Great Staughton, Rectory Manor, has a complex history. The building, which bears the current name of Rectory Farm, was the historic vicarage that Rev. James Pope found in a dilapidated state in 1796. In old documents the original rectory is shown as the Hermitage. The Rectory Manor, with lands extending into Dillington and Beachampstead, dates back to the thirteenth century.

In 1381, Richard II granted the rectory to the Charterhouse, a Carthusian monastery in London and this became the patron of the living giving the right to appoint the vicar. Staughton House (now known as the Manor), standing near the church in a park of 500 acres, was built as the manor house of the rectory in the early part of the eighteenth century, but incorporated elements of a seventeenth-century building.

The third of Great Staughton's four manors, Dillington (Dellingtune, Dilincthon (eleventh century), Dylington (thirteenth century) was named after the Anglo-Saxon Dilling or Dyling tribe. Dillington was granted to the abbey of Ramsey, together with the manor of Great Staughton, who held it until 1581. The manor of Dillington was for nearly 300 years the domain of the Engaynes whose ancestor, a military engineer, came over with William in 1066 and was richly rewarded for his loyalty and service. It was the Engaine family who built the moated manor house of Gaynes Hall. The family is also commemorated in the Gaynes Chapel in St Andrew's Church.

The fourth of the manors is Beachampstead (Bechansted 1141–53, Bychamestede 1227, Bechamstede 1341, Beauchampstede 1484, Beachamstede 1577). After the Conquest, William granted to his loyal followers lands that became known as the Manor of Beachampstead. In the *Hundred Rolls*, Geoffrey Beaufuy owned 180 acres of land and a messuage (dwelling) in the manor and this probably refers to the original moated Manor of Beachampstead, which seems to have been destroyed by fire sometime around 1376 and never rebuilt; only the moat remains and is still to be seen. After those of Cretingsbury, Gaynes Hall and Place House, Beachampstead is the fourth of the medieval moats in Great Staughton.

Staughton's Oldest Parish Name

These are the four principal manors of Great Staughton but there is one further manor at Lymage Farm, which appears in thirteenth-century records as Lymmynge. It is the earliest attested place name in the parish of Great Staughton and probably derives from *Hlymne* or *Limen*, meaning in Old English 'river'. An earlier form of the name was *Liminingas*, the suffix *-ingas* denoting 'the tribe that dwelt by the stream'. The manor was granted by King John to Earl David of Scotland and for three centuries ownership passed through the Hastings, Engayne and Burgoyne families. During the eighteenth and nineteenth centuries the manor was in the hands of various mainly London-based merchants.

Three other districts in the parish of Great Staughton have an interesting history. The hamlet of Agden Green (Akeden, thirteenth century) appears from earliest times in Great Staughton history as one of the principal districts in the parish. In the Domesday Book of 1086, it is recorded as being held previously by Edward the Confessor. In the *Hundred Rolls*, the tenant is given as William Aungevin who rented the land from the lord of the manor, Adam de Creting. La More (Staughton Moor) appears in the *Hundred Rolls* when it formed part of Adam de Creting and Anselm de Gyse's extensive landholdings.

The Modern Parish

Today, Great Staughton parish is one of the largest in the county, extending to over 6,400 acres of mostly arable land. The forests that once covered this area and Huntingdonshire in general have long since been cleared to make way for agriculture. The oldest district is the Town, a name probably derived from the Old English *ton* or *tun* as in Stocton, one of the Anglo-Saxon names of the village, meaning a fortified (Stok) settlement (ton). It is easy to see why the original settlement would have been built here; the river Kym was a source of water and the surrounding land, thickly wooded up to the medieval era, provided pasture, timber and hunting for the powerful landlords who have exercised power over Great Staughton throughout its history.

A Little Village in Huntingdonshire

3 *The Town*

The Districts of Great Staughton

The Town is a cluster of houses around the church; opposite is Place House; to the south is Staughton House (now the Manor) and the rectory. A mile to the south-west on a ridge overlooking the village is the thirteenth-century motte and bailey castle of Sir Adam de Creting.

Three-quarters of a mile to the north-east of the Town lies Agden Green, more populous in previous centuries than now. The Highway, the principal thoroughfare through the village, has also been its commercial heart since at least the sixteenth century.

To the north of the Highway is the ancient hamlet of Dillington, recorded as far back as the seventh century; it was for three centuries the domain of the Engaine family as was the hamlet of Perry and the mansion that commemorated their name, Gaynes Hall. The woods here, known as Perry Woods, are all that remains of the forest, which, at the time of Domesday, clothed the entire area. In 1154, Henry II decreed that Huntingdonshire should be a hunting park, reserved for the king and his retinue.

Finally, to the south of the village is Staughton Moor, an isolated hamlet referred to in the *Hundred Rolls* as *La More*.

The Pre-History of Great Staughton

The recorded history of Great Staughton may be said to begin with the discovery of a Roman villa dating back to the third century AD. Prior to this, there is no evidence of any permanent prehistoric settlement in what is now Great Staughton, although there are numerous traces of a prehistoric presence in and around the present village. Artefacts are much rarer but the few that have been discovered in Great Staughton are interesting. On what is now the Highway a beautifully shaped tranchet axe or adze made of flint from the Mesolithic era (c. 10,000–4,000 BC) has been excavated. Judging by the very limited wear on the blade, it is thought that the axe may have been intended for ceremonial rather than practical use.

4 *Tranchet Axe Head*

Neolithic Traces

The Neolithic (New Stone Age) era, c. 5,000 to 2,000 BC heralded the introduction of agriculture, which had spread westwards from the 'fertile crescent' of Mesopotamia. One interesting example of Neolithic technology was the discovery on Staughton Highway of a polished greenstone axe. For archaeologists, the interest of this 5,000-year-old tool lay as much in its provenance as its purpose. Greenstone is not found in the lowlands of Huntingdonshire and if our prehistoric ancestor had obtained the greenstone at its source, he would have had to undertake an arduous round trip of some 500 miles. The origin of this stone was almost certainly the axe 'factory' excavated in the Langdale Pikes area of the Lake District, particularly the slopes of Harrison Stickle and Pike o' Stickle and its appearance in Great Staughton confirms the extensive trading and communication networks in the Mesolithic era.

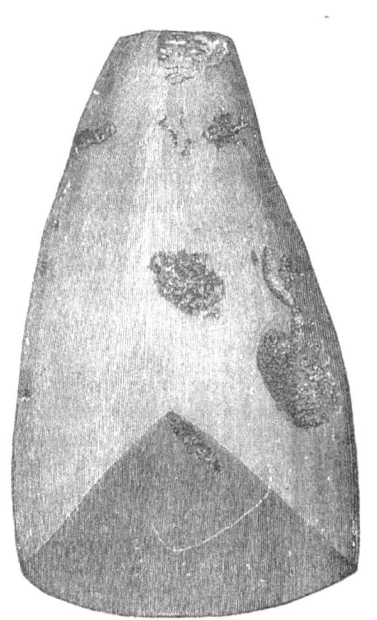

5 Greenstone Axe

Great Staughton and its People

The Beaker Folk

From c. 2,500 to 650 BC a major demographic change occurred with the arrival into Britain of the Beaker Folk, so named after the distinctive design of their pottery. They brought with them a revolutionary development that was to transform civilisation in this country: metal working. They knew how to combine copper and a small amount of tin at high temperature to produce bronze, from which they could fashion weapons, farming tools and elaborate personal decorative ornaments. They also worked in gold. They made the first woven garments found in Britain and it seems likely that they also brewed the first alcoholic drink, mead. One of the big cultural changes they introduced, evidenced by the finds in Staughton, was bowl and barrow mounds that were either used to bury their dead or which served as ceremonial focal points.

Two round barrows from this era have been excavated on the Highway and they are thought to be part of a group of four; the other two barrows lying to the south of the village have yet to be excavated. These barrows, surrounded by a three-metre-wide ditch and dating from 2,400–1,500 BC, may have served a ceremonial or a funerary purpose, in which cinerary urns (containing cremated ashes) were interred.

The Iron Age

Migrations did not stop with the Beaker Folk. The Iron Age (c. 800 BC to AD 43) was brought about by successive migrations of peoples, conveniently, but according to some historians, inaccurately called Celts, originating in c. 800 BC principally from the Rhineland and from north-western Gaul, in what is now Belgium. A tribe known as the Belgae arrived in southern Britain in c. 200 BC, testifying to the strong links between the Celtic tribes of mainland Europe and their British neighbours. These peoples brought with them the ability to work iron and one of the principal sources of iron ore was Britain. Evidence of the Iron

Age in Staughton is small but significant: an Iron Age hut was discovered on Staughton Highway and just a few hundred yards north of the spot, in Dillington, an Iron Age coin was unearthed. A rectilinear enclosure typical of Celtic culture has been excavated in Staughton, together with a number of Iron Age bowls.

The Roman Influence

More valuable than these physical artefacts is the fact that we also have, for the first time, a written record of the various tribes that had migrated to the country, thanks to Roman historians such as Tacitus and Dio Cassius, military leaders such as Julius Caesar and the geographer Ptolemy. According to these various authorities, the ruling Celtic tribe in Bedfordshire and Huntingdonshire appears to have been the Catuvellauni, whose leader until AD 9 was Tasciovanus. When Emperor Claudius' appointed general, Aulus Plautius, at the head of an army of 50,000, began the invasion of Britannia in AD 43, resistance was led by Caratacus, one of the sons of Tasciovanus. The date of the invasion, AD 43, is usually heralded as the end of the Iron Age in Britain. One Romanised Celt chose to build his villa in a settlement south of the river Kym. It was to be another sixteen hundred years before the Roman villa of Great Staughton yielded its secrets.

2

The Church of St Andrew

Great Staughton's rich and varied history is inextricably linked, as it is for most English villages, with the church. There has been a church in the village since at least the Domesday Book of 1086, but it is conceivable that a simple place of worship, probably constructed of timber, was built here a century before William the Conqueror, although it is not recorded in the earliest documentary record of the village, called '*Stoctune*' in a tenth-century Anglo-Saxon will.

The church of St Andrew is populated by the ghosts of the people who have shaped Staughton's history over a period of a thousand years and who are commemorated in the memorials, tombs, tablets, brasses and monuments placed there over the centuries. Some record only dates of birth and death; others offer a pithy sentence on the person's life and deeds; a few are dignified with a florid verse (often in Latin) proclaiming their renown.

The present church was built between the late thirteenth and the fifteenth centuries. The chancel and part of the north and south arcades are from the late thirteenth century, whilst the north and south aisles and the south porch date from the fourteenth century. The windows in the north and south aisle date from the fifteenth and sixteenth centuries respectively.

The north vestry and the north chapel (now the Gaynes Chapel) both date from the early years of the sixteenth century.

Great Staughton and its People

6 *Church of St Andrew*

The nave mainly dates from the fifteenth century although the two bays nearest the chancel may have formed part of an earlier thirteenth-century design. The church underwent a significant reconstruction in the fifteenth century when the nave arcades were rebuilt, the clerestory added, the fifteenth-century rood staircase built, and the chancel remodelled with a new arch and east window.

The west tower itself, built in the early years of the sixteenth century, consists of three stages and the bell chamber, accessed by a clockwise newel staircase. Above the lancet windows, on each face of the tower is a quatrefoil frieze, which was added at the time of the building of the tower.

The main entrance to the church is through the sixteenth-century door of nail-studded battens and ornamental lock plate. The porch, originally built in the fourteenth century but much altered since, was known as the Marriage Door because it was here, in the medieval period, that marriages were contracted before the betrothed proceeded to the altar for the Nuptial Mass.

7 Church interior

Ahead, across the west end of the nave, is the thirteenth-century font; during the restoration of the church in 1866, the font was unceremoniously uprooted, turned upside down and used as a base for a smaller font. It took more than three decades for this historical slight to be remedied and for the original font to be returned to its rightful position.

Directly opposite the font, across the north aisle, is the one of the original doors of the church, dating from c. 1330 and now no longer in use.

The beautifully inscribed vellum Roll of Honour commemorates the 165 volunteers from Great Staughton who served in the Great War, thirty-six of whom failed to return home. Other memorials in the church commemorate those who fell in the South African Campaign and the Second World War.

The next section of the church is the Gaynes Chapel (formerly the north chapel), which dates from c. 1455 and commemorates the successive families who have resided in the 'magnificent mansion' of Gaynes Hall over a period of eight centuries. The Gaynes Chapel is dominated by the huge monument to the Handsyds, Thomas and his son Roger who served their entire careers in the army.

Gaynes Hall possesses one of the four moats that still exist in the parish.

The organ was built by Norman Bros. and Beard of Norwich. Next to it, a plain wooden door leads to the vestry, which was added in 1526.

The chancel is interesting for the light it casts on the history of the church; the lancet window in the north wall is the oldest remaining evidence of the thirteenth-century church. In 1291, during the reign of Edward I, the church was valued at £26 13s 4d when the advowson of the church (the right to appoint the vicar) was held by Sir Adam de Creting. He and his descendants, the Wautons (or Waltons) were lords of the manor of Staughton for nearly 300 years.

The most impressive historical feature in the church is the imposing double monument to Sir James Dyer, knight, and Margaret (Barrowe) his wife, facing each other in an attitude of prayer and opposite Sir Richard Dyer, knight, his great-nephew, and Marie (Fitzwilliam) his wife. Sir James Dyer introduced the

The Church of St Andrew

concept of legal precedents into English law whilst he was Lord Chief Justice of the Common Pleas 1559–1582.

The panelling around the altar was the work of Edward Webster of St Neots and is dated 1754. The roof of the chancel is modern but incorporates two magnificent fifteenth-century moulded tie-beams.

Four largely illegible memorial stones in front of the altar are dedicated to Robert and John Baldwin. On John Baldwin's memorial stone is the inscription to a 'well-read, cultivated, pious, just, sincere gentleman'. The inscription bears the initials J. G., a reference to John Gaule, vicar of St Andrew's who single-handedly destroyed the reputation of the Witchfinder General.

Three plaques, arranged vertically, are dedicated firstly to Rev. James Pope, vicar of St Andrew's 1796–1822, who played a part in unlocking a Great Staughton mystery. Rev. Pope is also commemorated in a stained-glass window in the south aisle. The third of the three plaques commemorates the achievements of Richard Walter, author of the best-selling *A Voyage round the World with Captain Anson*.

The south aisle dates largely from the fourteenth century; at its eastern end is the second great monument in the church, the fine tomb of Sir George Wauton, *eques auratus* (knight bachelor), placed there by his 'very dear friend' (*amicus optimus*) Sir Oliver Cromwell, uncle of the Protector.

His heir, Valentine Walton, has no such impressive memorial in the church. His signature appears on the death warrant of Charles I. The Wauton/Walton dynasty was Staughton's most powerful and influential family for over three centuries.

The west tower of the church, built in the Perpendicular style, was described by Nikolaus Pevsner as 'ambitious'; it was certainly in existence prior to 1550 when it required urgent and costly repairs.

The exterior west face of the tower records the tragic story of three people killed by a flash of lightning.

The Bells of the Church

The church has six bells hung in the tower and a sanctus bell is enclosed in a bell-cote above the eastern gable.

(1) The first bell is inscribed: ✠ *To the Glory of God and in memory of those from this Parish who gave their lives in the Great War, 1919.* J. W. Wragg, Vicar, C. W. Pearson, R. Ekins, Churchwardens.

(2) *I. H. S. Nazarenvs Rex Ivdeorvm fili Dei miserere mei*, 1633. (Jesus of Nazareth, Saviour of Man, King of the Jews, Son of God, have mercy on me.)

(3) The third bell is inscribed: 'Edmond Ibbott, Ralphe Paine, c. 1633.' Edmund Ibbott was the E. I. responsible for erecting the sundial on Staughton Highway in 1637. He was an important landowner and during the 1630s was one of the churchwardens.

(4) *Hac in conclaue Gabriel nunc pange suaue.* (Now in this loft high, strike the bell softly, O Gabriel). This bell is thought to have been cast by a bell makers' guild, which was active in London between 1395 and 1420. Specifically, it could have been made by William Dawe.

(5) 'John Appleby, Vicar, Edwd. S . . . A . . . & John Rose, Churchwardens.' This bell was cast in St Neots, Robt. Taylor fecit, 1787. The missing name is Shadbolt.

(6) The sixth bell was a gift of 'George Wauton Esquier, 1600'. The minister was George Walkre.

The second, third and sixth bell were cast at the celebrated Leicester foundry of Newcombe and Watts.

There is one other bell in the church, perhaps the most interesting of all. The sanctus bell is now thought to be one of the oldest church bells in the country, having been cast in London around the year 1280, when Sir Adam de Creting was lord of the manor and held the advowson of the church.

The west face of the tower displays an impressive clock that is held in a wooden-framed mechanism, of a type described as a 'four-poster'. It is believed to have been made by Thomas Powers

The Church of St Andrew

of Wellingborough sometime during the 1680s, although a clock was recorded in the churchwardens' accounts of the 1640s.

The church of St Andrew, Great Staughton was Grade 1 listed on 14 May 1959.

3

A Roman *Mansio*?

'I had long known that there was a settlement of the Roman period near the village of Great Staughton. On ploughland alongside the footpath about 1 mile south of the village, Roman pottery lay scattered over the field. Furthermore, two barrow-like mounds occurred on the hill above, suggesting burials from a more sumptuous household somewhere in the area.' Thus in the late 1940s, the indefatigable local historian C. F. Tebbutt had his attention drawn to fragments of pottery that were being revealed at Rushey Farm in Great Staughton as a result of ploughing and drainage work. His investigations revealed what appeared to be a substantial Roman building. The then Ministry of Works was brought into the case and two sites were excavated by a team led by Ernest Greenfield: Site 1 was excavated between June and August 1958, followed in May and June 1959 by site 2.

The sites lie one mile south of the Highway over a medieval ridge and furrow field system, across the river Kym and thence over the sixteen-acre Rushey Meadow. Some 150 yards to the west of the site runs Whitley Brook, a tributary of the Kym. In Roman times, the area was well-wooded, particularly with oak and hazel, providing fuel for the hypocaust heating system and timber for building. Rushey Meadow itself, watered by the river Kym, was an ideal pasture. As the excavation proceeded it quickly became apparent that there had been two villas on the site; the original substantial building dated from the second century AD, to be replaced a century or so later by a smaller winged corridor villa. The Roman buildings seemed to have been in continuous occupation for some 300 years and intriguingly, the archaeologists uncovered evidence of a Stone Age building, dating from c. 500 BC, under the Roman foundations.

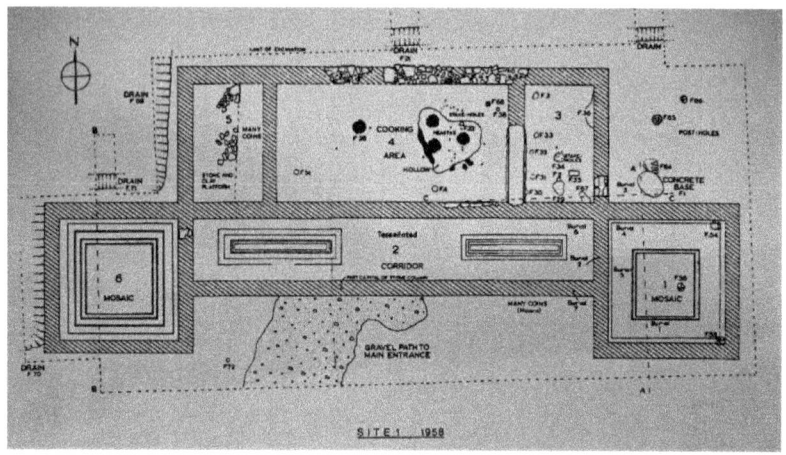

8   Roman Winged Corridor Villa

Site 1 revealed a substantial Roman winged corridor villa; site 2 was a bath house. The buildings were of substantial size; the first measured 150 ft in length (from east to west) and 105 ft in width (north to south); the second, slightly smaller, at 120 ft in length by 90 ft in width. The stone to build the villa came from a variety of sources: from Barnack (twenty-five miles north of the site), Yorkshire, and the Hitchin area. The villa itself consisted of six rooms, aligned east to west. The front of the house faced south and the east room was linked to its western counterpart by a corridor, hence the description of the villa as 'winged corridor'. The north side of the villa, overlooking Rushey Meadow and the river Kym, consisted of a large central room with a smaller room on either side.

Both the villa and the bath house were equipped with a hypocaust, the Roman underfloor central heating system. The main reception floors in the villa were supported on a series of pillars called *pilae*, creating a hollow basement through which hot

A Roman Mansio?

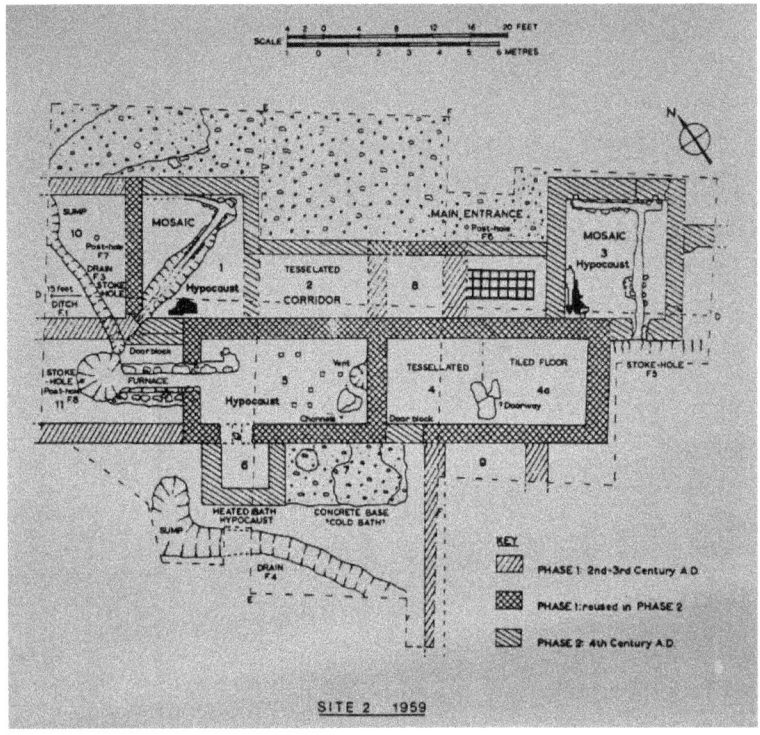

9 Roman Villa Bath House

air from the outside furnace circulated. Feeding the furnace was a costly and laborious task requiring a slave to stoke the fire continuously. Hypocausts were the preserve of the wealthy, testifying to the importance of the Staughton villa. It is said that the hypocaust system was invented by a talented hydraulic engineer named Caius Sergius Orata who lived around 95 BC. Central heating systems were not his only talent, as we shall see; he acquired a vast fortune breeding and marketing oysters, a staple for Roman citizens.

As with all the Roman villas excavated in Britain, the interior decoration of the public rooms was lavish and colourful. On the walls of the Staughton villa, fragments of painted wall plaster were discovered and unlike many of the finds, these can be precisely dated to the fourth century AD. The fragments are unfortunately tiny, but traces still remain of the colours used. The predominant colour was a vibrant purple and this would likely have formed the background onto which panels were painted. A fragment of a white floral pattern, on a background of deep purple, survived for 1,500 years buried under the ground. Red and yellow patterns were also uncovered, but so fragmentary that it is impossible to know what was pictured. There is evidence that the panels were bordered by red, yellow and blue bands. One of the most striking features consisted of swirls of purple, mauve and pink paint, which may have been a colourful covering of a bare wall or a window decoration.

Painted panels were not the only decoration. Numerous fragments of mosaic were recovered, which enabled the archaeologists to establish five distinct patterns that were used in the important rooms where guests were received. Only two surviving similar examples exist in England, at Lullingstone and Verulamium (St Albans). These mosaics were almost certainly created in the fourth century by the same craftsman and it was possible for the archaeologists to re-create the design. In the east wing of the villa itself, Room 1, measuring 17 ft by 17 ft, revealed a motif consisting of a 'star', formed of eight lozenges (essentially a square, rectangular or polygonal pattern), repeated sixteen times in four rows on a white background.

Whilst the public rooms of the villa featured elaborate, vivid designs, the 58-foot-long corridor linking the east and west rooms was decorated throughout its length by plain grey mosaics or, as the excavating team put it, 'decorated to a much more workaday standard'. Although, as noted above, the mosaics were of a relatively uncommon design for Britain, they were a common feature of villas excavated in Roman Gaul, Gallia Belgica and the German provinces and this led archaeologists to speculate that the owner of the villa belonged to a Romanised Belgic tribe who had migrated to Britain following the Roman invasion.

A Roman Mansio?

A more precise dating of the villa and its occupation came from the coins and other artefacts excavated at the site. The main villa yielded a substantial hoard of 850 mainly low-value coins originating from mints widely spread in the Roman Empire: Trier (Germany), Lugdunum (present-day Lyons in France), Arelate (Arles), Rome, Siscia (Sisak, near Zagreb in Croatia), Thessaloniki (Greece) and Amiens (France), a striking indication of the extent of Roman power and how it permeated down to even modest settlements such as Great Staughton.

Several coins bore the image of Constantine the Great I (AD 306–337), who decreed, by the Edict of Milan in February AD 313, that the Christian religion should be tolerated throughout the Roman Empire. Twelve years later, in AD 325, Constantine was instrumental in convening the first Council of Nicaea which led to the adoption of the Nicene Creed: 'I believe in one God.'

A number of artefacts, decorative, culinary and utilitarian, were uncovered by the excavations. Copper alloy ornaments and accessories included a bracelet, finger ring, pin and interestingly, a thin folded sheet decorated with an incised 'feather' or 'leaf' pattern. This was part of a votive plaque or leaf used for religious purposes and it is conceivable that the substantial quantity of coins may also have had a religious significance, as offerings to the gods. Iron objects uncovered by the excavation consisted mainly of tools or hardware: a complete knife, of a design that was common in Roman Britain, and a socketed instrument, which could well be a form of hammer and a chisel.

Other finds included fragments of Rhenish glass and a significant hoard of pottery, mostly Samian ware imported from south Gaul, more specifically from the vast pottery manufactories at La Graufesenque, near Millau, Lezoux and sites around Clermont-Ferrand, in Central France. Samian ware was also manufactured in eastern Gaul in Trier, Sinzig and Rheinzabern. From the second century AD in particular, Samian ware, prized for its quality and stylish design, could be found on every prosperous Roman's table. The dishes, bowls and other vessels were often painted in vivid red and decorated with mythic or pastoral scenes.

Not all the pottery was imported. The Nene Valley, close by, boasted an important centre of pottery production. For one pottery fragment, a mortarium (a kitchen vessel used for pounding or mixing foods), we even have the name of the maker. The bowl found in Staughton bears the stamp of Cattanus whose work is known from other examples in Northamptonshire, Hartshill and Mancetter and can be dated to AD 150–180.

The sites yielded an array of animal and bird remains. Birds were particularly well represented at the villa, with many unusual finds, including four peacocks, four geese (including merganser), six domestic fowl, two stock doves, one wigeon, one quail, one partridge, as well as more common varieties. Two of the above, quail and merganser, seem to be the first records of the species on Roman sites in Britain. The peacock was probably the most interesting find; for the Romans, the bird had a mythological and a religious significance.

The most numerous culinary remains in quantitative terms belong to shellfish and in particular oysters of which 1,544 shells had been discarded on site. Oysters were found all over the empire and it was one of the many foods enjoyed by the Romans, who believed that eating the molluscs increased their prowess on the battlefield and in the bedroom. Indeed, 300 years earlier, in 95 BC (according to the historian Pliny in his *Historia Naturalis*), an enterprising Roman called Gaius Sergius Orata (he of hypocaust fame), established a large and successful oyster cultivation bed in Lake Lucrine near Naples to exploit these riches of the ocean.

When they finally conquered Britain and established their capital in Colchester (*Camulodunum*), the Romans were delighted to discover that the estuary of the river Colne produced oysters of a quality to rival those of Gaius Sergius Orata. The fabled Apicius wrote what was reputedly the first cookery book *De re*

A Roman Mansio?

coquinaria (On cooking). In it, he gave a recipe for oyster sauce containing pepper, lovage, egg yolk, vinegar, liquamen (a fermented fish sauce), oil and wine. Apicius helpfully suggested that 'you can also add honey if you like'.

Oysters, stored in barrels of fresh seawater, would have been transported the eighty miles from the river Colne to the villa in Staughton on the Via Devana (the road that ultimately led to the Roman fort at Chester). At Godmanchester (*Durovigitum*) the oysters would be taken via Alconbury on the 173d road, which historians have suggested linked that settlement to Staughton.

One of the most surprising discoveries made during the course of the excavations was of the bones of up to twenty-four individuals, including seven complete human burials, which were not contemporary with the Roman occupation of the villa. They are thought to have been buried several centuries after the departure of the Romans in AD 410.

What was the purpose of the villa and what was its ultimate fate? One of the first tasks that the Romans undertook when Claudius' army invaded Britain in AD 43 was to construct a network of roads that would both facilitate the movement of troops and provide rapid communication links between their administrative locations, thus promoting trade and commerce. Typically, the roads were straight, avoiding hills and marshy ground and were anything from 20 ft to 100 ft wide. By the time of the construction of the villa in Great Staughton, some 2,000 miles of road had been built by the Romans. Thanks to an anonymous author of the second or third century AD, we know a considerable amount about the Roman road network in Britain. The work is entitled, *Itinerarium Antonini Augusti* (The itineraries of the Emperor Antoninus) and is a comprehensive account of all the roads in the Roman Empire; the section devoted to Britain is called the *Iter Britanniarum*. Dorchester-upon-Thames was one of the hubs of the Roman network and it was from this centre that roads radiated to the north, south and east. Two historians have postulated the existence of road 173d, running from Dorchester-on-Thames in the west, to Alconbury in the east. The road, if it did indeed exist, would have passed close to the Roman villa in Staughton and would provide an explanation for the location of the villa.

All Roman roads were equipped at regular intervals with staging posts (*mansio*) where soldiers, merchants and traders and messengers of the imperial postal service (*curus publicus*) could pause for refreshments and lodging, or the more elaborate *mutatio* (a changing post) where fresh horses could be secured if official, often military, business required urgent communication between far-flung military outposts. The official in charge of the *mansio* would have been designated as a guardian of the roadways (*curator viarum*), responsible for the good order of his section of the road and for providing food and lodging for travellers and officials of the empire. The cost of repair and maintenance was borne by the local population. It is highly likely that the villa in Great Staughton was such a *mansio*, and that its *curator viarum* was originally from a Belgic tribe in what is now Belgium or Central France.

The Staughton *mansio* was also conveniently located for access to Ermine Street, the principal north–south thoroughfare linking London and York (*Eboracum*) and nine miles from *Durovigitum*, a strategic crossing point of the river Great Ouse and an important junction of north–south and east–west roads, where a *mansio* has been fully excavated.

This brings us to the question: what was the ultimate fate of the *mansio*? The evidence of burnt areas and the discovery of a number of inhumations might at first suggest a violent end to the building but careful examination of the remains indicates that the villa was deliberately demolished or simply abandoned after falling into disrepair sometime in the fourth century AD. A further clue as to its fate is that in AD 296, little more than sixty years before the Staughton villa fell into ruin, the *mansio* at *Durovigitum* was raided and completely destroyed by fire, an act that was historically attributed to Saxon or Angle raiding parties, which were becoming an increasing threat during the early fourth century. It is likely that after the withdrawal of the Romans, the villa was dismantled and all the useful materials, such as bricks, timber and tiles, were salvaged and used to build new dwellings by local Romano-Britons.

4

Peoples From Across the Sea

By the beginning of the fifth century, the western Roman Empire had been fraying at the edges for a century or more under attacks from Vandals, Visigoths, Huns and Parthians, and Rome's northern outpost, Britannia, was not immune from the turmoil. In 367 the Roman garrison at Hadrian's Wall rebelled, which allowed marauding Scots and Picts to overwhelm the northern settlements. In what the historian Ammianus Marcellinus called the Great Conspiracy, Saxon and Frankish forces, in a concerted action, overwhelmed north and west Britannia, killing the Roman governors and destroying their cities and strongholds. It took a year and a substantial Roman army, commanded by Flavius Theodosius, to quell the barbarian incursions and re-establish the authority of Rome.

If there is a single date that can be said to symbolise the complete collapse of the Roman Empire, it would be 24 August 410, when Alaric and his Visigoths sacked Rome, the first time in nearly 800 years that the capital of the empire had succumbed to a foreign foe. The hapless emperor on whose watch this last and greatest disaster occurred was Flavius Honorius Augustus. When the Britons issued a desperate plea for help as the Roman army left Britain to defend the empire, Honorius was unmoved. In the words of the sixth-century Byzantine historian Zosimus, 'Honorius wrote letters to the cities in Britain, bidding them 'to guard themselves' and in what is called the *Rescript of Honorius*, the Roman emperor abandoned this distant outpost of empire to its fate.

Great Staughton and its People

The vacuum left by the departure of the Roman legions was filled over the next two centuries by movements of Germanic peoples whom Bede was later to describe as Angles, Saxons and Jutes. They are more familiarly known as the Anglo-Saxons, peoples from the north coast of Germany and Denmark. Not all contemporary historians viewed the Anglo-Saxon incursions with equanimity. The sixth-century monk, scholar and historian, Gildas, in his *On the Ruin of Britain* (c. 540), which he called the 'groans of the Britons', wrote a somewhat exaggerated description of the supposed malignant influence of these Germanic settlers. A century earlier, the British king Vortigern had enlisted the help of Saxon forces to stem the damaging raids of Picts and Scots into his kingdom. For Gildas, this represented the beginning of the decline of Romano-British civilisation. 'They [i.e. the effete and corrupt British kings such as Vortigern] sealed [the country's] doom by inviting in among them like wolves into the sheep-fold, the fierce and impious Saxons, a race hateful both to God and men, to repel the invasions of the northern nations. Nothing was ever so pernicious to our country, nothing was ever so unlucky.'

The Angles (from Angeln, a peninsula in present-day North Germany) had been present in East Anglia as early as the fourth century AD. It is thought that they had been hired as mercenaries by the Roman authorities. However, despite the qualms of Gildas and later historians, there is no evidence of a mass invasion or systematic slaughter of the native Britons by the Angles, Saxons and Jutes. Indeed, the newcomers seemed to have co-existed peacefully with the native Britons in the fertile river valleys of the Ouse and the Nene and quickly came to dominate politically and socially the territory that became known as the Kingdom of the East Angles. Little of the pre-Angle culture survives. The three important rivers of the region, the Nene, Colne and the Ouse, still retain their Celtic, or more accurately Brythonic names, but throughout the Kingdom it was *Englisc*, the language the Angles had brought over with them that prevailed and within two centuries it had become the lingua franca of all the Anglo-Saxon kingdoms.

One of the most interesting documents from the early period of Anglo-Saxon settlement is the Tribal Hidage, a list of the thirty-five tribes in what is now England and the number of hides they controlled. By the eighth century, seven powerful kingdoms, known as the Heptarchy and led by Mercia and Northumberland, struggled for dominance until in 927 Æthelstan united them into the kingdom of England.

Wulfhere may have been one of the Mercian kings behind the creation of the document. His kingdom was assessed at 30,000 taxable hides, as was the kingdom of the East Angles. The definition of a hide is still the subject of controversy amongst scholars; derived from the Anglo-Saxon word for 'family', a hide was the amount of land sufficient to support a family and it was the basis for the assessment of tax. Depending on the quality of the land, the hide seems to have represented between 60 and 120 acres.

According to the twelfth-century chronicler Hugh Candidus, the area around Ely and Peterborough (then called Medeshamstede) was occupied by a tribe called the Gyrwas, which meant in the Saxon tongue 'people who dwell in the fen'. The South Gywre were probably located around Ely, according to Bede in his *Ecclesiastical History of England*, but their lands extended as far south as the area around Great Staughton. Although the South Gyrwe was a small tribe, paying taxes, like the North Gyrwe, on a mere 600 hides, it had the distinction of possessing its own royal dynasty.

There is abundant evidence of an Anglo-Saxon presence in the area of Great Staughton, with examples of pottery found in Dillington. Elsewhere, coins, burial sites, cremations sites and an early cemetery have been recorded, all attesting to the settlement of the area by the incomers.

Great Staughton and its People

We do have evidence for the importance of the area of Huntingdon, including Great Staughton. The source of much of the information comes from the *Anglo-Saxon Chronicle*, a collection of annals created during the reign of the scholar king Alfred the Great in the latter half of the ninth century. It records, in *Englisc*, the history of the Anglo-Saxon tribes from the fall of the Roman Empire until the Conquest. In addition to the annals there are various charters (many of dubious authenticity) recording the granting of land to individuals or the church. In 656, King Wulfhere of Mercia granted extensive lands, which might have included what would eventually become Great Staughton.

Two decades after this entry in the *Anglo-Saxon Chronicle*, there is a charter dated 674 by which King Wulfhere granted to Berforde, his kinsman, for 30 mancuses of gold (a gold coin weighing around 4.25g), five 'manentes' (dwellings) at Dilingtun (Dillington) free of all but the three common dues. There is considerable doubt as to the authenticity of this charter, but it may nevertheless indicate that in the seventh century there was an organised settlement in Great Staughton.

The early Anglo-Saxon settlements mainly consisted of a small group of farmsteads, usually well protected against potential enemies and often located on pastureland in a river valley. The heavy clay soils of the area were difficult to cultivate and must have required considerable cooperative effort amongst the settlers to farm productively. Great Staughton was an attractive, well-wooded place to settle, with fresh water from the river Kym and Whitely Brook, substantial land for crops or pasture and a covering of dense woodland. In a tenth-century will, the village was called *Stoctune*, or Stockton.

One of the several manors of Great Staughton is Beachampstead and to investigate the origin of this 'lost place name in Huntingdonshire', it is not to archaeology nor to history that we must turn, but to philology. According to linguistic scholars, the name consists of two elements: 'Beach' is possibly a corruption of the Anglo-Saxon first name Bicca, or Bica, a masculine name probably meaning in Old English 'beak' or 'point'. The name is attested in a number of charters dating from the late seventh to the ninth century. The second element of the name 'hamstede' signifies a fortified farmstead. It is therefore not inconceivable that a group of East Angles, seeing the potential of an area watered by two rivers with ample land for pasture, established a settlement consisting of a number of farmsteads. These would be fortified against predatory incursions, particularly as there were constant hostilities between the kingdoms of Mercia and the East Angles in the late eighth and early ninth century. If this hypothesis is credible, it would suggest that originally the settlement that became Great Staughton was originally known by the name of Bicca's hamstede (Bicca's settlement) and it may over the years have become important enough to justify a church being built (a church is recorded in the Domesday Book of 1086).

Other localities in Great Staughton may also testify to an Anglo-Saxon origin: Agden is thought to derive from *Ac* = oak and *denu* = a vale or valley. In the *Hundred Rolls*, it is referred to as Akeden. Similarly, Perry has an Anglo-Saxon origin from *pirige*, a pear tree. Dillington is named after the Dylings, a Germanic tribe who inhabited the area.

It was not until the tenth century, however, that we have written evidence for the historical existence of the village of Great Staughton in the will of a Saxon nobleman, Ælfhelm Polga.

5

The Will of Ælfhelm Polga, 31 October 989

A mere sixty-eight wills survive from the Anglo-Saxon era. One was drawn up on 31 October 989 by Ælfhelm Polga, a *thegn* of King Edgar (reigned 959–974). Ælfhelm Polga's will seems to have belonged to Westminster Abbey or, as it was then known, St Peter's. This thousand-year-old document provides a fascinating insight into the life of Edgar's loyal *thegn* whose vast estates included the village of *Stoctune*.

Ælfhelm Polga had prospered as a minister under Edgar the Peaceful who granted him substantial lands in Huntingdonshire, Cambridgeshire and elsewhere in East Anglia, but by the time Ælfhelm drew up his will, Edgar had been dead for fourteen years and after the short turbulent reign of Edward the Martyr, Ælthelred 'the Unready' (978–1016), had assumed the throne and it was to him that Ælfhelm addressed his will. Ælfhelm's rank and title in society were that of a *thegn* and minister.

In the Anglo-Saxon period, *thegns* formed the backbone of a landowning warrior class on whom the king relied for financial and military support to maintain peace and stability in the kingdom. The *thegn* was a powerful local figure in his own right; his estates would provide accommodation and entertainment for the king as he and his retinue traversed the kingdom and the *thegn*'s company of warriors were at the king's beck and call during times of crisis. Edgar's reign ushered in a sixteen-year period of peace and stability in England. According to the twelfth-century historian Henry of Huntingdon: 'He … kept control … Over a kingdom that was in a most tranquil state ... His whole reign was tranquil. For he widely established the Christian faith in his dominions ... and his great concern was to promote peace among all the nations of his realm.'

Ælfhelm Polga's life can be followed both from his will and from the various charters to which he was a witness or of which he was a beneficiary. His will opens with a standard declaration of how he intended to dispose of his property in fulfilment of his duties to God and to his king. His principal obligation was to his lord, the king. To Ælthelred, Ælfhelm bequeathed 'the companions that ride with me' (*7 minan geferan healues þe me mid ridað*), the warrior retinue that the loyal *þegn* was obliged to provide in the king's service. The 'companions' were fully equipped, with two swords (*twa swurd*), four shields (*feorwer scyldas*), four horses (*feorwer hors*) two of which were harnessed (*twa gerædode*), and two unharnessed (*twa ungerædode*). In addition to this military hardware, Ælfhelm bequeathed to his king 400 mancuses of gold (a mancus of gold was equivalent to a soldier's monthly pay).

From his will we know that Ælfhelm had a large family, including, in addition to his wife, two sons, a daughter, three brothers, Æthelric, Ælfwald and Ælfhelm, and two nephews. He also had his own personal goldsmith, Leofsige, and at least one servant. Having proved his allegiance to his king, Ælfhelm now focused on his family, relatives and servants. To his wife, he confirmed her ownership of the *morgengyue* (literally, a morning gift, given upon marriage), namely various estates he had been granted by the king. The will continues: 'And when we first came together (*þa wyt ærest togædere*), I gave her the two hides at Wilbraham, and Rayne and whatever pertains to it.' Ælfhelm's wife is not named in his will, but there are reasons to suppose she may have been Æffa, a substantial landowner in her own right who is mentioned in another document as being the wife of a certain Ælfhelm who may be our man. Ælfhelm then made

The Will of Ælfhelm Polga, 31 October 989

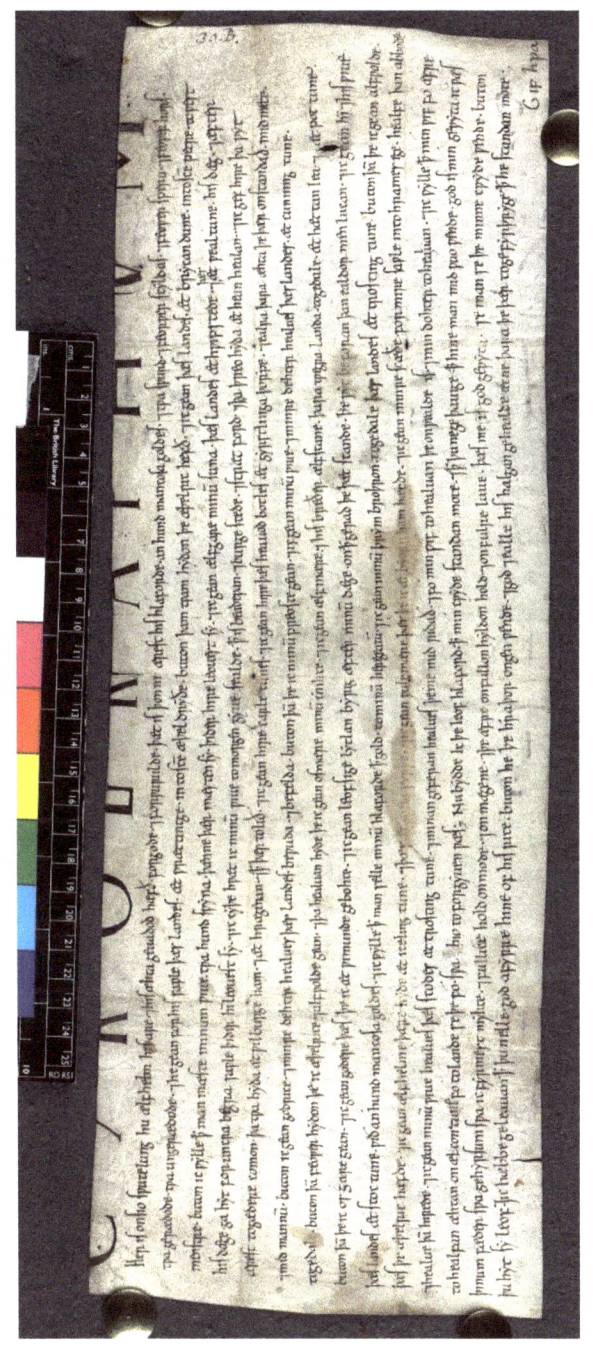

10 Will of Ælfhelm Polga

various bequests to his brothers, daughters, to his servant Osmær and son-in-law Godric.

For his soul (*sawle*), Ælfhelm granted his estate at West Wratting to *sancta Æpeldryðe* (St Etheldreda, founder of the Abbey of Ely), one of several bequests to religious houses. Ælfhelm Polga was particularly associated with two of the most powerful abbeys in England, Ely and Ramsey, and his will contains various bequests to these and other religious houses in England. To the abbey of Ramsey 'the earliest and most important of England's religious houses', Ælfhelm bequeathed his long-ship: *7 Ic gean minre scæðe. for mire sawle into Hramesege. healfe þan abbode. 7 healue þam hirede* ('And for my soul's sake I grant my long-ship to Ramsey, half for the abbot, and half for the community'). One of the purposes of the long-ship would have been to defend the abbey from marauding Danish raiding parties. Another cogent reason for the bequest was financial, to secure the lucrative tolls and duties that the abbey extracted from all river traffic passing along the river Great Ouse. An indication of the power and wealth of Ramsey Abbey is given in the Domesday Book of 1086, a century after the death of Ælfhelm Polga. The Abbot of Ramsey held no fewer than twenty-four manors in Huntingdonshire, including Great Staughton, in addition to numerous other manors in the eastern counties.

In the tenth century, before the draining of the fens, Ramsey (the isle of the ram) was a virtual peninsula, 'a hideous fen of huge bigness, oftentimes clouded with moist and dark vapours', according to the Ramsey chronicler. It was not a view shared by Bishop Oswald for whom the 'hideous fen', became, in his eyes, 'another Elysium'.

On 6 November 974, Ramsey Abbey was dedicated by Bishop Oswald in the presence of bishops from Dorchester and St Albans, as well as the abbots of Ely, Peterborough and Thorney. Amongst the bishops, nobles and other dignitaries who were present at the ceremony was Ælfhelm Polga.

The Will of Ælfhelm Polga, 31 October 989

Another important religious building was the subject of a further bequest. The *Anglo-Saxon Chronicle* for the year 962 recorded an outbreak of plague, followed by a fire that was possibly due to Danish raiders: 'there was a very great mortality, and the great and fateful fire occurred in London and the minster was burnt, and was rebuilt in the same year'. Ælfhelm Polga's will contained a bequest intended to support the rebuilding work: *ic gean þæs landes. æt Brycandune. into sancte Petre. to Westmenstre* ('And I grant the estate at Brickendon to St Peter's at Westminster'). This grant of land is the first documentary reference to the church of St Peter, now known as Westminster Abbey, after its re-foundation following the fire. Ælfhelm also stipulated that '200 pigs be fed for his wife's sake when mast [pig fodder] was available to benefit whichever foundation she desired'.

Ælfhelm's goldsmith Leofsige and his wife are the next beneficiaries of the will and this brings us to the first authentic documentary reference to Great Staughton: *7 ic gean him 7 his wiue þæs landes æt Stoctune. wið an hund mancosa goldes. 7 ic wylle þæt man selle minum hlaforde þæt gold. to minum heregeatum* ('And I grant to him and his wife the estate at *Stoctune* for a hundred mancuses of gold, and I wish that the gold be given to my lord in payment of my heriot'). In other words, Leofsige was obliged to pay 100 mancuses to the king to settle the heriot, in essence the death duty owed to the king. Leofsige and his wife received several further bequests of land and money in the will.

In the final section of the will, Ælfhelm Polga was keen to re-assert his loyalty to Æthelred. 'God is my witness that I was as obedient to your father [i.e. Edgar] as ever I could be' (*god is min gewyta ic wæs þinum fewer swa gehyrsum swa ic fyrmest myhte*). Ælfhelm may have had justifiable concerns that the terms of his will might not be respected. The king was within his rights to alter or annul the terms of a will if the *thegn* had incurred his displeasure, hence Ælfhelm's concern to prove his consistent record of loyalty to Edgar and his successors. The endorsement contained a warning against anyone tempted to tamper with the terms of the will: 'If anyone ever alters or removes anything in this will, may God's grace and his eternal reward be taken from him for ever.'

Whilst the powerful abbeys of Ely and Ramsey occupied much of Ælfhelm's attention, other religious houses were founded, or in the case of the priory of St Neots, re-dedicated. St Neots is a mere five miles from Ælfhelm Polga's estate at *Stoctune* and it is therefore unsurprising that he would have taken a close interest in the plan to re-dedicate the new priory in the town. The priory had a chequered history, distinguished by a paucity of historical fact and a wealth of legend and myth. Legend claims that the original priory was destroyed by Danish raiders in the ninth century. Historical fact states that the foundation of the priory can be dated no earlier than the reign of Edgar. The ceremony of dedication, which took place between 975 and 984, was performed by Æthelwold, Bishop of Winchester, in the presence of Æscwin, Bishop of Lincoln, Beorhtnoth, Abbot of Ely, Earl Ægelwin, Ædric Pape, and amongst the list of other signatories, Edgar's loyal *thegn*, Ælfhelm Polga. Sadly, this priory had a short history, which ended in 1010 when it was destroyed by the Danes.

It is not merely Ælfhelm's will that provides so much detail of the life and times of a *thegn* during the tenth century. He was a witness to numerous charters. These were elaborate affairs witnessed by numerous powerful figures of church or monastery often in the presence of the entire populace of the town. By a charter dated 966, Edgar granted Ælfhelm ten hides of land (in excess of 1,000 acres) in Parwich, Derbyshire. Three years later, in 969, this was followed by a grant of thirty hides (around 4,000 acres), with 'appurtenant meadow' in Witney, Oxfordshire. In 974, Edgar granted to Ælfhelm, his minister, 2½ hides of land at West Wratting, Cambridgeshire.

The Will of Ælfhelm Polga, 31 October 989

To the abbey of Ely, Ælfhelm bequeathed two hides of land at West Wratting, his estate some ten miles from Cambridge where he was to spend his last days. The Chronicle of Ely, the *Liber Eliensis*, describes the abbey in fulsome detail: 'Ely ... is the largest of the islands of the fens. It is magnificent in its wealth and its towns; equally praiseworthy for its woods, vineyards and waters; exceedingly rich in all fruit, live-stock-breeding and crops.' It took its name, according to Bede, from the abundance of eels that were caught in the same fens.

The *Liber Eliensis* contains two specific references to Ælfhelm Polga, both concerning his acting as a 'law worthy' witness to two charters. The first, held 'in the presence of the whole populace of the city of Cambridge', involved a certain Ælfric who found himself unable to pay his taxes. He offered to exchange two parcels of land, plus a sum of money, with the Bishop of Winchester and the Abbot of Ely. The Ely chronicler records that two Æelfhelms, 'one of whom had the additional name Polga', duly witnessed the transaction in the presence of Saint Æthelwold, Bishop of Winchester, Beorhtnoth, Abbot of Ely, twenty-four judges, twenty prominent landowners, including Ælfhelm Polga, and the entire population of Cambridge. The agreement was then ratified for a second time in the presence of twenty-one appropriately qualified 'law worthy' witnesses, amongst whose number was again Ælfhelm Polga.

The second case recorded in the *Liber Eliensis* concerned a certain Ælfwold, accused of illegally selling land for 20 mancuses of gold in order to raise money to free his wife and sons from slavery. At a general moot convened in Hertford, Abbot Beorhtnoth forced Ælfwold to acknowledge his guilt and the resulting judgement was duly signed by, amongst others, the 'law worthy' witness, Ælfhelm Polga.

Slavery was common in Anglo-Saxon England as the household accounts for Ely disclose. One document recorded the sale of a woman, as a slave: 'here are the things which have been supplied to Thorney [Abbey]: First, 2,000 herrings, from the North Sea, were bought with 40 pence ... A woman worth 5 oras was given to Stanground.' A further document records that the rent for a particular parcel of land in the fens owned by the abbey of Ely was 26,275 eels.

Perhaps the most famous charter witnessed by Ælfhelm Polga occurred at a general moot convened in London in 989 to condemn the crimes of a notorious villain, one Wulfbald. On the death of his father, Wulfbald had brazenly ransacked the estate of his stepmother and his kinsman Beorhtmær, seizing land, property and possessions, 'taking everything that he could find there, inside and out, small and great'. Four times the king commanded Wulfbald to make restitution by paying his *wergild* (blood money paid as compensation to victims of crime). Four times Wulfbald refused and the wergild was assigned to the king. At this juncture, King Æthelred and his queen Ælfthryth (Edgar's widow) lost patience and convened a great 'moot' in London to officially witness the charter, which condemned Wulfbald's crimes.

The moot was attended by all the king's councillors, both laymen and ecclesiastical; fifteen bishops, including the abbots of Ely and Ramsey, together with others from as far afield as Dorset, Hereford and Cornwall. Amongst the numerous other ministers and landowners who approved the judgement was Ælfhelm Polga. The king decreed that the lands feloniously seized by Wulfbald should be forfeited to the Crown and as for Wulfbald himself, he should be 'disposed of as the king desired either to remain alive or to be condemned to death'. To his dying day, Wulfbald remained unrepentant and after his death, his widow and her son continued the family tradition by slaughtering a number of Wulfbald's relatives and fifteen of his companions.

In 974, a year before his death, Edgar had granted 2½ hides of land at West Wratting to Ælfhelm. Edgar referred to his loyal *thegn* as 'his faithful minister' and sometime between 989 and the end of the century (Ælfhelm's actual date of death is unknown), it was at West Wratting that Edgar's faithful minister chose to spend his final days. The *Liber Eliensis* recorded the moment. Ælfhelm Polga, 'a certain knight possessed of much wealth', was near to death and wished to make his peace at the place with which he felt most closely associated, West Wratting. His local church, dedicated to St Æthelthryth, was 'positively coruscating with miracles and mighty works', thanks to the beneficence of 'the lady saint'.

Ælfhelm had bestowed upon the church many gifts, duly fulfilling his religious duties and obligations and over the years, had intervened in legal matters and undertaken business transactions for the benefit of the church, and, as the chronicler put it, 'for the benefit of his own soul'. As death approached, Ælfhelm was comforted by the thought that 'he who honours God's saints appeases God himself'. Having satisfied his spiritual longings, his thoughts turned to the physical well-being of Ely Abbey and in his will, he bequeathed the vill of Wratting 'apart from two hides' to the abbey of Ely. A little over a century later, on 10 November 1056, a bequest was made to Ramsey Abbey, by Leofgifu, widow, who granted land in Stocton, Dilinton and Gilling (Yelling) to the abbey. Leofgifu is thought to have been a descendant of Leofsige, Ælfhelm Polga's goldsmith.

In 1066, the Anglo-Saxon kingdom of England was destroyed by the Norman invader. The chronicler of Ely voiced his despair at the brutal destruction of all traces of a civilisation that had endured for 500 years. He expressed his horror at the vengeance wreaked by the Norman hordes on the Saxon nobility, who were disinherited or expelled from their lands, cast into extreme poverty, and subjects of scorn by the gouging out of their eyes or the amputation of their limbs. 'What am I to say about England? What am I to say to future generations? Woe to you, England, you who in former times were sanctified by your angelic progeny, but are now utterly distraught with groans for your sins.

You lost your native king and in war … became subject to a foreigner. Your sons were miserably slain … and your councillors and leaders … overwhelmed, or put to death or deprived of their inheritance.'

The age of the Normans had begun.

6

Tochestone, Huntedunscire

If evidence were required to confirm William's comprehensive subjugation of the Anglo-Saxon kingdom of England, it is only necessary to examine the names of the overlords of this little Huntingdonshire village in 1086: William de Eynesford, Hugh de Beauchamp, William Herengaud, William de Auberville, Nicholas de Crioll, Eleanor de Vaux. It had taken fewer than twenty years for William and his Norman army to dismantle utterly an Anglo-Saxon kingdom that had existed for 500 years. With astonishing speed, the Ælfhelms and the Edgars had given way to the Williams and the Richards. The upheaval was complete and enduring.

At Christmas 1085, King William convened a meeting of his chief counsellors at Gloucester. The Anglo-Saxon Chronicle of the same year explained the reason: 'Then, at the midwinter, was the king in Glocester with his council … After this had the king a large meeting, and very deep consultation with his council, about this land; how it was occupied, and by what sort of men.'

By 1086, 'the prolix and tedious' work had been completed. Officially known as the *Liber de Wintonia*, the Book of Winchester was the first detailed description of the village of Great Staughton, its inhabitants, the land they tilled and the amount of tax due to the king and how much the value differed from the time of Edward the Confessor in 1066. Writing a century later, the treasurer of England under Henry II, Richard FitzNeal, coined the term by which the *Liber de Wintonia* is best known: 'its sentence cannot be quashed or set aside with impunity. That is why we have called the book "the Book of Judgement" … because its decisions, like those of the Last Judgement, are unalterable.' Thus was born the Domesday Book.

The Domesday Process

The Normans did not have to start from scratch in compiling their 'Inquest'; their Anglo-Saxon predecessors had long collated data on the landholdings in England, providing a valuable aide-memoire for the legati (royal officials charged with collecting the data). Once collected, all relevant information was submitted for approval in the local administrative district, known as the Hundred, to specially convened juries, consisting of six Normans and six English. The legati would then send the completed returns to Winchester, the Norman capital, for final revision and publication.

Tochestone

William organised the collection of data according to a meticulous programme. There were seven great circuits encompassing the entire country and Huntingdonshire was included in the circuit that covered the large area of Derbyshire, Lincolnshire, Nottinghamshire and Yorkshire.

Huntingdonshire was divided into four Hundreds (an area of land encompassing 100 taxable hides) and *Stoctune* was part of the Hundred of Toseland, along with nearby towns and villages such as Godmanchester, Hail Weston, Little Paxton, St Neots and Yelling. The returns for each Hundred were sworn by the twelve local jurors. *Stoctune*, according to the Domesday entry for the village, came under: TERRA EPI LINCOLIENSIS. TOSELUND HUNDRED, i.e. the village was claimed by the Bishop of Lincoln, a claim that was disputed by the abbot of the powerful abbey of Ramsey.

In Tochestone, the Bishop of Lincoln had 6 hides taxable. Land for 15 ploughs. Now in lordship 2½ ploughs;

Tochestone, Huntedunscrire

16 villagers, and 4 smallholders who have 8 ploughs.
A priest and a church.
Meadow, 24 acres; woodland pasture, 100 acres.
Value before 1066 and now £10.
Eustace holds from the Bishop.
The Abbot of Ramsey claims this manor from the Bishop.
(Translation by John Morris)

Quite how, and why, the Anglo-Saxon settlement of *Stoctune* was transformed into the Norman French Tochestone is an enduring mystery and likely to remain so. There are two theories: one is that the Old French-speaking scribe simply misheard the name and despite the numerous hands through which the document passed, it remained unnoticed and uncorrected when the final version of the book was compiled in Winchester. A second hypothesis was that the scribe may have found the pronunciation of the English 'st' too foreign and to overcome the difficulty he came up with his own idiosyncratic linguistic solution.

The term 'hide' dates back to Anglo-Saxon times and seems to mean two things: the amount of land required to support one household, usually calculated at 120 acres, a figure that often varied by Hundred. The hide was also the basis for levying the geld (tax). Other historians have suggested that a hide represented the amount of land that a plough team of eight oxen could plough in a single day. The meaning here then is that the Bishop of Lincoln held enough land to support six households and tax would be paid to the king on this amount.

Land for 15 ploughs. This is a measure of how many ploughing teams, consisting of eight oxen, were required to cultivate the land and was the basis for calculating the total amount of tax owed.

Now in lordship 2½ ploughs. The tenant-in-chief owned land, which required 2½ ploughing teams to work it.

Villanus. Villagers, also translated as villein, villain, or villan. Like many of the terms used in the Domesday Book, 'smallholder' for example, this term is ambiguous and capable of a number of interpretations. Villeins owed labour services to the lord of the manor and depending on their status, were obliged to work a certain number of days per week for their lord.

Bordarius. Usually translated as bordar or smallholder, the term refers to a more prosperous rank of peasant, distinguished by the amount of land he could hold, up to five acres. They have eight plough teams between them.

With *meadow 24 acres* we are, so to speak, on firmer ground. South of the village, between the river Kym and the barrow on which the Romans built their villa, is an extensive meadow and this may be the meadow that is being referred to. It could also refer to the extensive pasture lands to the north of what is now Staughton Highway.

Woodland pasture 100 acres. From prehistoric times, Great Staughton was richly endowed with woodland, only a small part of which now survives as Perry Wood to the north of the village. At the time of Domesday Book and in subsequent centuries, ownership of woodland was highly prized and often disputed; woodland provided timber for building, wood for fuel and, perhaps more importantly, a rich hunting ground for the king or lord of the manor, jealously protected, with the most severe of penalties for any who dared trespass in its grounds.

A priest and a church. Perhaps the most significant entry in the document. It is tempting to speculate that the church may have been there when Ælfhelm Polga owned the estate. The lord of the manor was responsible for presenting the vicar and villagers would contribute a tithe to pay for the priest and for the upkeep of the church.

Value before 1066 and now £10. The value of the land was unchanged from the time of Edward the Confessor (reigned 1042–1066).

Eustace holds from the Bishop. Eustace de Lovetot, the sheriff, was one of the many knights who came over with William and was rewarded for his loyalty with grants of land throughout the county and beyond. The sheriff ('shire reeve') was a vital cog in the Norman administrative machine, involved in the management of the royal landholding, which provided lucrative opportunities for the sheriff to siphon off wealth as they went about their tasks. Eustace was notorious for his rapacity and greed. Unsurprisingly, sheriffs were frequently amongst the wealthiest of the king's courtiers. Prior to the Conquest, Eustace is not recorded either as landowner or tenant. There are suggestions that he may have been a native of Abbeville, in the Somme *département*. After the Conquest, by 1086, he owned twenty-seven separate lands and manors, principally in Huntingdonshire, but also in Northamptonshire. The vill of Great Staughton was claimed by the Bishop of Lincoln, but exploiting the power of his office of sheriff, it is likely that Eustace was illegally claiming ownership or at least enjoying the fruits of ownership.

The Bishop of Lincoln had 6 hides taxable. The Bishop referred to was Remigius, literally 'a man from Rheims' in France, yet another indication of the influx of French lords and ecclesiastics who were now securely embedded within the new regime. The Bishop of Lincoln also claimed other lands in Great Staughton, namely the manor of Blasworth, modern day Blaysworth, and the More, otherwise Staughton Moor.

The Abbot of Ramsey claims this manor from the Bishop. The disputes over land and endowments between religious houses such as Ramsey, Ely, Thorney and Lincoln were bitter and long standing and their conflicting claims were very often left unresolved.

From the details given in the Domesday Book, it is a reasonable hypothesis that the total population of the village, taking into account children and people no longer able to work, might have been in excess of 100 people.

Great Staughton and its People

Two further hamlets in the parish of Staughton are recorded in the Domesday Book:

Dillington
In Dellinctune, 6 hides taxable. Land for 12 ploughs. Now in lordship 2 ploughs;
16 villagers who have 10 ploughs
Meadow, 8 acres; woodland pasture 1 league and 2 furlongs long and 1 league wide.
Value before 1066 £6; now £4.

One league was equivalent to 12 furlongs, or about 1½ miles. The value of the land was less in 1086 than 1066. No church is mentioned.

The manor of Dillington was granted to Ramsey Abbey and for 250 years it was part of the landholding of the Engaynes who held it on behalf of the abbey. The Engaynes had come over with William the Conqueror and had been awarded lands in Huntingdonshire and elsewhere. The original meaning of their name was akin to 'engineer', which may signify the original bearer of the name was responsible for engines of warfare. One of the family, Vitalis or Viel Engayne, obtained a licence in 1238 to build a chapel in his manor of Dillington. The most illustrious member of the family was Sir John de Engayne, a contemporary of Sir John de Creting and both fought at the siege of Caerlaverock in 1300. One other legacy that the Engaynes did bestow upon Staughton was their principal manor, known as Gaynes Hall, which survives to this day, although not in its original form. Amongst the landholdings in their manor was Littlehey Park, whose name is still preserved in Perry. Here is the 1086 record for Perry:

In Pirie (West Perry) Alwin Devil had 1 hide taxable.
Land for 2 ploughs. Now in lordship 1½ ploughs;
6 villagers with 1 plough. A church.

Meadow, 4 acres; woodland pasture 1 league long and 4 furlongs wide.
Value before 1066 and now 40s.

The interesting item in the entry for Perry is the personal name, recorded in Domesday as Alwin but which may actually represent the Old English name Ælfwine, or Ælthelwine. If this is the case, he would be one of the very few local survivors of the now displaced Anglo-Saxon landowning class. His family name, noted as Devil, was in all likelihood originally Deule.

The Norman Legacy
Over the next two centuries, land dealings reveal the extent of Norman dominance and authority not only in Great Staughton but in the entire country. The Bishop of Lincoln continued to maintain his overall ownership of the land and the under-tenants came from the ranks of the Norman aristocracy who had come over with the Conqueror and were now enjoying the fruits of their loyalty.

One of the most powerful local landlords was William de Eynesford, who, in 1166, as under-tenant of the Bishop of Lincoln, held six knight's fees in Staughton. A knight's fee was nothing to do with money, but referred to the amount of land necessary to support a knight and his extensive retinue in the service of his sovereign. The quality of the land and the resources it contained, such as rivers, forests or mineral reserves, would determine the amount of tax the knight was obliged to pay either in money terms or more commonly in days of military service he owed the king. William de Eynesford was possibly the sheriff of Huntingdonshire at some time between 1100 and 1133.

For the next two centuries, the Norman overlords consolidated their landholdings by fortunate marriages. In 1265, national history intervened in the story of the village with Nicholas de Crioll and William Heringaud or Herengod, who

11 Domesday Book: 'Tochestone'

were suspected of supporting Simon de Montfort and the barons against King Henry III at the battle of Lewes in 1264. When de Montfort's rebellion was crushed at the battle of Evesham in 1265, Nicholas de Crioll and William Heringaud could have seen their lives, lands and property forfeited to the Crown but they seemed to have returned to their Staughton estates unharmed and untroubled.

Nicholas de Crioll went on to marry twice, but it is the children of his first wife Maud – probably the daughter of William de Eynesford – who are of most interest for the history of Staughton. Nicholas' eldest daughter, Nicholaa, married Adam de Creting, whose life and career will be described in the following chapter. By 1279, Adam and his brother-in-law Anselm de Gyse were in sole possession of the manor of Great Staughton, but legal disputes during the 1280s culminated in a hearing in Westminster before the justices of assize. By 1286, in a series of conveyances, the whole manor and the advowson became the sole property of Adam de Creting and Nicholaa his wife.

7

Sir Adam de Creting
Knight of Edward I

Of Adam de Creting's date and place of birth and parentage, history is silent. It seems clear that he took his name from the village of Creeting St Mary in Suffolk, near Needham Market and Stowmarket. His date of birth is uncertain but it is likely to have been c. 1255, given that his son John was born in 1276.

Adam must have descended from a wealthy landowning family. In the Inquisition (a coroner's inquest to determine the tax due on the deceased's estate) held after his death in 1295, Adam's landholdings were revealed to be extensive, encompassing manors in Huntingdonshire, Essex and Suffolk and including the manor of Barrow, near his probable birthplace, which he held of Walter Giffard. According to the Barrow records, Sir Adam de Creting (his name is spelt variously as Creeting, Cretyngge or Cretyng) held jointly with his wife Nicholaa half a knight's fee of the Giffards (between 500 and 2,500 acres).

What is certain is that by 1274, he had married Nicholaa, one of the three heiresses of Great Staughton's most powerful landowner, Nicholas de Crioll (or Kyriel) who had died in 1273. It is highly unlikely that Adam would have come empty-handed to this union; he would almost certainly have brought estates equivalent to those he would acquire by marriage. Legal disputes over the inheritance of Magna Stokton manor occupied several years but by 1279 (as recorded in the *Rotuli Hundredorum* or Hundred Rolls), Adam was in lawful possession (was seised) in the Manor of Stocton together with his brother-in-law Anselm de

Gyse, who had married Beatrice, the third daughter of Nicholas de Crioll.

The most impressive and still surviving testament to the presence and influence of Adam de Creting in Staughton is the motte and bailey castle on a ridge overlooking the village a mile south-west of the church. Cretingsbury, as it became known, is surrounded by an inner and outer moat, one of four such moats in Staughton, though none are as impressive as Adam's. The manor is sufficiently large not only to sustain a knight's retinue of men, horses and an armoury, but to host an agricultural community.

The domain of Cretingsbury measures some 800 ft long by 500 ft wide; its interior contains six substantial fishponds, the largest being 30 ft wide, 350 ft long and 6 ft deep, although it is now thought that these may have been constructed in later medieval times. There were farm buildings associated with the manor and sheep and cattle were raised there. Cretingsbury was to remain the Manor of Staughton for the next four centuries. Adam also held the manors of Blaysworth and *La More* (Staughton Moor). We do not know exactly the extent of the land he held in Staughton, but it may have been upwards of 4,000 acres.

The knight was expected to provide military service for as much as forty days per year per knight's fee. Many knights preferred to commute military service by paying a tax in lieu (homage and scutage), but Adam de Creting did not shirk his duties and remained in the king's active service until his death in 1295.

Adam de Creting, Knight of Edward I

It seems likely that by 1274, Adam was already in service to the newly crowned Edward I, the 'great and terrible' king and would have been dubbed a knight, eligible therefore to be known as Sir Adam de Creting. The rank of knight could be achieved on the

Sir Adam de Creting, Knight of Edward I

12 Cretingsbury Moat

battlefield in the king's service but the king could also dub as knights individuals who had lands with a substantial taxable value. In 1296 for example, Edward ennobled en masse several dozen men: 'On 24 Nov. 1296 ... the Justice of Chester was ordered to proclaim that all having £30 per annum lands or a Knight's Fee worth that sum, and who ought to be Knights, shall take up Knighthood before Whitsuntide.'

The formidable Edward I (reigned 1272 to 1307), known as 'Longshanks' and 'Hammer of the Scots', wasted no time in proclaiming his key policies: the subjugation of Wales and Scotland, bringing both under English rule and the wresting of the Gascon territories from Philip IV of France. In 1277 Edward made the first move in furthering his territorial ambitions, assembling a large army to invade Wales and bring the country under the English yoke.

We know that in 1276, Adam was already preparing to accompany the king and his army in the Welsh campaign. He and his wife Nicholaa were in Strowgul (modern Chepstow) in that year and it was there that Nicholaa gave birth to their son and heir, John. On 25 June 1277, the king granted Adam letters of protection, which gave him safe passage as he went about his diplomatic business in Wales on behalf of the king. A typical letter from a later period gives the scope of the protection offered: '[H]e is to be maintained, protected and defended from injury and violence, and amends should be made to them for any forfeitures that they have suffered without delay' (dated 15 March 1325). Sir Adam de Creting's fellow landowner in 'Magna Stouton', John de Engaine, was also summoned to serve against the Welsh on 1 July 1277 and again on 17 May 1282. By 1283, Wales had been brought under English rule.

13 Adam de Creting Coat of Arms

14 Engaine Coat of Arms

The Hundred Rolls (Rotuli Hundredorum) of 1279

Lib'e ten' Prior' de Huntingd' in elemōia de feodo d'ni Ade de Creting' in Stoutton'.

Wills fil Gregor' ten₃ de dco Priore di' v^rg' ℔re cū mes' & redd eid p ann' vj s.

Wills le Moyne t₃ di' v^rg' ℔re de dco Prior' & redd eid p ann' v s. & vj d.

Wills de Biffemede Rog̃s le F^emā & Angn' de Bockefworþe tenēt de dco Prior' di' v^rg' ℔re & redd eid p ann' v s. viij d.

Rog̃s Canoun ten₃ de dco Prior' di' v^rg' ℔re in villenag' & redd eid p ann' v s.

Wills fil Marfile de Mora t₃ & defend fextā ptē feod milit' de dno Ada de Creting' p homag' & fcutag' q^ndo accid & ht in dnico x ac^s ℔re j ac^am p^ati dimid ac^am bofc' & j rodā paftur' fepabit.

15 Illustration of 1279 Hundred Rolls, transcribed 1818

Edward's ambitions were not wholly confined to military campaigns. In March 1279, the king commissioned a great survey of landholding in England. Had it been completed, it would have been greater in scope and scale than the Domesday Book compiled 200 years previously. Only a few of the *Hundred Rolls* (so called because the rolls were arranged by Hundreds) were completed, but fortunately for the historian of Great Staughton, the *Hundred Roll* for the county has survived. It gives a fascinating picture of rural society in Great Staughton in the thirteenth century, with details of not only the major landowners but the names of peasants, villeins and cottars, the size of their holding, the taxes to which they were liable and the obligations they owed to the lord of the manor, in this case, Sir Adam de Creting.

The record for Great Staughton begins: *Magna Stouton cum Hamelet Blaysworth & Mora* (Staughton Moor). The Bishop of

Lincoln claims the manor of Dylington, and Hem'ingford abbis (Hemingford Abbots) as it did in the Domesday Book.

Adam's name features prominently throughout the record, which occupies three pages and which details the vast amount of property that he and Nicholaa held, sometimes wholly, sometimes partly from either the king or the abbey of Lincoln. *Adam de Cretingg in STOCTON. Dns Adam de Cretinges tens & defend in villa de Stouton iiij feof milit Epo Linc & Epo de Rege* (Sir Adam de Creting holds and maintains in the village of Staughton four knight's fees from the Bishop of Lincoln and from the King's Bishop). His landholding included thirteen acres of meadow, four dwellings, forty acres of woodland and seven acres of pasture. Many of the tenants on land held by Adam owe him homage and scutage; they included Alex le Sire, William and Eustace le Moyne, William Aungevin and Thomas de Beachampstead. There is also an intriguing mention of Galfre de Befeu who may be a member of the Beaufoys family who occupied the manor of *Bich'mstede*.

Adam's land dealings are recorded in a document known as the Feet of Fines. These were records of freehold or copyhold property being conveyed from one party to another on payment of a sum of money. In 1285, Adam and Nicholaa took possession of a messuage (dwelling) and two carucates of land (approximately 240 acres) in 'Magna Stocton'. With this landholding came the advowson of the church. In the same year, according to the Close Rolls, Adam extended his landholdings in a far corner of England, when Peter de Grenham granted him Woburneford Manor, Devon, on 27 December 1285. Another important transaction took place in 1287 between Willelmus de Kiriel (William de Crioll, Nicholaa's brother) and Adam de Creting and Nicholaa of 2½ virgates of land (approximately 30 acres), four acres, three and a half roods of land, an acre of meadow, three acres of pasture, 40 acres of wood and a moiety (half share) of the manor of Magna Stokton.

Sir Adam de Creting, Knight of Edward I

Like many nobles before and since, Adam de Creting, knight, occasionally had money troubles: according to the Patent Rolls of 1278, he owed various sums in Norfolk, Suffolk, Essex, Huntingdonshire and Kent. He faced a more serious charge of robbery in Suffolk on 25 May 1284. In April 1292, he appeared before Ralph de Sandwich, Warden of London, and John de Bakewell, Clerk, when a writ for payment of £200 was served on him by John de Bruges and Walter de Maidstone, acting as executors for Sir Gregory de Rokesley, deceased, citizen of London. It was a significant sum of money: a pound sterling would maintain the lifestyle of a peasant for six months and support a knight for a week.

Honours

Adam's military duties were to take him to Ireland in 1292, but before he left for that country, he exercised his right (advowson) to nominate the parish priest in Great Staughton. Accordingly, in 1290, Adam de Creting presented Richard de Insula to the worshippers of 'Stouton'; he was to serve the parish until his death in 1322. The same ceremony also confirmed Adam's claim to his landholdings in Great Staughton.

Sometime during 1291, Adam's wife Nicholaa died and between 11 December 1291 and 16 February 1292, Adam took as his second wife Juliane Fitz Maurice (born c. 1266, died 24 September 1300), widow of Thomas de Clare, lord of Thomond in Connaught and daughter of Sir Maurice Fitz Maurice, 4th Baron of Offaly and Maud de Prendergast. With the marriage, Adam inherited the lands of Thomas de Clare. Adam de Creting and Juliane Fitz Maurice were granted letters of protection on 2 May 1292 as they were going to Ireland.

Events moved quickly for Adam in the following years. In 1293, he was appointed Sheriff of Cork and a year later Edward confirmed him as Marshal of the Army in Gascony. Edward had claimed the province of Gascony for England, but France's powerful king, Philip IV 'the Fair' held sway and Edward was obliged to acknowledge the French king as overlord. Sporadic fighting occurred between 1294 and 1297, which explains Adam's appointment and his presence in the province.

A Death in Gascony

In 1294 Edward summoned Adam and John de Engaine and their knightly retinues to Portsmouth to take part in the king's military campaign in Gascony. Adam de Creting never returned. Sometime on or before 8 November 1295, he was killed in Risonce by the treachery of one Walter Giffard, according to William Rishanger's Chronicle *Acta Edwardi Primi* ('Deeds of Edward I') written around 1312. Scholars have subsequently cast doubt on Rishanger's authorship of the Chronicle but the account of the fatal skirmish that killed Adam almost certainly has a factual basis, particularly concerning the details of the capture and ransoming of his companions.

Rishanger's (or pseudo-Rishanger's) Chronicle described the circumstances in which Adam met his death. Charles, brother of the king of the French, invaded with his army and besieged Risoncium (present-day Rions in Gascony). A skirmish followed in which Adam and his band were routed, forcing them to seek protection in the town but they were overcome by Charles' forces, as a result of which John of Brittany, Robert Tipetot, Radulph de Touy (or Tony), Aumary de Saint Amand and his brother Radulph de Gorges, Roger de Leyburne, and Adam's son John de Creting together with forty-three other soldiers were taken prisoner and sent to Paris to be ransomed. Of Adam de Creting's fate, the Chronicle offers a succinct account. *Occisus est ibi Adam de Cretynge, miles admodum probus, proditione cuiusdam militis, nomine 'Walteri', cognomento 'Giffardi' qui, factus transfuga, moratus est in Galliis annis multis* (There [at Risonce] Adam de Creting, a most excellent soldier, was killed by the treachery of one Walter Giffard who, having committed the deed, remained in France for many years.)

Sir Adam de Creting, Knight of Edward I

The prisoners, including John de Creting and John de Engaine, had to wait three years before they were released from captivity. On 24 September 1298, notification was received that John de Creting was in good health. By March 1299 he had been released and had done homage for his English and Irish lands, meaning that he had raised money from his lands to pay the ransom demanded by his French captors. Whilst he was being held prisoner in France, custody of Adam's lands was granted in 1296 to Thomas de Creting.

By 1299, the prisoners in Paris had been discharged having paid their ransom. Pseudo-Rishanger gives details of the release of prisoners. *Nobiles vero viri Anglicani, utpote Dominus Johannes de Sancto Johanne, et Dominus Almaricus de Sancto Amando, cum pluribus aliis capti et incarcerati, liberati sunt.* (English nobles, such as Sir John of St John and Sir Amaury de St Amand, captured and imprisoned along with numerous others, were freed.) Amongst the 'numerous others' were John de Engaine and John de Creting. Most of these soldiers were to see action again in Edward I's expedition to Scotland.

The King's Gratitude

Edward clearly regarded Adam de Creting as a loyal, assiduous and faithful retainer, because we read that on 15 November 1302, seven years after Adam's death, the king granted £200 from escheats (reversion of land to the king in the absence of legal heirs) to Adam's daughters Margaret and Katharine in gratitude for Adam's loyal service in Gascony. He repeated his generosity three years later when he granted Katharine 50 marks 'until she shall be suitably married' and on 8 May 1305 added a further 150 marks to her marriage portion, a handsome sum enough to support a knight and his retinue for a year.

The Inquisition of Barrow, 1296

After the death of a lord of the manor, an Inquisition (a coroner's inquest) was convened to determine the landholdings they held, the value and tenure, together with the names and ages of the heirs who laid claim to the money and land. An Inquisition was often initiated by the heirs of the estate to ensure that they obtained legal possession and to prevent the property reverting to the Crown by default. One of Adam's manors was Felton in Norfolk, which he held in 1274 jointly with Nicholaa, having been acquired from the Giffards. The Inquisition gives a fascinating glimpse of his holding. The extent of the manor was 240 acres of arable land with a taxable value of 60s (3d per acre) and 1½ acres of meadow valued at 3s; half an acre of pasture valued at 6d, 23 acres of wood of which eight acres one rood could be cut every year, valued at 24s 9d per acre; and one windmill valued at 10s. From his tenants he claimed payment in hens, 1 lb of pepper at Christmas and eggs at Easter. The capital messuage (principal residence) and dependent outbuildings and land were found to have a taxable value of 4s. All these lands were held from William Giffard, on payment of a 'sixth part of one knight's fee'. Adam also held 44 acres of land from the sacrist of St Edmund in Saxham and had other landholdings in Fornham, Risby and Barrow. Adam's heirs were his son Sir John de Creting and John's wife Hawise. Adam's brother, Sir Edward de Creting, was tenant for life of the manor by gift from his deceased brother and held the fee until 1346.

Edward I's Campaign in Scotland

The contribution of the de Cretings in the service of the king did not end with the death of Adam. In late 1297, Edward concluded a truce with Philip IV of France, bringing to an end to the war and Edward's claim to Gascony. Edward's more pressing concern was to avenge his army's defeat at the Battle of Stirling Bridge at the hands of the Scottish leader William Wallace. The moment came on 22 July 1298, at the battle of Falkirk, where John de

Engaine and his retinue served as part of the King's Battalion. It was at this battle that John de Engaine received the first of two mentions in despatches or, more correctly, in the Falkirk Roll of Arms, composed shortly after the battle and consisting of the blazoned shields of the 111 knights who fought for the king on that day. It is the oldest known English roll of arms.

The Song of Caerlaverock
In July 1300, Edward marched north with an army of 3,000 men to bring Scotland under English rule. His army included eighty-seven of the Barons of England, almost the entire peerage, amongst whom were Sir John de Creting and Sir John de Engaine.

One of the first stumbling blocks to impede Edward's progress was Caerlaverock, literally 'lark castle', a formidable moated fortress some seven miles from Dumfries. Edward immediately laid siege to the castle but in the face of determined resistance by the sixty-strong garrison, he was forced to bring up one of the largest trebuchets (a giant catapult) ever used to bring the siege to an end. Despite Edward's promise to spare the garrison, he wasted no time in executing all the ringleaders. Present at the siege, or certainly a confidant of people who were there, was an anonymous poet, claimed by some historians to be the cleric Walter of Exeter, who was moved to celebrate this great victory by composing the Song or Roll of Caerlaverock, a lengthy tribute in verse to the valour of each of the nobles and knights who had distinguished themselves in the battle. The verses were decorated at the appropriate point in the narrative with the coats of arms of each of the knights.

The poem begins: 'In the year of Grace one thousand three hundred, on the day of Saint John, Edward held a great council at Carlisle, and commanded that in a short time all his men should prepare to go together with him against the Scots'. It must have been a colourful sight, as the eighty-seven knights paraded proudly before their sovereign, *Meint beau penon en lance mis, Meint*

16 Caerlaverock Castle

banier deploié (Many a beautiful pennant affixed to a lance, and many banners displayed). *E li Roys o sa grant maisnie/Tanttost se vunt vers les Escos,/Non pas en cotes e sourcos,/Mès sur les granz chevaus de pris./Por ceo q'il ne seussent supris,/Armé ben e seurement* (And the king and his great household, immediately proceed against the Scots, not in coats and surcoats, but on mighty and costly chargers so that they would not be taken by surprise, well and securely armed).

The poet depicts the leaders of the great army in heroic terms: *Henris li bons Quens de Nicole, Ki provesté enbrace e acole* (Henry, the bold earl of Lincoln, who proclaims and embraces valour). Here is *Lui Robert le fiz Water, Ke ben sout dez armes le mester* (And with him, Robert Fitz Walter, who well knew the mastery of arms). William the Marshal is next to be depicted *Dont en Irlande ot la baillie* (who held chief command in Ireland). And so the glowing tributes continue, down to the lesser knights about whom sometimes the poet finds it difficult to summon suitably heroic lyrics to embellish their deeds. Veterans of the campaign in Gascony in 1295, which saw the death of Adam de Creting, are

Sir Adam de Creting, Knight of Edward I

now on the field of battle to deliver Caerlaverock for the king: John of Brittany, Amaury de Saint Amand, Radulph de Gorges, Radulph de Touy, John de Engaine and John de Creting. The poet finds little worthy of note to say about John de Engaine *Johans de Engaigne le ot jolie. Rouge dance de or croissillie.* (John de Engaine had an elegant [banner], of red crusily (crosslets) and a dancette of gold). John de Creting merited a slightly more dashing entry in the poem:

Or je vis Johan de Cretingues / Where I saw John de Creting
En peril de perdre un cheval / In danger of losing a horse,
Kant sur li un vint contre val / When one came down upon him
Esperonnant au saietiz, / Spurring like an arrow;
Mès pas ne semble estre saintiz, / But he did not seem to be feigning
Ki tant se haste au fait atteindre / So great was his haste to attain his object.
En son blanc escu ot fait teindre / On his white shield he had had engraved
Un chievron rouge o trois molettes / A red chevron with three red mullets.

Thus, so far as history records, the military career of Sir John de Creting ended and he returned to his estate at Great Staughton. Like his father Adam, John held the advowson in his manor church and in 1322 he presented Radulphus de Malton to the church. John de Creting was summoned to parliament on three occasions in 1332 and created Baron Creting by Edward III. The title became extinct when John de Creting died in that same year.

His comrade-in-arms Sir John d'Engaine took part in Edward II's campaign against the incursions of Robert the Bruce in 1311. Subsequently, John d'Engaine retired to his estate where he is thought to have died sometime around 1322.

8

From Waweton to Walton: Birth of a Staughton Dynasty

For three centuries, from the mid-1400s to the restoration of Charles II in 1660, the Waweton/Wauton/Walton dynasty was the most powerful family in Great Staughton. Their story begins around the year 1339 with the birth of the founder of the dynasty, John Waweton.

John Waweton, described in the historical records as being of Great Staughton and Somersham in Huntingdonshire, Basmey in Bedfordshire and Stowe Wythe in Cambridgeshire, was born c. 1339, the fourth son of Robert and Maud Waweton of Stowe Wythe. He married Parnell, by whom he had two sons and a daughter. John Waweton represented Huntingdonshire in ten parliaments from 1365 until 1395. How he came to acquire the manors of Staughton and Basmey in Eaton Socon is not recorded, but there is an unverified account suggesting that a daughter of one of the last of the de Cretings (perhaps Sir Edmund) married into the Waweton family in the late 1340s and John Waweton may have thereby inherited the manor of Staughton.

The fourteenth century, aptly described by one historian as 'calamitous', was the ominous backcloth to the rise of one of Staughton's most influential families. The calamities of the fourteenth century began with the onset of the Little Ice Age and the ensuing great famine of 1315–1317. Twenty years later and two years before the birth of John Waweton, Edward III declared war against the French to recover lands lost by his father Edward

II. It was the beginning of the Hundred Years War. When John was nine years of age, the bacterium *Yersinia pestis* arrived in England and the subsequent Great Mortality wiped out an estimated one-third of England's four million population. The shortage of labour resulting from the Black Death was to cause serious social unrest culminating in the Peasants' Revolt of 1381. John Waweton lived and was politically active throughout the entire period.

One of the greatest revolutions in English history did not however involve civil unrest, wars or famine and John Waweton, Member of Parliament for Huntingdonshire, was present when it occurred in 1362. More accurately called the Pleading in English Act 1362, the Statute of Pleading was passed into law, stipulating that henceforth all pleas in the English courts 'shall be pleaded, shewed, defended, answered, debated, and judged in the English language'. After 300 years, Norman French was to be replaced in the courts and in Parliament by 'the vulgar tongue'. Edward III became the first monarch to address Parliament in English. By 1385, English had become the language of instruction in schools. As a final example of the triumph of English over the 'enemy language' French, Henry V, king of England, began writing his official correspondence in English on 12 August 1417.

In a diligent but somewhat colourless career as the representative for Huntingdonshire between 1365 and 1395, John Waweton served three sovereigns; Edward III, Richard II and Henry IV. Throughout his tenure as Lord-Lieutenant of the County from 1367 to 1399, John Waweton was obliged under the Commission of Array to raise troops in the event of a national emergency. As an assize judge, he was considered sufficiently qualified to lead an official inquiry in March 1367 into the crimes of one William Burton. He served as a Justice of the Peace for Huntingdonshire from November 1369 to 1374 and from November 1397 to February 1405.

His sole military exploit in the service of his king was in 1370 when he was part of a disastrous foray into French territory led by Waweton's almost exact contemporary Sir Robert Knolles (c. 1325–1406) whose freebooting character was matched only by his gross military incompetence. By 1370 the Hundred Years' War had been reduced to a succession of minor skirmishes followed by volleys of diplomatic invective. Knolles, at the head of an army of 6,000, was commanded to push into French territory and capture strategic towns on the way. It was a disaster. His generals lost confidence in his strategy, particularly when he declined to engage in battle the formidable French commander Bertrand de Guesclin and he finally abandoned his army to its fate.

Retribution for Knolles quickly followed; he was stripped of his lands and fined 10,000 marks (perhaps £2m today). Waweton was one of the few to survive the debacle and the experience did not seem to halt his modest rise up the political ladder.

A testing moment for Waweton came in the wake of the Peasants' Revolt in 1381 when riots broke out in Huntingdon as agricultural labourers pressed for higher wages. John Waweton did not hesitate in taking the necessary steps to 'suppress the insurgents'. In the same year, he was obliged to 'enforce labour services' i.e. force the labourers on the Ramsey Estates to return to work. Waweton came to the aid of his neighbouring landowner, William Gamboun, and the subsequent relationship he developed with Gamboun was especially fruitful. In 1401, Waweton, having obtained the wardship of William Gamboun's son and heir Richard, promptly married off his daughter to the young man, to the great benefit of his wealth and landholding.

The trickiest moment of John Waweton's career came in the final years of Richard II's authoritarian reign. Waweton had long enjoyed the confidence of the king but elsewhere in the kingdom revolt was brewing which came to a head when Henry de Bolingbroke deposed Richard and installed himself on the throne as Henry IV. He reinforced his authority a year later by allegedly having Richard murdered. If Waweton thought that his loyalty to Richard would count against him, he must have been relieved to retain the favour of the new king. The last mention history has of John is in 1412, when he is named in tax returns. He may have died shortly after that date, leaving a widow, Parnell, who held the estate in Staughton. After much litigation the estate passed to John's son Thomas.

Thomas Waweton was born in 1370 in his father's manor in Great Staughton. His rapid rise to power in Huntingdonshire politics owed much to his father's influence and to his own energy, ambition and purpose. In 1495, at the age of twenty-five, he was appointed alnager in Bedfordshire. The position carried weight. An alnager was responsible for ensuring that woollen cloths, 'shall be of the same width, to wit, of two ells (an ell was roughly a yard) within the lists, and of the same goodness in the middle and sides'. If fault were found with the cloth, it was forfeited to the Crown. The title testified to the importance of the wool trade in England's economy at this time.

Two years later Thomas Waweton was elected to represent Huntingdonshire in Parliament and he quickly acquired important responsibilities: collector of taxes in 1404 and Justice of the Peace for Huntingdonshire and Bedfordshire at various times between 1405 and 1448. His personal circumstances changed; in 1406 Thomas made the manor of Great Staughton his principal residence and upon the death of his father in or around 1412, Thomas took possession of the manor of Basmey in Eaton Ford, which handily gave him the residence qualification he would require if he chose to stand for Parliament for Bedfordshire.

Thomas Waweton's parliamentary career spanned the first four decades of the fifteenth century during which time he represented Huntingdonshire on several occasions between 1397 to the late 1420s. In the elections of 1413 and 1414 he was returned as the Member of Parliament for Bedfordshire and in

1415 he was appointed sheriff for that county. Knighted in 1418 and styled 'chivaler' (knight), he was again elected as MP for Bedfordshire in 1419. In 1420 and 1422, he reverted to his former constituency when he was returned as MP for Huntingdonshire. He was again appointed sheriff of Bedfordshire in 1422. More honours followed when he became chamberlain of North Wales, thus rising in both royal and national ranks.

The pinnacle of Thomas Waweton's career came in 1425 when he was appointed Speaker of the House of Commons. In an entertaining and sardonic look at the eminent worthies who have held the office, one writer had some caustic observations about Sir Thomas Waweton who seemed to have held no legal appointments, nor was he even 'learned in the lawes', which would normally be expected of the holder of such a high office. Indeed, Waweton seemed to owe more to 'fortunate matrimonial alliances with eminent lawyers' than to any exceptional forensic and diplomatic skills normally considered appropriate to the office.

Waweton was also witness to one of the most curious ceremonies to have attended a State opening of Parliament. After the early death of his father Henry V, the victor of Agincourt, his new-born son Henry VI succeeded to the throne at the age of nine months in 1422 and at the age of two he opened Parliament, seated on the lap of his twenty-year-old mother, Catherine of Valois.

More parochial matters may have claimed Waweton's attention in 1420, when a new church bell was delivered to the vicar of Great Staughton, John Teesdale, and duly installed in the church tower. The bell is thought to have been cast by a bell makers' guild, which was active in London between 1395 and 1420.

Noteworthy though Thomas Waweton's parliamentary career may have been, it was not without blemish. Throughout his forty-year career Thomas Waweton often showed a reckless disregard for electoral law.

Great Staughton and its People

17 Henry VI

Waweton's illegal machinations were to catch up with him in the summer of 1429, when, in the space of two weeks, he made two outrageous attempts to influence the outcome of two elections. The first egregious disregard of electoral law came on 20 August 1429, in the elections for Huntingdonshire. Waweton was determined to foist his relative William Waweton, who was not even resident in the county, and his wealthy neighbour Robert Stonham in place of his close friends, Roger Hunt and Nicholas Styuecle. Waweton meant business; with a body of armed men, 'visitors from Bedfordshire', he stormed into Huntingdon town hall and forced the terrified sheriff and his entourage to return Waweton's two choices. He repeated the ploy in the elections for the sheriff of Bedfordshire. An official royal commission into the latter affair concluded that Waweton had acted in defiance of the law and the original candidates were reinstated. Waweton did not escape unscathed; brought before the courts, he was fined £100 for contravening the Statutes of 1406, 1410 and 1413.

Despite his behaviour, Waweton became sheriff of Bedfordshire in 1432, a period that coincided with an upturn in his fortunes when, after the death of Maud, he married Alana, a widow and daughter of Sir Simon Felbrigg, a standard-bearer of Richard II. No doubt as a result of his now regal connections, Waweton was summoned to attend a great council at Westminster in the spring of 1434. On 15 November 1435, in an indication of his power, wealth and influence, Waweton was asked by the king for a loan of £50 in support of the French war.

For the remainder of his days, Waweton withdrew from political life and devoted himself to his property holdings. The date of his death is not known but it must have been around this time, when he would have been over eighty years of age. He was buried in the church of Great Staughton. His wife Alana died in 1458 and was buried in the parish church of Eaton Socon. They left two sons and two daughters. The Waweton line continued into the following century when the Manor of Staughton passed to George Wauton in 1555.

One of the more interesting of Thomas Waweton's extended network of friends and acquaintances was Sir Robert Stonham, another neighbour in Staughton and said to be one of the wealthiest individuals ever to represent Huntingdonshire, where he was elected MP for the first time in 1421. He was born c. 1390 to Robert Stonham of Stonham Aspall in Suffolk and Katherine, daughter of Sir William Burgate. His path to riches began around 1415, when he married a well-connected lady of the shires, Mary, daughter of a wealthy landowner, Sir John Bernak, or Barnack, of Saxlingham, Norfolk. This promising start was continued when, in an extraordinary stroke of good fortune (at least for Robert Stonham), Mary's two brothers and co-heirs both died in infancy within days of each other, leaving Mary and Robert in possession of estates extending across several eastern counties.

When Mary's sister and co-heir Joan died in 1420, Mary and her husband thus inherited a number of estates in Eastern England, including the Manor of Dillington and hence Gaynes Hall. Their good fortune continued when his mother Katherine married her second husband, John Spencer, keeper of the wardrobe to Henry V. Through his influence, Stonham was introduced to royal circles, but it was Katherine's third husband, John Tyrell, a distinguished Parliamentarian and treasurer of the royal household, who secured a permanent place for Stonham in the king's intimate circle.

For all the good fortune and helping hands that came his way, Robert Stonham was not without his own considerable merits. In 1415, he joined Henry V's campaign in France, but dysentery forced his early return to England and thus he missed the slaughter of Harfleur and the triumph of Agincourt.

Stonham entered Parliament as the MP for Huntingdonshire in 1421 and in 1432 and 1436, he was appointed sheriff of Cambridgeshire and Huntingdonshire. Subsequently, Stonham served in at least nine further parliaments and occupied various official positions: collector of taxes, Justice of the Peace 1437–1443 and again in 1450 until his death in 1454.

He accompanied the newly crowned Henry VI on his visit to France and obtained letters of protection in May 1430. He was still abroad in November 1431, presumably in France and the letters of protection were renewed. In February and March of 1431, the trial took place in Rouen of Joan of Arc and after being found guilty by an English judge and jury, she was burnt at the stake in May of that year. Were the letters of protection issued to Robert Stonham to enable him to be present at the trial and subsequent execution of the 'Maid of Orléans'?

Robert Stonham died on 27 February 1454 and was buried in the panelled vault of a specially built chapel in the parish church of Great Staughton. In his *History of Great Staughton*, H. G. Watson stated that in Camden's *Visitation of Great Staughton* in 1613, an inscription existed in the church relating to the Stonham family. It read:

> Here lies Robert Stonham Esquire and his wife Mary, which said Robert died the 27th day ... [text missing]. ... Barnack knight, died the 23rd day of the month of September A.D. 1454. May God have mercy on their souls.

Watson (1919) suggested that on the chancel floor there was a matrix of a brass that may have corresponded to the above inscription. It is no longer extant. In the vault of what is now the Gaynes Chapel in St Andrew's Church, there are shields bearing the arms of the families of Stonham, Barnack, Noone, Engaine and Burgatt.

9

'Pray For the Good Astate of Olyver Leder'

Oliver Leder had to prove himself to be very sure-footed to negotiate one of the most turbulent and transformative eras of English history, a period of political divisions, religious strife and social unrest. For more than forty years, Leder was a privileged witness to the events that shaped England and for many of those years he was an active participant in both local politics and national affairs of state.

Oliver Leder came to prominence in the 1520s as a protégé of Cardinal Thomas Wolsey, Henry VIII's powerful Chancellor of the Exchequer. During the king's expensive and protracted divorce from Catherine of Aragon, Leder was one of the financial backroom boys helping to raise taxes in the quaintly named Court of First-fruits and Tenths of Spiritualities. Henry's equally messy divorce from the Roman church saw Leder occupying several key roles in the state. After Wolsey's downfall, Leder moved seemingly without effort to become a trusted confidante of Thomas Cromwell, and unlike either of his two mentors, Leder managed to preserve his head. He saw the establishment of the Church of England with a liturgy and doctrine provided by Thomas Cranmer and a Bible in English placed in every church. He charted a skilful path through the fanatical Protestant dogmatism of Edward VI and the immediate reversion to Catholic orthodoxy that followed the accession of Mary I and Philip II. He was witness to the social unrest brought about by two different causes, namely unlawful enclosures (Kett's Revolt) and Thomas Cranmer's *Book of Common Prayer* (the Prayer Book Rebellion). Oliver Leder died in 1557, on the cusp of the next great period of English history, the age of Elizabeth.

How did this man from a Huntingdonshire village come to occupy such prominent roles of state? By c. 1497, when Leder was born, the Leder family had been established in Great Staughton for more than a century and a half since their antecedent, Thomas Leder, acted as attorney for Sir Edmund de Creting in the 1340s. Subsequently, the family was involved in the legal affairs of the Waweton/Wauton family who exercised their power and influence from their Manor of Staughton at Cretingsbury.

As a young man, Leder had followed in the legal footsteps of his forebears and in 1514 he was admitted to the Middle Temple. He was quick to rise through the ranks and very soon he was rubbing shoulders with the most powerful man in the kingdom after the king himself, Cardinal Thomas Wolsey, Henry VIII's closest and most trusted confidant. Wolsey's confidence in his young colleague was shown in contemporary records: in 1517–18 the 20-year-old Leder owed Thomas Wolsey the not inconsiderable sum of ten shillings on 'bills and obligations'. Already Leder was establishing the credentials he would need to climb up the social and political ladder. The law was not the only source of income for Leder; he had strong connections in trade and commerce. In 1526, for example, when he was in his late 20s, he was made a freeman of the Fishmongers Company and he was also said to have owned a share in a pepper factory in Spain.

Leder's growing influence in the political circles of Huntingdonshire was steady and uneventful. In 1524, he was Commissioner for Subsidy in Huntingdonshire, responsible for the collection of taxes. Great Staughton at this time was one of the largest and wealthiest villages in the shire, contributing annually £21 15s 4d in taxes. (For comparison, Godmanchester, a much more important commercial and trading centre, contributed £35 11s 6d.)

'Pray For the Good Astate of Olyver Leder'

Leder's good fortune continued when, also in 1524, he was appointed one of Six Clerks in Chancery, an important public legal office responsible for commissions, patents and other instruments of business that formed part of the English Court of Chancery. For a twenty-month period, the Court was controlled by Leder's ally and patron, Thomas Cromwell. In accordance with Catholic doctrine, the clerks of chancery were obliged to observe the vow of celibacy but when this law was abolished, Leder seized the opportunity to marry Frances, daughter of Thomas Baldwin, a wealthy, lately deceased London draper.

1527 saw Leder in the thick of Henry's plotting to be rid of Catherine of Aragon who had borne him a daughter, Mary, but not a son and heir. In that year Henry had unsuccessfully petitioned the Pope for an annulment to his marriage, but it was not until 1533 that Henry's wishes were granted.

The doctrinal and political struggle with papal authority came to a head in 1534 when the Act of Supremacy was passed, making Henry 'supreme head on earth of the Church of England', in the process disregarding any 'usage, custom, foreign laws, foreign authority or prescription'. Oliver Leder was soon to find himself party to this protracted break from Rome. In 1535, he had been appointed to the Court of First-fruits and Tenths of Spiritualities. This curiously named body was responsible for setting and collecting taxes on benefices. The First-fruits were the initial taxes on the income of a benefice, the Tenths were the proportion of taxes on income due in subsequent years. The taxes duly collected were then normally remitted to the Papal Exchequer. After his excommunication by the Pope, Henry saw no reason why the taxes collected by the Court of First-fruits should go to Rome and he therefore diverted the monies to fund his new Church of England. Henry's determination to stamp his authority on his new Church and his rejection of the Pope's authority was confirmed by the introduction into English churches of the *Book of Common Prayer*, which had been compiled by Thomas Cranmer. This

18 Thomas Cromwell, Earl of Essex

became a compulsory part of the liturgy of the Church of England in the Act of Uniformity passed by Parliament in June 1549 in the reign of Henry's successor, his son Edward VI.

The upheaval in the church was not welcomed by all in the population; as early as 1536 there were a number of uprisings in the north of England, known as the Pilgrimage of Grace, protesting against Henry's rejection of the Catholic faith.

Meanwhile, Oliver Leder, 'gentleman', had not been slow in acquiring land in 'Magna Stoughton'. In 1535, he purchased 20 acres of land and an acre of meadow in the parish.

In July 1539, with the Dissolution of the Monasteries, Oliver Leder purchased the Rectory Manor for £1,430 and various other parcels of land. In due course Leder sold off many of the peripheral lands and settled with his wife in the Rectory Manor, which became for a time his principal residence. The Leders did not long remain here. Sometime after 1539 and before 1543, Leder built 'Place (or 'Palace') House' opposite the church of St Andrew, on the site of the Charterhouse monastery. This was the house that 'at the dayes of their deaths they (the Leders) did inhabit'.

19 Place House built c. 1539

Leder's purchases of land did not always proceed without incident. There were riots in protest at his enclosures in his parks of Rushoe and Whitley in 1554 during his time as sheriff in the shire. So serious were they that Leder brought proceedings against one Robert Sapcote and his band of followers, whom he accused of breaking down hedges 'in a warlike manner' and shooting with crossbows at the keeper and his wife who, terrified by the onslaught, were forced to take refuge in their lodge. Servants encountered by the insurgents were given equally short shrift, being hounded into the moat. Finally, the most serious criminal act: they had killed and maimed deer on the estate.

The last decade of Leder's life saw an England riven by political divisions, religious factions and social unrest that greatly eclipsed the damaging conflict that had followed Henry VIII's rupture with the Church of Rome. Henry had died in the summer of 1547 and was succeeded by his son, Edward VI who was imbued with a single, all-consuming ideal: to rid the church of any remnants of its former Catholic faith.

On 3rd March, 1551, the Privy Council, commanded by Edward, ordered that Commissioners were to be appointed to carry out an inventory of the ornaments in every parish church in the land. Ostensibly, the principal reason was to prevent church goods being embezzled by private individuals following the Dissolution of the Monasteries. Severe penalties awaited any person 'that hath sold, alienated, imbezilled, taken or carried away, and of such also as have councelled, advised and commanded any part of the said Goods, Plate, Jewels, Bells, Vestments, and Ornaments to be taken or carried away, or otherwise imbezilled'. There was however a rather more pressing concern: 'the Kinge's Majestie had neede presently of a masse of mooney, therfore Commissions shulde be addressed into all shires of Englande to take into the Kinges handes suche churche plate as remaigneth, to be emploied unto his hignes use'. Thus were Edward's religious piety and his financial demands deftly combined.

The Commissioners, Sir Robert Tyrwhit, knight, Thomas Audeley, Thomas Cotton, William Laurence and Robert Rowley duly arrived at the church of St Andrew in Great Staughton on 28 July 1552 where they were met by the three churchwardens, Roger Harrison, Thomas Barrowes and Thomas Peyte. Before they could commence their work, however, the churchwardens submitted a document asking the Commissioners to take into account the dilapidated condition of the church tower that was in imminent danger of collapse. Money had already been donated for repairs but more would be needed and would the Commissioners therefore be prepared to give any monies raised from the sale of any ornaments to help with the repair? The churchwardens made a compelling case: 'And we the sayd churchewardens of the sayd churche of Moche Stowghton … ar redy to prove that the roof of the sayd churche fell downe to the grownde this last yere past.' Parishioners readily contributed to the repair, notably Oliver Leder: 'lent by Olyver Leder esquire, for and towerd the reparacions'. He paid 21s to 'Myddelton of Kymbulton, carpenter' towards the repair of the roof and 20s was paid for 'tymber delyveryd by the sayd Olyver'. He also paid 'to the sawyers for sawyng of the same tymber, 20 shillings'. The Commissioners, having received the bill, then proceeded to carry out their Inventory.

'[This inventory] indentyd [made the] xxviij day of Julij 1552, between Robert Tyrwhyt, Thomas Audeley, Thomas Cotton, William Laurence, Robert Rowley; Roger Harrison, Thomas Barrons [Barrowes] and Thomas Peyt. churche wardyns of all mannour goodes and ornamentes &c.'

The Commissioners made a substantial haul in the church including altar cloths, 'olde towyls', a cross of copper, a canopy, a 'crosse clothe of greyn seylk', four candlesticks and various items of clerical regalia. The Commissioners noted the existence 'in the stepull iiij belles', but removing four weighty bells from the tower for melting down would have involved strenuous effort and costly labour so they were reprieved.

Their work 'in thys churche of Myche Stowghton' completed, the Commissioners signed their names on the document and left the churchwardens with the responsibility of selling off what remained. The three churchwardens duly set about selling the church property, which included 'three olde candellstickes' and did so 'with th' assent of all the parochineres'. The proceeds were duly allocated to the 'necessarie repaires of ther churche'.

A year after the Inventory, tuberculosis brought the reign of Edward VI to an end and he was succeeded by a monarch with very different ideas about the church and religion. In her short reign (1553–1558) Mary I, daughter of Henry and Catherine of Aragon, lost no time in reversing all of Edward's policies and restoring the primacy of the Catholic church in England, which led to her being nicknamed Bloody Mary for her ruthless policy of executing Protestant martyrs. The austere Protestant John Foxe, in his *Book of Martyrs*, made plain his dismay at this religious volte-face: 'the gospel and true religion were banished, and the Antichrist of Rome, with his superstition and idolatry, introduced'.

This may at first have caused a frisson of alarm to Oliver Leder but his forthrightness may now have come to his aid. The accession of Mary coincided with Oliver Leder and Lawrence Taylard being elected again as Members of Parliament for Huntingdonshire. Mary and her ministers were not slow in compiling a list of members who were noted, ominously, as having 'stood for the true religion', namely Edward VI's Protestantism. The list did not include either Leder or Taylard, indicating that the queen and her ministers were prepared to accept that Leder and Taylard were most definitely not of a venomous Protestant stripe. A year after the accession of Mary, in 1554, Leder was rewarded firstly with his appointment as sheriff for the second time, and a year later, on 2 February 1555, he received a knighthood from Mary's consort, King Philip of Spain, testimony to the esteem in which he was held by both royalty and parliament.

His acceptance of the religious and political realities of Mary's England did not prevent Oliver Leder from following his own path when it accorded with his principles. There was the case of a well-known local Protestant, by name Thomas Mountain, a fervent supporter of Edward's evangelism – he had been cast into gaol on the serious charge of heresy in this now Catholic land. Leder graciously entertained Mountain, presumably at his residence in Place House, prior to discharging his responsibilities

'Pray For the Good Astate of Olyver Leder'

20 Mary I

as sheriff for the shire in conducting his prisoner to Cambridge to face his judges. Upon arrival, Leder had to apologise to the judges as he had unfortunately forgotten to bring with him the writ that laid out the charges against Thomas Mountain, who was promptly released from custody.

Sir Oliver Leder died at his estate in Great Staughton in 1557, to be followed a few months later by his wife of over thirty years, Frances, née Baldwin. The Leders are remembered to this day in the church of St Andrew. At the west end of the nave is an oak screen, inscribed 'Of your Charyte Pray For The Good Astate Of Olyver Leder and frances hys Wyfe, Anno Domini 1539.'

21 Oliver Leder inscription

Sir Oliver Leder's will, drawn up on 21 September 1554, is a touching document. He asked his wife to execute his numerous charitable bequests, with the rider that 'not for that I do trust to my works, as some prating preachers have lately borne us in hand'. He left all his estates to her. In a heartfelt tribute to Frances, he wrote: 'being very sorry that for her wise and womanly governance and most loving and honest behaviour ... I have not ten times so much to give unto her'. Oliver Leder also provided generously for three nieces, but his nephew was not quite so fortunate, Leder describing him as 'a very unthrifty lad ... of a lewd life', who had already cost him 200 marks, presumably to bail him out of trouble with the law.

Sir Oliver Leder was buried in Great Staughton churchyard on 6 March 1557. His wife Frances also died in that year before her husband's will was proved and the substantial estates went to her uncle Thomas Baldwin, who lost no time in selling them, in July 1558, to Sir James Dyer and his wife Margaret. With the arrival of Sir James Dyer, the Lord Chief Justice of the Common Pleas, another chapter was about to open in the history of Great Staughton.

10

'… that famous and most reverend judge …'

Thus, Sir Edward Coke (1552 – 1634), England's celebrated seventeenth-century jurist, paid fulsome tribute to Sir James Dyer, one of his predecessors as Lord Chief Justice of the Common Pleas. There is a more visible testament to the fame and reputation of Sir James and it is to be found in St Andrew's Church in Great Staughton. The impressive double monument next to the altar, erected some twenty years after his death, shows him appropriately clad in his coif of office, kneeling in an attitude of prayer and facing his wife, Margaret. To the right is his great-nephew and heir Sir Richard Dyer, gentleman to the privy chamber of James I, and his wife Marie. The inscription above the monument reads in part: 'Here lieth Sir James Deyer, Knight, sometime Lord Chief Justice of the Common Pleas — and Dame Margaret, his wife: which Dame Margaret was here interr'd the six and twentieth day of August, 1560, and the said Sir James, upon the five and twentieth of March, 1582.' A florid Latin verse eulogises his fame.

Coke was not alone in praising the life and achievements of James Dyer. George Whetstone was a prolific minor poet, biographer and sometime soldier whose tenuous claim to fame rests upon the alleged resemblance of his epic play *The right excellent and famous Historye of Promos and Cassandra: devided into two Commicall Discourses*, to the plot of Shakespeare's *Measure for Measure*. Shortly after Sir James Dyer died in March 1582, Whetstone was moved to write a eulogy in praise of this eminent officer of the law. This

22 The Dyer Monument

was no routine obituary, which might be penned on the passing of a prominent figure, but a tribute, born of respect and admiration for the reputation and personal qualities of a man who had occupied, for over twenty years, the highest legal position in the land. Whetstone's lament, written entirely in verse and dated 17 May 1582, was entitled, *A remembraunce of the precious vertues of the Right Honourable and Reverend Judge, Sir James Dier, who disseased at great Staughton, the 24th of Marche, 1582.* The poet praises Dyer's honest character, integrity and professional competence:

> The deapth of law he searcht with painefull toyle
> Not cunning quirks, the simple man to spoyle

Who was James Dyer and what prompted this outpouring of praise and respect? James Dyer (his name is also spelt Deyer or Dier) was born c. 1510 in Wincanton, Somerset, to Sir Richard Dyer of Roundhill and Wincanton and his wife Lady Elizabeth, from a long-established and well-connected family. Dyer was

'...that famous and most reverend judge...'

educated first at Broadgates Hall Oxford (now Pembroke College) and later at the Strand Inn, Middle Temple.

James Dyer's life spanned four very different reigns (five, if Lady Jane Grey is included): Henry VIII, Edward VI, Mary I and Elizabeth I. Like Oliver Leder, his Great Staughton near contemporary and neighbour, Dyer, in common with many who rose to prominence during this stormy decade, had to tread a very careful path between the religious and political factions that dominated English society from Edward VI's accession to the throne in 1547 until Elizabeth restored some semblance of harmony and stability to the country when she began her long reign in 1558.

23 Edward VI

Dyer's beginnings in 1536, when he was practising at the King's Bench, were not auspicious: he was described as 'not very rapid for both his parts and acquirements are said to have been more solid than brilliant'. Nonetheless, Dyer was able to cultivate useful contacts amongst the established figures of the time, including Sir William Fitzwilliam, Earl of Southampton, who left him a legacy in 1542. It was in this year that Dyer began writing reports on the cases in which he was involved. Dyer's reports gave rise to the principle that obliges judges to respect a legal precedent established by previous court judgements and decisions. Thus was born the law of legal precedents, backbone of English Common Law for over 400 years. The man responsible for establishing this important principle was James Dyer of Great Staughton.

The number of court positions Dyer occupied bears witness to the esteem in which he was held. He was practising at the Middle Temple by 1530 and called to the bar in 1537 in his mid-20s. In 1542 Dyer was elected Member of Parliament for Wells in Somerset. On 9 February 1547 Dyer married Margaret à Barrow, widow of the philologist Sir Thomas Elyot of Long Combe, Oxfordshire and Carlton cum Willingham, Cambridgeshire who had died just eleven months previously. Elyot was the author of *The Boke named the Governour*, a manual instructing the gentry on how to conduct themselves in the exercise of public office, a book that Dyer may well have profitably consulted. This fortunate alliance, which brought land in Cambridgeshire as part of the dowry, undoubtedly moved Dyer further up the social ladder and would later prompt him and his wife to purchase property in Great Staughton. In the subsidy rolls of the county of 1547, he was assessed on lands worth £200 a year. In that same year he was appointed Justice of the Peace for Cambridgeshire.

Henry VIII died in 1547 and was succeeded by his nine-year-old son Edward. This must have been an unsettling time for Dyer. A new regime was often accompanied by dramatic changes to the status quo. The new king outlined his aim of having a Parliament 'composed of men endowed with good and great abilities to consult with him on the pressing affairs and difficulties of his kingdom'. He wished to surround himself with 'men of learning and wisdom' to ensure that 'this assembly [would be] of the most choicest men in our realm for advice and counsel'. James Dyer became one of the 'most choicest men' around the king.

Dyer found himself caught up in Edward's machinations to ensure that his doctrinal legacy was preserved. His success at navigating the political crises between 1552 and 1557, from Protestantism to Protestantism via Catholic orthodoxy, demonstrated both Dyer's diplomatic skills and the high esteem in which his legal prowess was held. Dyer became Autumn Reader at the Middle Temple in 1552, an important and ancient honour. Having delivered the lecture, it was the custom to exchange rings; contrary to tradition, Dyer had the rings engraved with a motto *Plebs sine lege ruit* (Without the law, the people will founder.) In that same year he was appointed Serjeant-at-law, and appointed knight of the shire for Cambridgeshire in 1547 and 1553. In that year he became Speaker of the House of Commons and on 4 March was said to have made 'an ornate oration before the king'. He must have won the respect of the king, for he was knighted in April 1553 in recognition of his legal expertise and for his services as Speaker of the House of Commons. On 21 June 1553, a month before his death, Edward signed his will, known as the *Letters Patent*, the intention of which was to prevent the accession of the Catholic Mary. Dyer was invited to be a signatory of the *Letters Patent*. It must have given him pause for thought, for he was in effect endorsing Edward's Protestant doctrine. Edward VI died on 6 July 1553 and was succeeded (after Lady Jane Grey's brief reign) by his half-sister Mary I and Philip II of Spain.

The Catholic Mary was confronted by the fact that James Dyer, one of her senior legal officers, had signed Edward's *Letters Patent*. The new queen wisely chose the path of magnanimity when she came to review the qualities and competencies of the public servants she had inherited. On 19 October 1553, just months after succeeding to the throne, she appointed Dyer as one of her serjeants and commissioners. In that year he became a member of the Order of the Coif, an elite group of senior lawyers, never more than ten in number, drawn from the four great Inns of Court, who alone had the right to be appointed Justice of the Common Pleas. As a symbol of their office, they wore a coif, a cowl or hood, which exposed only the face.

Dyer's crowning achievement as a law officer began on 8 May 1557, when he was raised to the bench of Common Pleas.

On 17 November 1558, Mary died and was replaced by the Protestant Elizabeth. The transition from the Catholicism of Mary to the Protestant Elizabeth did not appear to harm James Dyer's reputation for on 22 January 1559 he was promoted to Chief Justice of the Common Pleas, a position he was to hold for over two decades. The Court of Common Pleas was established to examine civil actions, mostly involving property disputes and other civil matters and during Dyer's time, it was an exceptionally busy place. The reports, summaries of previous historical cases that Dyer had been compiling for over twenty years, were now used by him in his new position. Dyer's collected law reports, numbering over 1,000 entries and going back to 1513, were published in a single volume in 1585 and reprinted in 1592, 1601, 1621 and 1672.

Three attributes that characterised Dyer's conduct in his cases were integrity, impartiality and a commitment to law and justice. One example of how Dyer made use of his reports is in a lurid murder case that took place in Easter Term 1574. The facts of the case were straightforward. A wife conspired with her servant to have her husband murdered. To provide herself with an alibi, she specified the time and date at which the crime was to be committed. At this point, Dyer consulted his reports and discovered the case of Saunders and Browne of London. Mrs Saunders solicited a stranger, Browne, to murder her husband. The judge in that case found that such a 'third party murder' was 'petty treason, notwithstanding the wife was not present, by the

'...that famous and most reverend judge...'

opinion of diverse Justices'. In the record of the trial, Dyer appended a marginal note, stating: 'A wife conspiring with a servant to kill her husband, though he be killed in her absence by the servant, is guilty of petit treason. Sicus of such as (i.e. similar to) conspiring with a stranger.' Dyer used the Saunders' precedent to find the accused guilty of murder.

24 Sir James Dyer: a man 'of a handsome reverend and venerable countenance and personage'

A case brought before Dyer at the Warwick Assizes, also in 1574, demonstrated his punctilious impartiality in interpreting the law. He 'ruled by laws and listned not to arte', as George Whetstone wrote. A poor widow alleged that a rich knight of the shire, Sir John Conway, in collusion with local magistrates, had conspired to evict her illegally for non-payment of rent. The widow successfully brought an act for trespass against the knight. Sir John, aided by a body of armed men, subsequently resisted the sheriff's attempts to uphold the law in favour of the widow, causing a riot in the process. The magistrates, presumably cowed by the power and wealth of Sir John Conway, failed to deal with the riot. Disregarding the high status and influence of the knight of the shire, Sir James Dyer lambasted the magistrates for dereliction of their legal duties in supporting someone of their own class rather than upholding the law. He then personally drew up the bills of indictment against several of them because the widow had neither the resources nor the legal knowledge to do so. The magistrates did not take this lying down but reported Dyer to the Privy Council. This august body wasted no time in rebutting these charges and duly punished the author of the attack 'that depraved the good judge Sir James Dyer'. The widow won her case.

In 1558, the year that Dyer was promoted to the Queen's Bench, saw him purchase Place House from the estate of Sir Oliver Leder. The chief messuage also included substantial land holdings, including parks, cottages and houses and 100 acres of pasture. Two years later, in 1560, Dyer's wife Margaret died and was buried in Great Staughton.

Dyer began buying land elsewhere in Huntingdonshire and further afield in Kent and Leicestershire. More ambitiously, in 1562 he purchased the Earl of Westmorland's mansion house near St Bartholomew's Hospital in the parish of St Sepulchre, London.

In early 1582 Dyer fell ill. Just before his death, a curious incident occurred. A Northamptonshire man had made some foolish remarks about him and was sentenced to lose both ears, pay a heavy fine and remain in the Fleet prison until he had obtained Dyer's forgiveness. Demonstrating a magnanimity of spirit, Dyer duly forgave the man.

'…that famous and most reverend judge…'

On 13 March the Chief Justice of the Common Pleas made his last will and testament. Sir James died on 24 March 1582 at Place House in Great Staughton and was buried in the churchyard of St Andrew's Church next to his wife Margaret. The entry in the Great Staughton parish registers reads: Burials, March 25 1582 Dyer James Chief Justice of the Bench.

He directed in his will 'that a grave stone be layde uppon her corps and myne there withe oure names and stiles to be engraven with the daies and tymes of our deathes'. The Dyers had no children.

Queen Elizabeth received 'my ring with a diamond' for 'the great goodness and benefits which she hath freely bestowed on me since her coming to the crown'. To his 'singular good lord' the Earl of Leicester, Dyer left his 'best stoned horse or £20 in money', whilst his 'very good friend and neighbour' the Bishop of Lincoln was left a gilt cup. His mansion, Place House, and his estate, descended to Sir Richard Dyer, his great-nephew.

Sir Edward Coke, Dyer's younger contemporary, author of *The Institutes of the Lawes of England* and one of Dyer's successors as Chief Justice of the Common Pleas, was lavish in his praise of the fame and reputation of Sir James. He wrote: 'A judge of profound knowledge and judgment in the laws of the land, and … of great piety and sincerity, who in his heart abhorred all corruption and deceit; of a bountiful and generous disposition … and of a fine, reverend and venerable countenance and personage.'

11

George Wauton's 'trayned band' and the Armada

For twelve days from late July to early August 1588, England found itself facing its greatest military peril since 1066, in the formidable shape of the Grande y Felicísima Armada, the 'Great and Most Fortunate Navy'. This mighty invasion fleet consisted of 125 galleons, 16,000 soldiers and 7,000 sailors under the command of the Duke of Medina Sidonia. By contrast, England's defences were patchy, dependent on 'trayned bands' comprising yeomen and tradesmen, ordinary citizens, often 'of the meaner sorte', and cavalry made up of the local gentry. In Huntingdonshire, there were two such 'trayned bands'. One was led by the scion of the Cromwell family, Sir Oliver Cromwell, uncle of the Protector. The other had as its captain George Wauton of Cretingsbury Manor, Great Staughton. It was destined to be Wauton's finest hour and his achievements are commemorated by an elaborate tomb in the church of St Andrew, paid for by his great friend and comrade-in-arms, Sir Oliver Cromwell.

George Wauton was born in 1534, the son of Thomas and Elizabeth Wauton; his forebears included John Waweton and his buccaneering son Thomas. When George Wauton's father Thomas died in 1555, the 21-year-old George inherited the Manor of Staughton. He was educated at Trinity College, Cambridge, leaving without taking a degree, a common occurrence for those not intending a career in the church. George Wauton made his first, undistinguished entry in the history books in 1562, when as a callow, naïve young man, 'void of learning and knowledge in the common affairs of the world' he came close to losing his and his family's inheritance, the Manor of Cretingsbury, when the 'crafty and subtyll' Thomas Beverley almost persuaded the young Wauton to part with it. Wauton managed to extricate himself but was obliged to grant Beverley a 21-year lease of the manor. It was poor deal, Wauton's share of the bargain being '£50 in hand, 2 nags worth 5 marks and a lute worth 5 shillings'. Beverley's descendants would emerge a century later from historical obscurity to rebuild Gaynes Hall.

If this transaction was a blow to Wauton's self-esteem, not to mention his finances, he did not appear to show it and he quickly recovered, developing business and personal relationships with some of the powerful political figures of Huntingdonshire. When he had property difficulties again in 1582, Wauton was an older and much wiser man. The cause on this occasion was a property Wauton had leased to Sir James Dyer and subsequently, on the distinguished judge's death in that year, to his heir Richard, 'a gentleman of the royal chamber' of James I. According to court proceedings instituted by Richard Dyer, George Wauton had forcibly entered Dyer's principal dwelling, Place House, and in so doing had damaged the conduit and watercourse, which George's mother Elizabeth had, in the words of the court documents, 'suffered the late Sir James Dyer to quietly hold'.

Wauton made slow but steady progress up the Huntingdonshire political hierarchy. His political ambitions were indubitably helped by his close friendship with Oliver (later Sir Oliver) Cromwell. Oliver was the son of Sir Henry Cromwell, 'the Golden Knight', so called because of his habit of distributing gold coinage to the populace as he passed by in his carriage. Sir Henry was unsurprisingly a popular figure in the county. He had several children, one of whom was Oliver, who became the *amicus optimus* (very dear friend) of George Wauton.

George Wauton's 'trayned band' and the Armada

From 1583 to 1587 Wauton served as a Justice of the Peace and in 1586 was returned as Member of Parliament for Huntingdonshire. His one contribution of note was a complaint he made against a certain Mr Wingfield, who, according to Wauton's own testimony, had offered 'to draw his weapon upon him and gave evil language'. This was Edward Wingfield, who lived three miles away in Kimbolton, a fellow knight of the shire whose father had contrived to lose the family castle and estates on account of his leading 'a wasteful course of life'. Happily, the relationship was to be repaired little more than two years later, thanks to the King of Spain's decision to attack England.

England was not wholly unprepared for a Spanish invasion. It was known that the Armada had departed from Lisbon on 28 May 1588 and was heading for the English Channel. Two weeks later, responding to the gravity of the threat facing the country, Elizabeth I issued a proclamation: 'We give our dyrections for the preparing of our Subjects ... to be in redynes and defence against any attempt that might be made against us and our realm'. She called for 'the better sort of gents' to defend the country against the Spanish threat. Elizabeth's call to arms was quickly taken up in every town and village; preparations were rapidly put in place, led by the prominent men in the locality. Huntingdonshire was no exception and Sir Henry Cromwell, the Golden Knight, his son Oliver and George Wauton set to work to mobilise resources, men and weaponry.

Beacons were erected on every prominence, to be lit when the Spanish forces were sighted. With no permanent standing army, the defence of the country rested on 'trayned bands' recruited or conscripted from the ranks of the yeomanry and tradesmen. They were equipped, mostly at their own expense, with a variety of weapons, swords, maces and clubs. These relics of fourteenth-century warfare were increasingly redundant as qualivers, arquebus (early forms of musket) and muskets themselves became commonplace on the battlefield. Lower down

25 Elizabeth I. The portrait painted to celebrate the defeat of the Spanish Armada

the military hierarchy, 'the meaner sorte of gentlemen' responded swiftly and willingly to the call to arms. For mere tenants (copyholders), there was no choice; they were bound by feudal law to serve their lords in time of war, as Sir Henry reminded them in forthright terms: 'There is a statut y doth Compell every Coppiholder ... to serve their Land Lord in person at any tyme of invasion or Rebellion uppon the forfeyture of this Land'. And just in case there be any misunderstanding, he rammed home the point: '[T]hat you are my Coppyholders in my mannor of Ramsey to provid your selves with sufficient warlike furniture ... and to be redy at one howers [hour's] warning'. Signed, 'Yor frynd, H. Cromwell.'

Preparations were often ad hoc and improvised, but England held three significant trump cards that were to be deployed against the would-be invaders. The first was physical: better, faster ships armed with lighter, more effective canon. The other two were beyond human agency: the sea and the weather.

The Marshal of the county was Sir Henry Cromwell of Hinchingbrooke and Ramsey, then fifty years of age and his captains were his son Oliver and George Wauton of Staughton Manor.

On 18 June, when the Armada was sighted in the English Channel, a proclamation was issued to every Lord-Lieutenant by Queen Elizabeth from the 'Cort' at Greenwich: '[W]e have therefore thought mete to wyll and requyre you to call together … the better sort of gents' to meet the threat 'now burst out in upon the seas tending to a proposed conquest'. If Spain should succeed, the 'trew and sincere Religion of Christ' would be overthrown.

The situation was daily becoming more urgent. Lord St John, Lord Lieutenant of Huntingdonshire, requested Sir Henry to 'send me a note how your present bandes are furnished and … also what store of bows and bills Remain in the County'. The High Constables of the County were ordered to supervise the beacons erected on every hill, to be lit 'by men of honest credit' when the hour of need came. Sir Henry wrote instructions to the 'gentlemen of the county', which included George Wauton 'to mete me at the George in Huntingto [sic] on Munday next in the morning betymes being the first of July'. Sir Henry Cromwell wrote personally to George Wauton expressing his gratitude for the exemplary way in which the Staughton man had fulfilled all his commitments to Queen and country by providing the necessary 'trayned bands'. He went on: 'I do heare ye, you and your officers have taken great paynes with those uninstructed shotte [musketeers, &c.] … And so at this time I bid you hartily farewell being desirous of your good company.'

The threat from the Armada was focused on an invasion attempt, which would be concentrated on Tilbury and it was to that town that the 'trayned bands' of Wauton and Cromwell would direct their men. Wauton was appointed captain of the trayned bands covering the Hundreds of Leightonstone and Normancross. It included a number of men from Great Staughton who marched to Tilbury in defence of the realm: John Bullmer and Thomas Money were equipped with pike and arquebuse; Thomas Ibbott (who may have been an antecedent of the Edmund Ibbott who erected the sundial on Staughton Highway fifty years later); John Rogers and William Cosen with qualiver and arquebus; Thomas Burton, John Banker, Robert Lylford with qualiver and sword; William Glover, Francis Smyth and John Anewes with pike, (an 18- to 20-foot-long spear) and sword. Sir Richard Dyer was charged with supplying one 'launce' and two 'light horse'. Amongst the 'private gentlemen of the Courte and yeomen of the better sort, there are John Badwyne (Baldwin) gent, and Owyn Biggs' (a major landowner in Dillington).

George Wauton commanded a troop of 200 trained men, whose weaponry and armour included 100 qualivers, 20 muskets, 80 corsletts (body armour) and four furnished carts to carry provisions and ammunition. His troop also included fifteen highly specialised pyoner (sappers). On 29 June, the Lord-Lieutenant wrote to Cromwell, requesting that Wauton's band be assembled for his inspection. 'I pray you therfore give warning accordingly to Mr. Walton [*sic*] on munday following for his band, and thus till then I Leave further to troble you'. Sir Henry addressed his trayned bands, urging them to remember what was at stake. 'Genttillmen, The cause of o' assembling here this day … Concerneth matter of no small importance, her majesty doth requier at our hands for the defence of our owne Lyves, liberties, wyves, wealth, children & contrey & especially the true Gospell of Christ.' Should Spanish force prevail, he warned, they would 'supplant the devellishe suppersticon of the pope and now are abroad uppon the seas for this purpose'.

News reached Cromwell and Wauton on 24 July 1588 that the Armada had been sighted off Plymouth and they should make haste to Tilbury. 'A perfect muster roll of all such soldiers as were mustered trayned and delivered before the Right Hon. the Lord St John, Lord-Lieutenant of the County of Hunts, Geo. Wanton [*sic*] Esquire, their Captain and Captain Oliver Cromwell the Mustermaster, with all such furniture as belongeth to the seyd souldyers as Pikes, Halberts, Muskattes, and Quallivers the 2 August in the yere of our Lord 1588'. On the same day, 2 August, Sir Henry Cromwell, knight, 'rid toward London with tene Launces, tene Light horse & tenne Carbines to serve her majesty all of his owne'.

The immediate threat from the Armada was swiftly lifted. By 4 August, the more manoeuvrable English ships had repulsed the Spanish fleet. The weather then took a hand, storms driving the Armada to seek shelter off the Isle of Wight. By 5 and 6 August, the worsening weather forced the Spanish to seek refuge from the elements off Calais where the decisive battle took place. Sir Francis Drake launched eight devastating fireships amongst the Spanish fleet causing panic and disrupting the Armada's formation. The wind changed and the Armada escaped to the North Sea and thence returned home via Scotland and Ireland. It is unlikely that Wauton and his band of Staughton brothers were present when, ten days later on 18 August 1588, Elizabeth belatedly addressed the assembled troops in Tilbury. 'I know I have the body of a weak, feeble woman,' the Queen proclaimed, 'but I have the heart and stomach of a king, and of a king of England too.'

Although the Armada had been successfully routed, the threat to the security of the nation and to Elizabeth's throne had not disappeared and in the following year Cromwell wrote to George Wauton asking him to have the infantry of the Hundred of Normancross mustered at Stilton on 18 February and those of Leightonstone at Spaldwick on 19 February 1589. 'I will acquaynt you with the causes which doth urge her majestie thus speedily to put all her forces in a redlines.' Wauton and the other captains were urged 'to take some paynes by continuall practis to attayne the weight and perfect use of your weapons I comytt you all to God'.

The drama of the Armada was the high point of George Wauton's career. Thereafter, he remained on his estate at Great Staughton, occupied with the official positions to which he had been appointed. From February to November 1594, and again in 1604–5, towards the end of his life, he was escheator for Cambridgeshire and Huntingdonshire, responsible for co-opting juries to conduct an *inquisitio post mortem*, carried out on the death of a lord to determine the tax due to the king. The position was potentially a lucrative one, worth at least £20 per annum to the holder. In 1600, George Wauton donated a tenor bell to the church, which still gives good service today; four years later he was knighted by Elizabeth's successor, James I.

George Wauton died on 4 June 1606. His estate included the manor house, a substantial amount of land, three windmills and a dovecote. In his will, dated 18 January 1607 and proved on 14 June, Wauton remembered at least eight household servants, a miller, a shepherd, a brewer and a herd boy, the poor of Great and Little Staughton, Kimbolton and St Neots and the prisoners in Huntingdon gaol. The Parish Register of Burials in St Andrew's Church, Great Staughton, contains this entry: 'Sir G WAUTON was buried the 4th day of the month of June who bequeathed ten pounds to the poor of this parish and by his will ordained that it should thus remain for their use for ever that is manifest in the transcript.'

George Wauton's 'trayned band' and the Armada

26 Tomb of Sir George Wauton

Oliver Cromwell, the executor, his 'honourable good friend', received Wauton's goods, 'to this end and purpose, that hospitality shall be kept in the manor house of Great Staughton ... for the space of three years next after my decease'. Sir Oliver paid for a more lasting testament to their long-standing friendship, which can still be seen today in St Andrew's Church. It is the elaborate tomb decorated with the Wauton coat of arms and bearing an inscription in Latin, which reads in part:

GEORGIUS WAUTON Eques auratus
Egressus ex hac vita quarto nonas Junii
Anno parte salutis millesimo sexcentessimo
Sexto statis sue septuagesimo secundo

Oliverus Cromwell miles de la Bathe
Amicus optimus optimo amico in mutui
Amoris, vereque gratitudinis

GEORGE WAUTON, knight bachelor
Departed this life on the second of June
In the year of our redemption 1606
And of his age seventy-two

This [monument], Oliver Cromwell, Knight of the Bath
A very dear friend to a very dear friend
In token of their mutual affection and in sincere gratitude

George Wauton died without issue and his estate passed to the cousin of his grandfather, the then twelve-year-old Valentine Wauton who was to acquire a very different national reputation.

12

Valentine Walton: Curriculum Vitae of a Regicide

As one of the fifty-nine signatories of King Charles I's death warrant, Valentine Walton is, unsurprisingly, not one of English history's heroes; indeed, in his home village of Great Staughton, there are no statues or memorial plaques celebrating his life. He was the comrade-in-arms (and brother-in-law) of Oliver Cromwell, the Lord Protector. From the beginning of his political career, when he was imprisoned for non-payment of tax, Valentine Walton was a staunch Parliamentarian who believed that the power of the monarch should be curtailed by elected members of Parliament representing the views of their constituents. As such, he was one of the architects of Europe's first revolution. He was also a regicide, one of the killers of the king.

Valentine Walton was born c. 1592, the son of Nicholas Walton, a member of the lower gentry in Huntingdonshire and at the age of twelve, in 1604, he inherited the Manor of Staughton from his grandfather's cousin, Sir George Wauton. The young Valentine seems to have been a ward of Sir Oliver Cromwell, *amicus optimus* of George Wauton and spent his childhood at the Cromwell's family seat at Hinchingbrooke House in Huntingdon. At the age of twenty-five, in 1617, Valentine Walton married Margaret Cromwell, sister of the future Protector. The marriage registers of St John's Church, Huntingdon recorded the occasion: Anno Domini 1617, Mr Valentyne Walton, and Miss Margarett Cromwell, marry'd the XXth day of June.

Walton's First Steps to Power

When King Charles I needed money to fund the so-called Bishops' Wars in 1639, his solution was to re-introduce a tax known as Ship Money, originally levied for the defence of coastal towns to protect their coastline. To extend the tax to inland areas was considered an affront by many, including Valentine Walton, who was gaoled for refusing to pay the tax, amounting to 2s 6d, a move that burnished his anti-Royalist credentials. In 1640 he was elected Member of Parliament for Huntingdonshire.

Described by one observer as 'a private obscure gentleman' Walton sat together with his brother-in-law on a number of committees, mostly concerned to ensure the preservation of 'the true Reformed Protestant Religion in His Majesty's Dominions established'.

The Affair of the Cambridge Plate

By 1642, with the country moving inexorably towards civil war, King Charles I was in need of money and a useful source of funds was the silver plate held by the Cambridge Colleges, valued at £20,000. Parliament was equally determined to thwart the king's plans and delegated Oliver Cromwell to take the necessary steps to prevent the plate falling into the king's hands. Realising that he would need reinforcements, Cromwell called upon his brother-in-law, Valentine Walton, to raise a militia in Huntingdonshire. Walton encountered stiff resistance from his constituents. A certain John Merrill wrote: 'the town of Huntingdon is so disaffected to Capt. Walton, that when he sent out his warrants to raise 200 of the "train bands" … very few of the train men would come at time.' Mr Heyton, one of the Chief Constables of the county, informed Walton in no uncertain terms that 'he would not obey the Parliament for he had received a warrant from the king'.

Matters came to a head on 15 August 1642 in a skirmish at 'Lowler Hedges, betwixt Cambridge and Huntingdon'. The spectacle attracted a huge band of Cambridge citizens, keen to witness the action. There were marching men, brandishing banners and beating drums, troops of men equipped with musket and pike and a procession of cavalry. Oliver Cromwell commanded 'a disorderly Band of Peasants on Foot'. At his side was Valentine Walton and together they prevented the plate from reaching the king. There were casualties amongst the spectators: Richard Langley, a seventy-six-year-old from Hemingford Grey, prosecuted for being present at the incident, pleaded that his only 'delinquency' was being a spectator as the two sides fought over the spoils.

Outbreak of the First Civil War
The first major battle of the Civil War was fought at Edgehill on 23 October 1642. Captain Walton, in command of a troop of horse, arrived too late to play any significant role in what turned out to be an inconclusive engagement. However, he had the misfortune to be captured by Royalist forces and was imprisoned in Oxford (a Royalist stronghold) in the care of the Master of Balliol College, Thomas Laurence. Walton was forced to endure his Oxford sojourn until July 1643, when the House of Commons *Journal* reported: '8 Julii, 1643, Exchange of Prisoners … That my Lord General shall be desired to exchange Sir Tho. Lunsford, Colonel, Prisoner in Warwick Castle, for Captain Walton, Prisoner at Oxon.'

Battle of King's Lynn
In September 1643, Captain Walton informed Parliament of Royalist plans to capture King's Lynn and Crowland. The enemy, he reported, had 'an eye especially on the Isle of Ely'. This would have been disturbing news for Oliver Cromwell who had moved to Ely with his family in 1631. King's Lynn was a key strategic port, a vital supply route for food, weapons and ammunition and it was situated on the high road that connected it directly with London. It was a prime target for both Royalists and

Parliamentarians. Although the town was held by Parliamentary forces, danger threatened from within from the considerable local sympathy for the Royalist cause. Walton began to organise the town's defences 'in putting the Isle of Elye — the south part — into a posture of defence, caused breastworks to be made upon other places, and all great boats upon the fresh rivers'. Leading the Royalist faction in the town was Sir Hamon l'Estrange and in August they seized the now strongly defended port.

Captain Walton, Governor of King's Lynn

The Parliamentarians could not afford to ignore the threat of not only King's Lynn but much of East Anglia falling to Royalist forces. A large force of 5,000 men, under the command of Edward Montagu, earl of Manchester, Walton's neighbour in Kimbolton and Oliver Cromwell himself was despatched to quell the insurgency and retake the town. Brute force, rather than a lengthy siege, was the Parliamentarians' decided course of action. The bombardment by the Parliamentarian canons caused immediate panic amongst the population. Rev. Hinson, delivering his sermon in St Margaret's Church, was rudely interrupted by a canon shot crashing through the window; his congregation 'departed in a most confused manner … some leaving their hats, some their books, and some their scarves'.

The Parliamentarians drew up their Horse and Foot regiment in the meadows before the town, then, 'with beating drums and sounding trumpets, as if we had been presently to march into the town', Colonel Russell, leading, with Captain Walton in the rear, marched on foot to the East Gate and forced their way into the town, to a subdued reception from townspeople, fearful of what might ensue. The siege of King's Lynn finally ended on 16 September, but the newly promoted Colonel Walton found himself being accused of embezzling £300 allocated for the town's defences. Nevertheless, he became governor of the town and numerous official documents record his efficient management of the financial and material needs of this vital port. The documents all bear his signature: Valentine Walton.

Death of Walton's Son
The battle of Marston Moor, on 2 July 1644, was one of the bloodiest engagements in the whole of the Civil War. It was described by Thomas Carlyle in his biography of Cromwell, as 'the most enormous hurly-burly, of fire and smoke … the end of which … was four thousand one hundred and fifty bodies to be buried'. Amongst the many fallen was Valentine Walton, the son of Colonel Walton.

His death prompted the famous consolatory letter from Oliver Cromwell to his brother-in-law, simultaneously reporting on the triumphant God-inspired outcome of the battle and breaking the news of the 20-year-old Walton's death. Cromwell had lost his own son Oliver (though not on the battlefield) and this must have been on his mind as he wrote his letter, expressing his heartfelt grief but reminding his brother-in-law that his son's death was for the greater glory of the Puritan cause. 'You know my own trials this way … Let this drink up your sorrow; seeing these are not feigned words to comfort you, but the thing is so real and undoubted a truth. Let this public mercy to the Church of God make you forget your private sorrow'. After these consolatory words, Cromwell gets to the heart of the matter; 'Sir, God hath taken away your eldest son by a cannon shot, it brake his leg, we were necessitated to have it cut off, wherof he died … He was a gallant young man, exceeding gracious … he was a precious young man, fit for God. … You have cause to blesse the Lord, he is a glorious saint in heaven, wherein you ought exceedingly to rejoice'. Cromwell's eulogy concluded: 'Let this public mercy to the church of God make you to forget your private sorrow. The Lord be your strength, so prays your truly faithful and loving brother, Oliver Cromwell'.

27 Oliver Cromwell

The letter ends somewhat prosaically: 'My love to your daughter and my cousin Percevall, sister Desbrowe and all friends with you.' Comrades of the fallen soldier duly made their way to Great Staughton to offer their condolences to Valentine's mother on the loss of her son. Two years later, in 1646, Margaret Walton died.

A Threat from Sir Hamon l'Estrange
In December 1644, Colonel Walton had to face another Royalist threat as governor of King's Lynn when Sir Hamon l'Estrange entrusted his highly indebted, feckless son Sir Roger with a bold plot to secure the town for the king. The 'trusty and well-beloved Roger le Strange [*sic*]' managed to win over the king with a foolhardy plan to retake King's Lynn for the Royalists. A fatal flaw

in Roger le Strange's plot was his failure to take into account that he would need money and men to succeed: 'he knew not where to get the men'. The plot was an ignominious failure. Walton's men, disguised as 'poor old seamen' seized the plotters. Roger l'Estrange escaped the gallows thanks to the influence of his father.

The security of King's Lynn was a continuing preoccupation for Parliament. *The House of Commons Journal* recorded: 'Die Lunæ (Monday), 20 Septembris, 1647 Order for £1,500 for the Garrison of King's Lynn. It is this Day Ordered, by the Lords and Commons, That the Treasurers do forthwith pay unto Colonel Valentine Walton, Governor of King's Lynn, or his Assigns, the Sum of Fifteen hundred Pounds, upon Account, towards the present Relief of the said Garison of King's Lynn.'

Army or Parliament?
At the height of the first Civil War, in 1645, Parliament passed the Self-Denying Ordinance, forbidding any member of either House of Parliament from holding a position in the army, and Valentine Walton promptly relinquished his military duties. A fervent supporter of the authority of Parliament, Walton, in common with many republicans, deeply distrusted the increasing power of Cromwell's New Model Army.

The Desperate Flight of the Monarch 1646
By April 1646, things were going badly for the king in the west. Strongholds such as Bristol, Winchester and Basing House had been taken. Royalist forces fell back to Oxford and by the end of the year the king had been soundly defeated in the area and forced to hide out in this, his last redoubt. Flight was the only option and thus it was, that at three o'clock in the morning of 27 April 1646, Charles I, king of England, in the demeaning disguise of a humble servant, prepared to set off on a hair-raising and eventful journey across England to seek the safety of his Scottish allies encamped

at Newark. Parliamentary agents, prominent among them Valentine Walton, having got wind of the king's intention, redoubled their efforts to capture him but the king succeeded in reaching safety. Valentine Walton and the recorder of King's Lynn, Miles Corbet, submitted a laconic account to Parliament of the affair: 'Sir, Since our coming to Lynn we have done what service we were able.' It was not enough; the king had slipped through their fingers.

The 'Battle' of St Neots

It was July 1648 and in St Neots, five miles from Walton's Manor at Cretingsbury, all was not well. The remnants of a Royalist army, led by the Earl of Holland and numbering about 100 men, entered St Neots. Colonel Scroop and his Parliamentary forces, encamped forty miles away in Hertford, quickly marched north to deal with the threat. The ensuing battle was short and, for the Royalists, disastrous. Driven back into the Market Square, the battle, described in contemporary accounts as 'hot', was quickly over. Thus ended St Neots' sole military contribution to the Civil War.

Pride's Purge

On 6 December 1648, Colonel Thomas Pride burst into the House of Commons and forcibly ejected those he arrogantly regarded as not only opponents of the army, but also as rather too keen on seeking peace with the king. Valentine Walton escaped the Purge, possibly because of his closeness to Oliver Cromwell, but the incident may have tested his loyalty to his brother-in-law.

The Second Civil War

A prelude to the outbreak of the second Civil War was a series of uprisings of 'malignants' (Royalist supporters) that took place throughout the eastern counties. There was a violent uprising in Norwich, riots in Colchester and Bury St Edmunds, followed by serious unrest in Thetford. Finance to help quell the insurrection was urgently required and in February and March 1648 Huntingdonshire was to receive 'the monthly sum of Six hundred eighty-seven pounds, three shillings, five pence, three farthings'. On 20 January 1649, the king was brought from Carisbrooke Castle on the Isle of Wight to London to face trial.

'A Wicked Design'

The charges against the king were laid out in 'An Act of the Commons of England assembled in Parliament for erecting a High Court of Justice for trying and judging of Charles Stuart King of England, Jan. 29 1648: That Charles Stuart, ... hath had a wicked Design totally to subvert the antient and fundamental Laws and Liberties of this Nation.' Amongst the Commissioners and Judges appointed to judge the king were Oliver Cromwel [*sic*] and Valentine Wallton [*sic*]. Of the 135 Commissioners appointed, fewer than half were to attend the hearings. One of the most dedicated was Valentine Walton, who attended all but five of the hearings, missing days 12, 17, 18, 19 and 24.

Sentence is Pronounced

On 26 January 1649, Charles I, King of England, was condemned to death by the court. The following day, Walton was present when the death sentence was pronounced. 'That the court being satisfied that he, Charles Stuart, was guilty of the crimes of which he had been accused ... to be put to death by the severing of his head from his body.' The death warrant was 'sealed and subscribed' by fifty-nine of the Commissioners, amongst whom was Valentine Walton. The official record tersely describes the event, unique in English history, of the killing of the lawful king of England: 'his Sacred Majestie was brought unto a Scaffold and there publiquely murthered before the Gates of his owne Royall Pallace'.

Walton's signature is to be found at the foot of the fifth column of the death warrant. Throughout his career, in all the

Great Staughton and its People

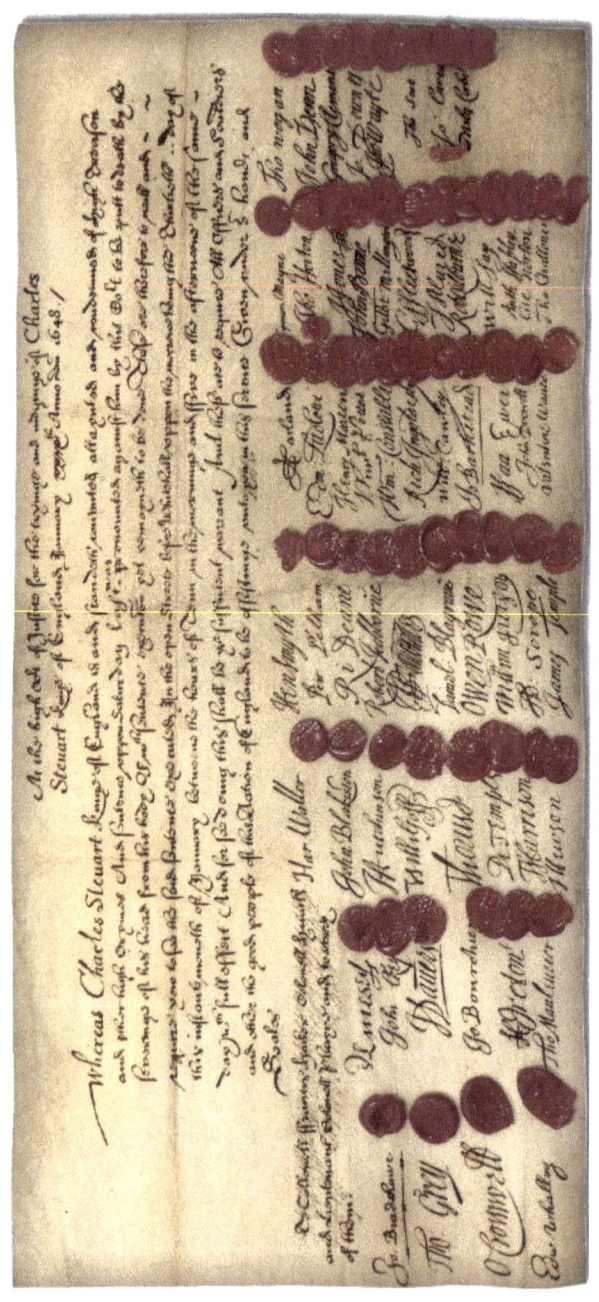

28 *Death warrant of Charles I. Valentine Wauton's signature appears at the foot of column 5*

numerous official documents he had signed or where his presence was recorded, his name was given as Valentine Walton. Exceptionally, on the king's death warrant, he signed himself, in an uncharacteristic scrawl, with the old form of his family name, Valentine Wauton. Did he hope that this modest orthographic subterfuge would shield him from any retribution which might be brought by those still loyal to the monarchy?

The Triumph of Parliament

A month after the execution of the king, other significant constitutional changes were passed in February 1649, when a Council of State was appointed. Valentine Walton was one of thirty-seven councillors convened to the first meeting of the Council of State, chaired by Oliver Cromwell. Under the Commonwealth, Walton served on all five of the Councils of State appointed by Parliament in 1650, 1651 and 1652. In addition, he retained the position of Governor of King's Lynn and Croyland (Crowland).

The Protectorate

On 16 December 1653, Oliver Cromwell dissolved the Rump Parliament and established the Protectorate, proclaiming himself Lord Protector. Valentine Walton grew increasingly uneasy at what he considered Cromwell's assumption of almost regal powers, 'king in all but name' and retired from public life for five years. He found a more profitable use of his time in the marshlands of the Fens, familiar to him from his time in Kings Lynn.

Valentine Walton, 'adventurer'

As early as 1650, Walton was turning his attention away from Parliament, focusing instead on a scheme for self-enrichment. A scheme was proposed by William, earl of Bedford, to form a consortium of 'Adventurers' (venture capitalists) whose business mission was 'to drain the Great Levell of the Fennes'. On 29 September 1656, Walton, along with some thirty other petitioners, made a claim before the Commissioners for 'dreyning of the Great Levell of the Fennes, extending itself into the counties of Northants, Norfolk, Suffolk, Lincoln, Cambs, and Hunts'. The Commissioners found in favour of the applicants and Valentine Walton Esq. became the legitimate (and profitable) 'owner of 500 acres' of newly drained fens.

The End of a Political Career

In September 1658, Lord Protector Oliver Cromwell died and was replaced by his son Richard who was unable to control serious discontent amongst the ranks of the army and the internecine squabbles in Parliament's ranks. The Protectorate collapsed, to be replaced by a Committee of Safety, which included Valentine Walton who had resumed his seat in the Rump Parliament. However, Walton found himself caught between a rebellious army and the political manoeuvring of General Monck. Unconvinced that Walton was 'one of us', Monck summarily dismissed him from command, thus bringing to an abrupt end Valentine Walton's political career.

The Restoration of Charles II

King Charles II returned from exile in Holland, on 25 May 1660. He entered London on 29 May 1660, his thirtieth birthday and was crowned at Westminster Abbey a year later on 23 April 1661. Almost his first move was to instruct Parliament to bring an Act into force 'for the Attainder of severall persons guilty of the horrid Murther of his late Sacred Majestie King Charles the first', committed, in the words of the Act 'by a party of wretched men desperately wicked and hardened in their impietie'. The Act then goes on to name the guilty men: 'And whereas Oliver Cromwell deceased ... Valentine Wauton ... (and some 50 other regicides) ... are notoriously knowne to have beene wicked and active

Valentine Walton: Curriculum Vitae of a Regicide

Instruments in the prosecution and compassing that traiterous Murther of His late Majesty.'

The regicides' lands were to be immediately sequestrated: 'as followeth; viz. Lincolne, Valentine Walton, Manor of Crowland, part of the Manor of Spalding. Huntingdonshire, Five manors of Somersham, with the parks and chase'. Many of the regicides, including Walton 'shall by vertue of this Act be adjudged to be convicted and attainted of High Treason'. All English ports were to be closely watched so that none of the regicides 'may make Escape beyond the Seas'. Valentine Walton and five others are named specifically.

A Burgess in Hanau
Walton, realising the fate that awaited him, fled 'from Justice, not dareing to abide a Legall Tryall' to Hanau, in the Landgraviate of Hessen-Kassel in Germany. The town was a bustling international centre of trade and commerce and Valentine Walton became a burgess (freeman) of the town, a position that required both money and influence to achieve. However, the Queen of the province was not pleased to learn that her realm was harbouring a regicide and Walton was forced to flee again. He took refuge in Flanders, where he spent the few months left to him 'in the greatest privacy' according to one of Cromwell's biographers, who recorded what he claimed were Walton's final days: 'finding himself ill and at the point of death, he discovered himself, and desired that after his death his relations in England might be acquainted of it'. He sagely concluded that Walton's death was 'probably occasioned by disappointment, anxiety, and dread of a violent and ignominious end'.

The Testimony of an Oxford Antiquarian
A contemporary source gives more details of Walton's end. Anthony Wood (1632–1695), an Oxford antiquary, kept a detailed record of his life and the events around him. His life covered the

entire period of the two Civil Wars to the restoration of Charles II. His *The Life and times of Anthony Wood* gives a graphic and perhaps somewhat fanciful account of the end of Valentine Walton. It begins with a description of the miserable end of Walton's second wife: 'Friscis, daughter of Pym of Brill in com. Bucks, widdow of . . . Austen of Brill, the wife of collonell Valentine Walton the noted regicid, died a little better than in an obscure condition in the house of Anne Lichfeild, a printer's widdow, in Cat Street, 14 Nov. 1662 (of the [small]pox as they say), and was buried in St. Marie's church, Oxford.'

Wood records that he had received a report of Walton's end from a friend of Mrs Walton, before her death in November 1662: 'to save himself from hanging, fled into Flanders or the Low Countries, and having skill in gardning and manuring hired himselfe with a certaine gentleman, there for that imployment; but falling sick and seing his time draw neare, sent for his (master's) wife and told that he had bin a man of fashion etc. and desired that after his death his wife and relations may be acquainted with it, etc'.

Valentine Walton, regicide, died in Flanders, an impoverished gardener. It was claimed that at his death, Walton left behind a now vanished manuscript containing his account of the Civil War including many letters from Cromwell. It was last reported to be in existence in the eighteenth century but is now lost to history. Valentine Walton's estates in Great Staughton, including Cretingsbury, were subsequently sequestrated by the Crown.

13

John Gaule: 'Preacher of the Word at Great Staughton'

In the mid-1640s, a wave of moral hysteria swept with devastating rapidity throughout East Anglia, a stronghold of strict Puritanism and home to the Parliamentary cause. Wherever it manifested itself, it caused panic in some, rejoicing in others. It originated in Manningtree in Essex and over the course of two years, it spread eastwards, reaching as far as Huntingdon, St Neots and Kimbolton and it was only due to one man that it did not blight the village of Great Staughton. The author of this moral panic was Matthew Hopkins, the self-styled Witchfinder General and in the havoc he wreaked, he was ably accompanied by his loyal henchman John Stearne. The only man who possessed the necessary courage, resolve and the intellectual armoury to stand up to this collective madness was the priest-in-charge of the church of St Andrew in the Huntingdonshire village of Great Staughton. His name was John Gaule.

John Gaule was born in Lincolnshire in 1603 or 1604. About his parents and childhood nothing is known. As all men of the cloth were obliged to do at the time, he studied at both Oxford and Cambridge but left in 1623, at the age of twenty, without obtaining a degree. In 1625, he was ordained in Peterborough and employed as chaplain by Robert Bertie, 1st Earl of Lindsey, but his career began to prosper when he was taken on as chaplain to Baptist Hicks, 1st Viscount Campden, in 1629. When Baptist Hicks died in that same year, it was John Gaule who delivered the eulogy and a year later, his sermon was published under the title,

A defiance to death, Being the Funebrious Commemoration of … Viscount Camden. It was through the offices of Lady Campden, the widow of Baptist Hicks, and with the assistance and approval of Valentine Walton, then at the beginning of his political career, that the 29-year-old Gaule became curate of the parish of Great Staughton in 1632 and vicar five years later. On 2 June 1637, Lady Elizabeth, Viscountess Campden, conveyed the advowson of the vicarage to Archbishop Laud who immediately sold it in perpetuity to St John's College Oxford, in whose possession it remains to this day.

From an early age and throughout his life, Gaule was a prolific and industrious author. His interest in witchcraft, magic and astrology had first become apparent on 7 September 1628 when he preached a sermon at St Paul's Cross, entitled, *The practique theorists paneygyrick*. Between 1628 and 1630 he published several collections of what he termed 'votive speculations', the treating of significant episodes in the Bible: *Distractions, or the Holy Madnesse* (1629), *Practique Theories, or Votive Speculations, upon Iesus Christs Prediction, Incarnation, Passion, Resurrection* (1629), *Practique Theories, or Votive Speculations upon Abrahams Entertainment of the three Angels*, &c. (1630).

Until the mid-1630s, with the country riven by religious and political divisions, Gaule was shrewd enough to wear his Royalist sympathies lightly and was grateful for Valentine Walton's influence in gaining his benefice. When, on 3 May 1641, Parliament drew up a Protestation, obliging all citizens to swear an oath of loyalty to the 'true Reformed Protestant Religion, expressed in the Doctrine of the Church of England', it was dutifully signed by John Gaule and the newly elected Member of Parliament for Huntingdonshire, Valentine Walton.

At the time, John Gaule may not have been fulsomely enthusiastic about the Protestation, but if he did have any qualms, he swiftly suppressed them. Gaule's attitude to the religious and political divisions of the time seems to have been equivocal: in the

John Gaule: 'Preacher of the Word at Great Staughton'

1620s he favoured the Royalist cause, but political reality moved him to sympathy for Parliament. In a petition to Parliament during the Civil War, he claimed that he had been imprisoned on Cromwell's orders on a charge that he had declared the war against Charles I unlawful. The general of the army, Edward Whalley, had threatened to have him executed by firing squad, but 'a soldier prevented it'.

Over a period of two years, between 1645 and 1647, a mass witch-hunt occurred in East Anglia, organised by Matthew Hopkins and John Stearne. The two traversed the towns and villages of East Anglia offering to seek out and eliminate people, mainly old women as it turned out, who were thought to be possessed by evil forces in the shape of imps, familiars and devils. In the turmoil of the Civil War, a 'world turned upside down', it was perhaps not surprising that people resorted to superstition and witchcraft to explain the upheaval that was uprooting their lives. After the battle of Edgehill, for example, there were reports of a battle in the sky observed by numerous witnesses. Such was the concern that Charles I sent heralds to check the veracity of the account. There were other signs and wonders. A lake in Leicestershire was said to have turned to blood. Pamphlets describing terrible events were widely read. An example came in 1645, with the appearance of a pamphlet entitled, *Strange and fearfull newes from Plaisto, in the parish of West-Ham, neere Bow, foure miles from London.* The householder, a silk weaver by name Paul Fox, recorded that 'dayly to be seene throwing of stones, bric-bats, oystershels, bread, cutting his worke in peeces, breaking his windowes, stones of fifty wayt coming up the stayers, a sword flying about the roome, books going up and down the house'.

Innocent people were accused of witchcraft and many, mostly women, were put to death. Evidence to substantiate the accusations ranged from the improbable to the grotesque. Trials were hastily convened and even hastier judgements delivered, as a result of which people were hanged, burnt or sacrificed in the

29 Matthew Hopkins, a contemporary woodcut

so-called swimming test. For Hopkins and Stearne, it was an extremely lucrative enterprise. Like many in the population, Hopkins believed that certain women make a satanic pact with the devil, made evident by obvious marks on the body, through which 'familiars' (usually in the form of malignant beasts) and imps do the work of the devil. Evil was everywhere, in the form of witches possessed by the devil and Hopkins was the man to root it out. His prescription was simple: identify the witch, usually a woman, usually of low social status, usually over fifty years of age, often querulous and generally considered objectionable by her neighbours and townsfolk. Examine the woman for signs of satanic infection, take account of circumstantial evidence, gossip and innuendo, bring her to trial and submit her to horrendous treatment to extract a confession. A credulous public applauded and then asked for more.

Thus buoyed by popular acclaim, Hopkins and Stearne proceeded to expand the campaign to the rest of East Anglia. They were well paid for their work; 'his fees were to maintain his company with three horses'. he took 'twenty shillings a town'. In Stowmarket, Hopkin's fee came to £23 (some £3,500 by modern reckoning). Hopkins and Stearne claimed that their work was authorised by Parliament (it was not) and that they had letters of protection, ensuring that they could carry out their activities without interference or fear of molestation.

There were several methods employed to determine the guilt or innocence of a woman accused of witchcraft; most resulted in the death of the unfortunate victim. The most notorious method was the 'swimming test'. Since witches had renounced baptism, water would reject them. The accused was tied to a chair and submerged in the river. If they floated, they were witches and executed. If they sank, and drowned, they were innocent. A typical accusation and trial took place in July 1645. 'A true relation of the araignment of thirty witches at Chensford in Essex, before Judge Coniers, fourteene whereof were hanged on Friday last, July 25, 1645 ... Setting forth the confessions of the principall of them. Also shewing how the divell had carnall copulation with Rebecca West, a young maid.'

From his pulpit in Great Staughton, John Gaule observed the Hopkins phenomenon with increasing alarm. Whilst Gaule was a firm believer in witches and witchcraft, he was convinced that the present madness was driven by superstition and public credulity. His reasoning was that anyone who denied the existence of witches would then go on to deny there was a devil. From there it was an all too easy step to denying there was a God. Gaule was appalled that popular superstition, rather than biblical authority, was driving the witch-hunts. He poured scorn on those who claimed to be able to identify witches by quirks of physical appearance: 'They conclude peremptorily ... that ... every old woman with a wrinkled face, a furr'd brow, a hairy lip, a gobber tooth, a squint eye, a squeaking voyce, or a scolding tongue ... is not only suspected, but pronounced for a witch'.

John Gaule was no ordinary 'preacher of the word' although there are some who assert that he was little more than 'an unlearned and wearisome ranter', but he felt that the moment had come to confront this madness. He had been visiting a woman, Frances Moore, held in St Neots gaol, charged with witchcraft when, to his dismay, he learned that Hopkins was intending to investigate the case.

One Sunday in 1646, John Gaule stepped up to the pulpit in St Andrew's Church and began a lacerating series of sermons denouncing any witch-hunt not supported by biblical authority. He condemned in forthright terms the methods used to extract evidence. He poured scorn on the flimsiness of the so-called evidence. Most of all he condemned the actions of Matthew Hopkins and John Stearne. He was unsparing in his language: Hopkins, he maintained, targeted 'every poore and peevishe old creature'. The proceedings were based entirely on 'ignorance, humour and superstition'. Remarkably, for these times of intense religious fervour, Gaule cast doubt on the infallibility and reliability of the 'confession without fact', a bold move. He asked whether a confession possibly borne out of delusion, or forced under duress, could be admissible. He rejected the tedious stories of 'witches upon broomsticks' and other fantasies conjured up by fevered imaginations, but with an eye to monetary gain.

This was not just a single sermon; for a whole month his astonished congregation found their beliefs in witchcraft being comprehensively undermined and then utterly demolished. Gaule lambasted Hopkins for his excessive methods including his use of

John Gaule: 'Preacher of the Word at Great Staughton'

torture, at that time illegal, for obtaining evidence. It must have taken some nerve. He did not have long to wait for the inevitable response. Hopkins had heard of Gaule's sermons and his intervention with the unfortunate woman in St Neots gaol and on 30 June 1646, an incensed Hopkins wrote a venomous letter to someone, apparently in the parish of Great Staughton, known only by their initial M. N., although the initials match no known name in the Protestation Returns of 1641.

Hopkins stated his intention 'to come to a Towne called Great Staughton to search for evill disposed persons called Witches', braving the attacks of the minister 'farre against us through ignorance'. His visit would be unannounced: 'I intend to give your Towne a Visite suddenly' as he would be in Kimbolton the same week. 'Tenne to one but I will come to your Town first', he boasted but discretion proved more compelling than valour and the face-to-face confrontation with John Gaule did not take place.

Gaule did not let go. In a direct response to Hopkins, he vigorously protested that there were no such 'great enemies' in his parish and in 1646 unleashed the most devastating and withering riposte to Hopkins in a pamphlet entitled, *SELECT Cases of Conscience TOUCHING Witches and Witchcrafts*. So influential was this work that it was consulted half a century later at the time of the Salem witch trials. A prominent Puritan and theologian, John Downame (1571–1652), authorised the publication of Gaule's pamphlet 'finding it to bee very solide and seasonable, I allow it to bee Printed and published'. Gaule dedicated his work to Valentine Wauton [*sic*] Esquire, 'Colonell, and one of the Honorable House of Commons' and 'all the good people of the Parish of Great Staughton'.

In the pamphlet's exposition, Gaule sought to examine, in twelve questions of clinical brevity, whether witches actually existed, why they had turned to sorcery and whether they could be redeemed. He began with a fundamental question: *Whether it*

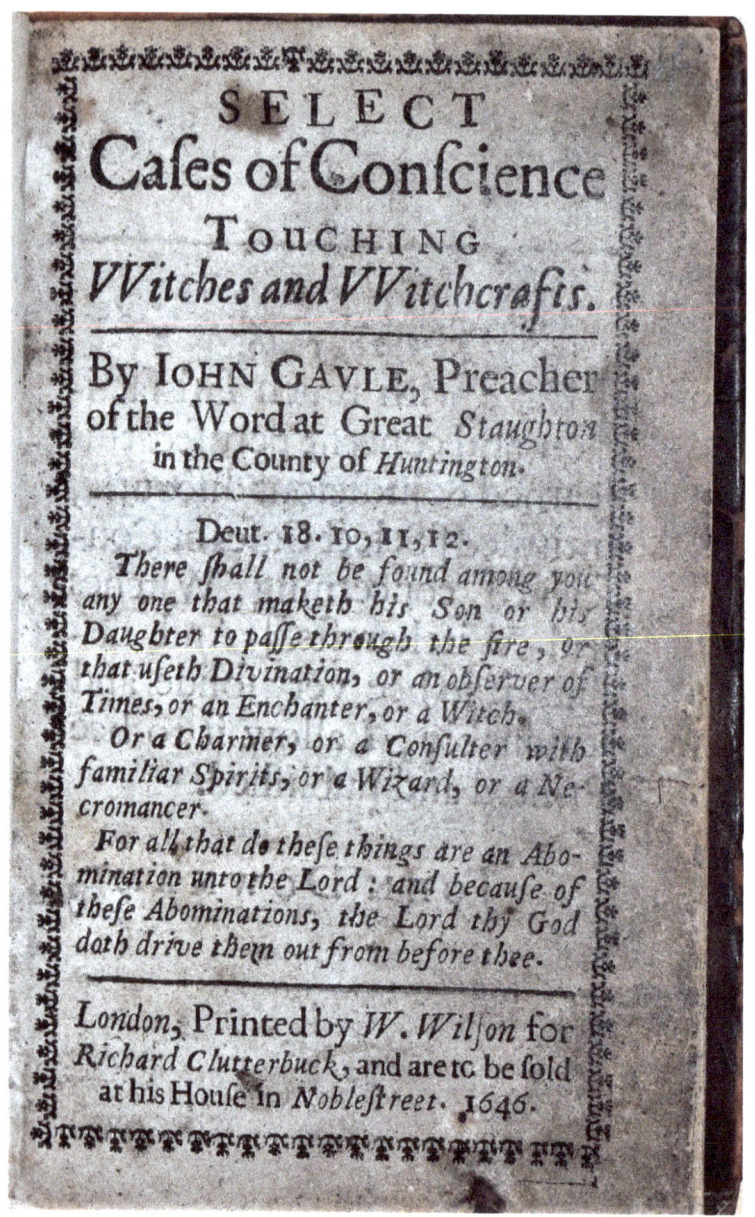

30 John Gaule's pamphlet helped end the Witch Finder General's murderous campaign.

ought to bee beleeved, that there are any Witches? If indeed there were witches, the next question posed by Gaule demanded evidence of their existence: *What are the signes and marks of a Witch, whereby such an one may bee rightly discerned, and so Censured?* With his next question, Gaule was in effect asking Matthew Hopkins to justify his campaign of terror: *Whether Witch-seeking or witch-finding be an Art, Vocation, Profession, Office, Occupation, or Trade of Life, allowable in a Christian Church, or State?* The answer to this question must have been clearly evident to Gaule's readers. The Witchfinder General had made a considerable business out of persecuting largely innocent women as alleged witches. Gaule posed one final question: *Whether a Witch may repent, and so be saved?*

Gaule's pamphlet attracted much favourable publicity and 'queries' began to be raised about Matthew Hopkins and whether he himself was a witch. His reputation was coming under fire and in response he published a self-serving justification for his campaign in *The Discovery of Witches*. The matter came to the attention of Parliament who noted that more witches had been executed as a result of Hopkins' campaign than at any other time in English history. Parliament also noted that Hopkins and his associates were making a tidy living from their activities. A special 'Oyer and Terminer' Commission was set up to 'hear and determine' the consequences of Hopkins' activities. Events overtook the Commission's deliberations. Matthew Hopkins died in 1647, apparently of consumption and was buried in August of that year. The reign of terror he instigated and successfully prosecuted gradually dwindled, although John Stearne continued his campaign for some years afterwards.

The successful campaign against the witch-hunt panic was the very considerable high point of John Gaule's career and thereafter he reverted to his role as priest-in-charge of a rural Huntingdonshire parish although he continued to publish pamphlets and preach sermons. One such, *A Sermon of the Saints judging the World*, was delivered at the Assizes in Huntingdon in 1649, the year of Charles I's execution. By the early 1650s he was very well aware of the political realities shaping the country and in an astute move, in 1652 he dedicated to Oliver Cromwell, then at the height of his power, his book, *Pusmantia, The Mag-Astro-Mancer, or the Magicall-Astrologicall-Diviner, Posed and Puzzled*, an attack on astrology and kindred magical arts, lamenting popular enthusiasm for consulting almanacs rather than the Bible. Gaule fiercely denounced the methods of the astrologers who took advantage of human credulity in an attempt to persuade people that the alignment of stars and planets would somehow predict the future success or otherwise of their children or ensure a prosperous marriage. In the dedication of his book, Gaule praised Cromwell for 'superabounding favours for those sundry favours past', favours he would have no hesitation in regretting less than a decade later when Charles II returned to England to claim the throne.

By 1659, shrewdly realising that England was close to abandoning its republican experiment, Gaule issued a fawning tract, *An admonition moving to moderation*, dedicated to the future king, deploring the excesses of the 1640s and 1650s. In the tract, he attacked all forms of what he now called 'immoderate belief' during the turbulent period of the Civil Wars and the Protectorate. Gaule was motivated by a desire to retain his living in Great Staughton and in this his obsequiousness was successful. Indeed, he was sufficiently emboldened in 1660, at a time when he was demonstrating his Royalist sympathies, to petition the estate of the now disgraced Valentine Walton for arrears on the grounds that the regicide had seized the benefit of his living, which was valued at £400 per annum, over a period of six years. After 1660, the pages of history concerning John Gaule are blank. He died in 1687 and was buried on 10 July of that year. He left three daughters, Elizabeth, Anna and Eleanor.

John Gaule's courageous stand against the prevailing orthodoxy has not gone unremarked in the present day, as is revealed from a surprising source, the engaging antiques dealer Lovejoy: 'Let's hear it for brave John Gaule of Great Staughton village ... a lion. What makes a wimp suddenly heroic? .... He'd fawned and grovelled, bowed and scraped. Until that fateful day when he became a lion. Light a candle to his courage. He deserves it.' Amen to that.

14

'Our Ideal Possession of the Peruvian Treasures'

In the chancel of the church of St Andrew, affixed to the wall opposite the impressive organ is a modest but elegant plaque commemorating Rev. Richard Walter MA. The plaque describes Walter as 'author of the well-known *Voyage Around the World*'. Walter was sometime Fellow of Sidney Sussex College, Cambridge; Chaplain of Portsmouth Dockyard (1745–1785) and Chaplain of HMS *Centurion* in Commodore Anson's Expedition. Richard Walter's account of his voyage around the world with Lord Anson was an immediate bestseller when it was published in 1748, running to four editions in that year alone and attracting several hundred wealthy subscribers.

> A VOYAGE ROUND THE WORLD, in the years 1740–4
> by LORD ANSON, COMPILED
> From Papers and other Materials of the Right Honourable GEORGE Lord ANSON, and published under his Direction, by RICHARD WALTER, M.A., Chaplain of his MAJESTY's Ship *Centurion*.

The years since have done nothing to diminish the book's appeal to the general reader or its influence on later authors of stirring adventures on the high seas. *A Voyage Around the World* turned out to be an epic adventure of fortitude and resolve in the face of ferocious tempests and mountainous seas; of crews ravaged by typhus and scurvy or driven by desperation to mutiny;

and above all the decisive yet compassionate command of Commodore George Anson (1697 – 1762). There were compensations: sojourns in tropical paradises, the discovery of hitherto unknown territories, surprise at the sight of unfamiliar flora and fauna and most enticing of all, the expectation of fabulous riches to be plundered from the Spanish ships transporting silver and treasures from Mexico and Peru to Spain.

Richard Walter was born in 1716 (there is some dispute about the date), the son of a London merchant. It is known that he was admitted to Sidney Sussex College Cambridge at the age of eighteen on 3 July 1735. Three years later he graduated with a BA degree, was elected to a fellowship and ordained deacon by the Bishop of Norwich in June 1740. Quite what inspired this 'puny, weakly man, pale and of low stature' to embark on a perilous voyage around a globe that was beset by England's fiercest enemy, the mighty Spanish empire, is a question to which Walter gave a positive response: 'a voyage round the world promises a species of information of all others the most desirable and interesting, since great part of it is performed in seas with which we are as yet but very imperfectly acquainted'. There was another, more commercial and political purpose; 'if faithfully executed, the more important purposes of navigation, commerce, and national interest may be greatly promoted'. There were other, less virtuous objectives, namely the prospect of plunder, or as Walter put it: 'our golden dreams and our ideal possession of the Peruvian treasures'.

In 1740, the British Admiralty had conceived a grand plan for an expedition around the world that would have three principal objectives: first, to bolster British trade interests in the South Seas; secondly, to disrupt and attack Spanish possessions on the South American trade routes; and thirdly to capture Spanish galleons laden with fabulous quantities of Peruvian silver. The military justification for this 'enterprize' was the war that had broken out with Spain when the unfortunate Captain Jenkins suffered

'Our Ideal Possession of the Peruvian Treasures'

unauthorised surgery to his ear at the hands of Spanish coastguards in what became known as 'The war of Jenkins' ear'.

The 'generous and good-natured' George Anson, a veteran of twenty years' experience, was chosen to lead the expedition. He was appointed Commodore of a fleet of six ships being brought together at Portsmouth. The flagship was HMS *Centurion*, with a crew of 400. The other five ships were *Gloucester* (300 crew), *Severn* and *Pearl*. Smaller were *Wager* and *Tryal*. Two merchant ships called 'pinks', *Anna* and *Industry*, carried provisions and other supplies.

31 George Anson, 1st Baron Anson.

The departure date was to be June 1740 from St Helens (now Spithead). The omens were not good. The 500 fit and capable fighting men who were supposed to crew the ship were actually inmates of the Chelsea hospital 'the most decrepid and miserable objects' pressganged into reluctant service, according to Walter's account. 'Most sixty years of age … or upwards of seventy', he noted gloomily and 'all those who had limbs and strength to walk out of Portsmouth deserted'.

Delayed by bad weather, the fleet did not put to sea until forty days later, on 18 September 1740. The delay meant that the fleet would be forced to navigate the treacherous passage round Cape Horn at the height of the ferocious winter tempests. Their first stop, however, was Madeira, held by England's oldest ally Portugal, where the fleet took on provisions. News came that the French had got wind of the expedition and had alerted the Spanish authorities who duly sent Admiral Pizarro with a squadron of gunships to lie in wait for Anson's fleet. For Walter, this first halt was an opportunity to satisfy his curiosity about the customs, people, flora and fauna of the territory. In Madeira, he enthused over its fine wines and its verdant scenery '[The hinterland] of Fonciale (Funchal)] is … cultivated and interspersed with vineyards: and in the midst of this slope the merchants have fixed their country seats, which help to form a very agreeable prospect.' After a week on the island Anson, mindful of the threat from Admiral Pizzaro, ordered the fleet to depart on 3 November 1740. Pizarro, however, was in no mind to pursue the English fleet. He forecast that the rounding of Cape Horn would, as Walter wrote, 'effectually baffle all our designs'.

The fleet headed for the Isla de Santa Catarina (St Catherine's), a Portuguese outpost off southern Brazil. On 16 November, one of the 'victuallers', *Industry*, requested permission to leave the fleet, having discharged its duties. Even at this early stage of the voyage, the fleet was beset by serious health problems,

'Our Ideal Possession of the Peruvian Treasures'

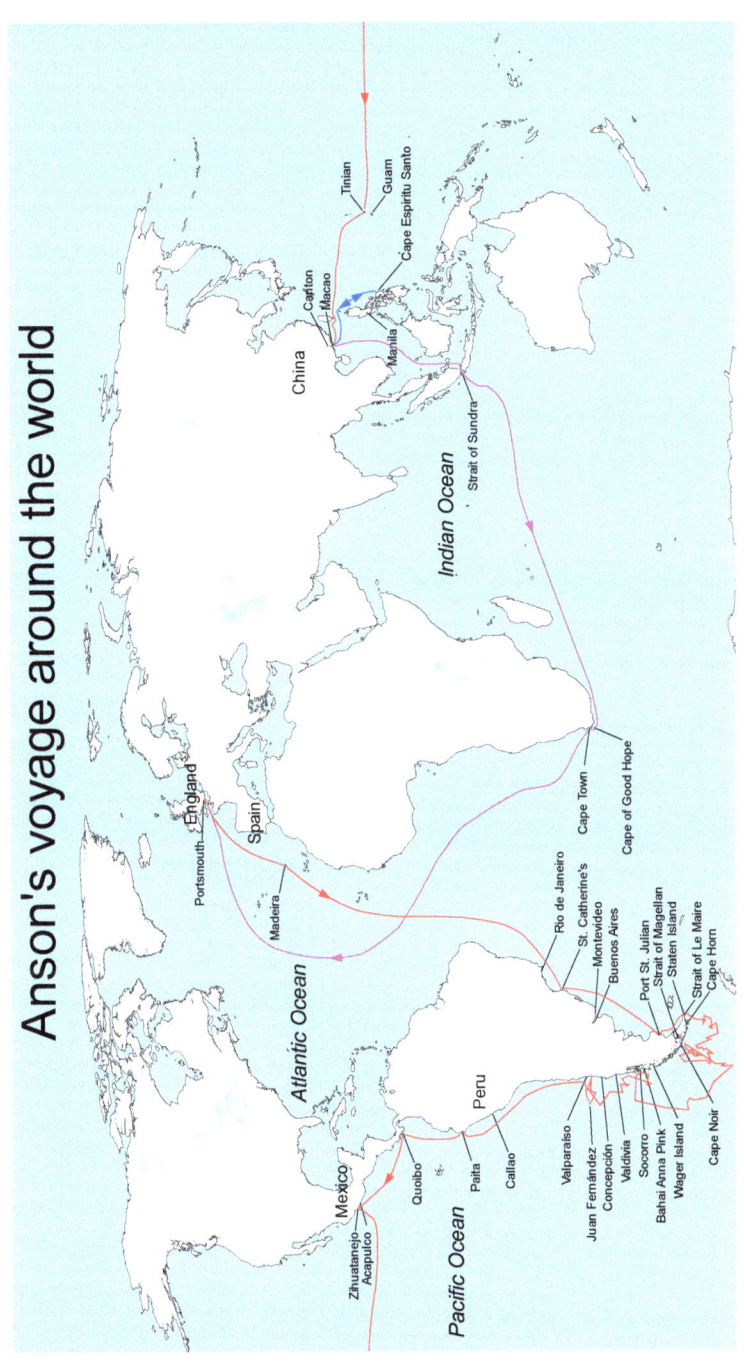

32 *Map of Anson's voyage*

as typhus (ship fever) and dysentery took hold. An infestation of flies and rotting food did not help matters. Walter wondered why all possible remedies were not investigated 'for maintaining a ship's crew in health and vigour'. He went on: 'it is surely obvious that our ships can be kept sweet and clean by a constant supply of fresh air'. It was not, in Walter's view, wilful neglect by the Admiralty, but the result of 'a settled contempt and hatred of all kinds of innovations, especial such as are projected by landmen and persons residing on shore'. It took a further month until 21 December for the fleet to reach the safe haven of St Catherine's Island, where Anson hoped to pick up fresh water and provisions and put the sick ashore for treatment (there were eighty sick crew from *Centurion* alone). There was repair work to be undertaken on the ships; rigging to be overhauled, decks and sides to be caulked, masts to be secured. The ships had to be thoroughly washed and cleaned with vinegar 'for correcting the noisome stench on board, and destroying the vermin'. A month was spent repairing *Tryal*'s broken mast.

Taking advantage of this unexpectedly lengthy sojourn on the island, Walter went off to explore; 'the island is truly luxuriant, producing fruits of many kinds spontaneously. Here is no want of pine-apples, peaches, grapes, oranges, lemons, citrons, melons, apricots, nor plantains ... [and] a great abundance of two other productions ... I mean onions and potatoes.' Fish were plentiful, 'exceeding good, and are easily catched'.

After a month on St Catherine's, the fleet set sail on 18 January 1741 bound for the island of St Julian located at the eastern end of the Straits of Magellan and the last major port of call before the passage around Cape Horn. For Walter, this was 'an hostile, or at best, a desart and inhospitable coast with a boisterous climate'. In a fierce storm, the *Tryal*'s mast again broke and *Gloucester* was forced to take her in tow. When the fleet finally made landfall at Port St Julian on the Patagonian coast on 19 February, it was to discover there was no fresh water and little

'Our Ideal Possession of the Peruvian Treasures'

salt. Once again, much of their time ashore was occupied in repairing the storm-damaged fleet and shortening the mast of the *Tryal*.

Walter again took the opportunity of continuing his engaging travelogue. He noted that the countryside was bare of wood but rich in pasture and quoted the words of a previous traveller to these parts 'he never saw a stick of wood in the country large enough to make the handle of an hatchet'. There were, however, abundant quantities of cattle brought over by the Spanish and Walter was horrified to learn of their brutal treatment at the hands of the horsemen as they brought down and killed the unfortunate beasts. He was, however, much more impressed with the gauchos' use of a piece of equipment, which the English 'generally denominate a lash. ... It is made of a thong of several fathoms in length and very strong, with a running noose at one end of it.' The gaucho is mounted on a horse and, grasping in his right hand the 'thong', which he has carefully coiled, he rides towards the cattle. When they get sufficiently close to the herd, 'they throw their thong at him with such exactness that they never fail of fixing the noose about his horns'. Walter marvelled at the skill involved: the whole process 'performed with a most wonderful and almost incredible dexterity'. Was this the first description of the lasso? One other creature caught his observant eye, which a previous traveller had 'whimsically likened ... to little children standing up in white aprons'. It was a penguin.

The passage around Cape Horn would be perilous and Anson foresaw that the ships might be separated. Should this occur, he ordered that the fleet should set a course for the island of Nuestra Señora del Socorro (now the island of Guamblin) at the southern tip of Chile, and await the rest of the fleet. If, after fourteen days, the fleet had not regrouped, the remaining ships should proceed to the island of Juan Fernandez. If all went well, the fleet should, in accordance with Admiralty instructions, seize the Spanish port of Baldivia (Valdivia) in southern Chile. The fleet left St Julian on 27 February setting a course for 'Streights le Maire' (Straits of Magellan). With 'the brightness of the sky and the serenity of the weather', the crew were in high spirits. With little wind to help them, they reached Cape Virgin Mary on 4 March, the northern boundary to the Streights le Maire. On 6 March they sighted Tierra del Fuego and on the following day they entered the Streights le Maire, passing through this boundary between Atlantic and Pacific without problem. But the earlier optimism of the crew turned out to be misplaced. A violent storm nearly cast the ships onto the rocks of Staten-land and it took all Anson's skill to navigate the fleet to safety. Walter's narrative sounds a sombre note of foreboding: the entire fleet was 'ignorant of the dreadful calamities which were then impending ... ready to break upon us; ignorant that the time drew near when the squadron would be separated never to unite again, and that this day of our passage was the last chearful day that the greatest part of us would ever live to enjoy'.

As if the weather and the raging ocean were not enough, a new horror swept through the crews already ravaged by typhus and dysentery: scurvy. Walter graphically describes the effects on the men 'they have become so feeble that they are unable to make the slightest of movements ... resolved to get out of their hammocks, have died before they could well reach the deck'. Walter recounts the astonishing case of one old man 'wounded above fifty years before at the battle of the Boyne, for though he was cured soon after ... on his being attacked by the scurvy, his wounds, in the progress of his disease, broke out afresh, and appeared as if they had never been healed'. For two weeks, capricious winds, flurries of snow and hail and tumultuous seas prevented the orderly setting of the sails, causing the ships to drift out of control.

Sleep was almost impossible and would often be attended by a deluge of freezing seawater flooding the decks and penetrating the sleeping quarters. A violent storm, almost a hurricane, was followed by a dense fog that enveloped the fleet. The firing of the ship's guns was the only means of communication between the ships. *Wager* and the *Anna pink* both suffered damage to their rigging in the storm and *Gloucester* reported that its mast had been broken in the violent winds. Three days later on 3 April came the storm of all storms, a violent combination of raging seas and venomous winds that continued for three days. Altogether, the storms had lasted for forty days and when the weather abated, the spirits of the men were buoyed by the hope that they were approaching the calmer seas of the Pacific Ocean. Their hopes were to be brutally dashed.

The next disaster to hit the hapless fleet was a navigational error. During the night of 13–14 April, the captain of the *Anna pink* was alarmed to note the steep cliffs of Cap Noir barely two miles distant. According to their charts they should have been proceeding northwards along the coast of Chile, instead of which they now found themselves back where they had started and almost 300 miles off course. Adding to the collective dismay, *Pearl* and *Severn* had not been sighted since 10 April and were presumed lost. Then *Wager* too was lost from sight and there was 'the uncomfortable prospect of ending our days on some desolate coast'.

On 8 May, *Centurion* reached the first proposed rendezvous, Socorro (Guamblin) island. It was not before time, as scurvy was continuing to take its toll of the crew. Nor did the storms abate; the Pacific Ocean was not living up to its name. A ferocious hurricane on 22 May caused such mountainous seas that it was feared the ship would founder, but despite the loss of sails and damage to the masts, *Centurion* struggled through. By the end of May, forty-three sailors had succumbed to scurvy. Anson anchored on the island for two weeks, hoping that the other ships in the fleet would make an appearance but his hopes were not realised. He therefore set sail for the third the agreed rendezvous, the island of Juan Fernandez, deeming a landing and the possible ransacking of Baldivia, amongst potentially hostile forces, too risky.

Anson's troubles continued to multiply. Once again, the Admiralty charts were to prove faulty. They showed the island of Juan Fernandez lying some 150 miles west of Valparaiso in Chile. In fact, the island is located nearly 400 miles west. In attempting to correct this error, Anson ordered the fleet to set a course eastward and the coast of Chile duly came in sight. Realising his error, Anson changed course and headed westward. It took nine days to get back to his original starting point. The nine days delay cost the lives of eighty men, but it also had a fortunate result. The Spanish squadron, alerted to Anson's successful passage around Cape Horn, had redoubled their efforts to find the English fleet but were foiled by Anson's unwitting navigational misjudgement. On 9 June, with a crew of little more than 200 men, *Centurion*, alone amongst the fleet, reached the safety of the island of Juan Fernandez. It was not until several days later that *Tryal* struggled into the harbour. Out of its eighty-six crew, forty-six had died, and only the captain, his lieutenant and three seamen were left standing.

HMS *Centurion* spent three months in the safe haven of Juan Fernandez, a time for recuperation, re-provisioning and burying the dead, an onerous task as an average of six men were dying every day. The disease was slowly stemmed as the sailors' diet was uplifted from rotten meat and stale bread to fresh fruit and vegetables and a steady supply of meat. The other ships were still missing but relief came on 21 June when *Gloucester* was sighted but strong gales prevented her from anchoring for a further month. The casualty rate amongst its crew was horrific: 254 were dead, leaving only ninety-two sickly men to crew the ship. Many of the sick were to perish on the island.

As was now his custom, Walter lost no time in exploring the island, with its excellent climate, lush vegetation, springs and waterfalls. He noted in particular the great variety of vegetables, including 'water-cresses and purslain, with excellent wild sorrel and a vast profusion of turnips and Sicilian radishes'. The terrain was difficult and hilly. One of the sailors, pursuing a goat, lost his footing and was 'dashed to pieces on the rocks below'.

Throughout his narrative, Walter constantly brought out the generous nature and humanity of the Commodore whom he always referred to as Mr Anson. Walter recorded how, to express his gratitude for their safe deliverance, Anson took some seeds and set rows of peach and apricot trees for the benefit of future travellers to the island, which, according to later testimony, were gratefully appreciated years later. The change in the sailors' diet had a significant beneficial effect on their health. Fish were plentiful, 'above all, a black fish which we most esteemed, called by some a chimney-sweeper, in shape resembling a carp'. Seal was a welcome addition, providing fresh meat and the fattest of them 'afforded us a butt of oil'. Walter was particularly impressed by the size and ferocity of the sealion, 'from twelve to twenty feet in length, and from eight to fifteen in circumference', he noted admiringly. Their hearts and tongues made for 'exceeding good eating'. The most famous earlier inhabitant of the island was next to capture Walter's attention: the Scotsman, Alexander Selkirk, allegedly the inspiration for Defoe's *Robinson Crusoe*, who had spent four years on the island forty years previously.

Spirits were lifted on 16 August when, to general astonishment and delight, the victualler *Anna pink* sailed into the harbour, apparently in fine fettle and with a remarkably healthy crew. The ship had become detached from the fleet and as a result of bad weather had found shelter for two months on the island of Inchin (off the southern coast of Chile), where there was an abundance of fruit, vegetables and meat, and plentiful water, thus allowing the crew to recuperate. The *Anna pink* itself, however, was not so fortunate. Upon inspection it was found that she was holed below the water line and incapable of being made seaworthy. Anson ordered her to be destroyed and the crew transferred to *Gloucester*. Three of the ships were now accounted for. What had become of *Severn*, *Pearl* and *Wager*? It was to be several months before Walter learned their fate.

One of the most dramatic episodes of the whole voyage was the fate of *Wager*, which reads like the preliminary sketch for a tale of sea-faring derring-do that a Conrad or an O'Brian might have penned. The severely damaged *Wager* became detached from the squadron off Cap Noir and desperately sought a safe haven. *Wager*'s captain, David Cheap, was seriously ill and confined to his cabin. His decision to head for Socorro, to rendezvous with the rest of the fleet, met with opposition from two of the crew, his lieutenant Robert Baynes and the gunner John Bulkeley, who believed the island of Juan Fernandez would be a more sensible destination. Cheap overruled them. What happened next was a shipwreck, a mutiny and a desperate voyage by fifty-nine of the crew in a makeshift boat piloted by two of the mutineers. They reached Rio de Janeiro four months later on 28 January 1742 and eventually made it back to England. David Cheap and the remainder of his crew were not so fortunate; it was not until 1744 that they managed to reach English shores.

By September 1741, the expedition was one year old and for Anson and Walter it was an appropriate moment to assess the lessons of the voyage thus far. The numbers were staggering. Walter wrote: 'We had buried on board *Centurion*, since our leaving St. Helens, 292, and had now remaining on board 214.' Of the 961 men on board who set out from England, no fewer than '626 were dead before this time'. With only 335 crew remaining, it was impossible to crew *Centurion* let alone the other ships. *Severn* and *Pearl* had abandoned the voyage, setting a course back to Rio de Janeiro, which they eventually reached on 6 June. Six months later, they set sail for England.

At the beginning of the month, a Spanish man-o-war approached HMS *Centurion* believing that the English ship was an escort vessel. Anson ordered the decks to be cleared to give the

'Our Ideal Possession of the Peruvian Treasures'

guns a clear shot at the enemy. The supposed man o' war turned out to be a mere merchantman, the *Nuestra Señora del Monte Carmelo*, commanded by Don Manuel Zamorra. Anson brought *Centurion* alongside and a whiff of grapeshot at the Spaniard's rigging was enough to force the Spanish ship to surrender. The *Carmelo*'s cargo included 'sugar, and great quantities of blue cloth made in the province of Quito [and] some tobacco, which, though strong, was not ill flavoured'. Slightly more interesting was the discovery of 'twenty-three cases of dollars, each weighing upwards of 200 lb. averdupois'. 'The prize', as captured ships were called, was immediately brought under English colours. Perhaps more valuable than the booty was the news that Admiral Pizarro had been forced to return to Rio de Janeiro having suffered the loss of two of the ships in bad weather. With the threat of Pizarro now removed, Anson realised that the chances of capturing a Spanish treasure ship were now greatly enhanced.

Intelligence received from the *Carmelo* indicated that the main channel for the galleons was the sea route between Callao (Lima) and Valparaiso in Chile and Anson therefore despatched *Tryal* on a reconnaissance mission off the coast of Valparaiso. On 19 September, *Centurion*, towing her 'prize' the *Carmelo*, left the island of Juan Fernandez to join *Tryal* in the hunt for plunder. A second 'prize' was swiftly captured, the *Arranzazu*, a Spanish merchantman with a healthy cargo of £5,000 of silver but the cost was high. The *Tryal* was so severely damaged that she had to be scuttled. The *Arranzazu* was duly designated as a frigate in his Majesty's service and became *Tryal II* (or *Tryal's Prize* as Walter named her). The next 'prize' to fall victim to the predatory English fleet was the *Santa Teresa de Jesus* bound from Guayaquil to Callao. The booty was meagre, amounting to no more than £170 worth of silver. The rather more interesting cargo was ten passengers, including three women, one of whom was a 21-year-old 'of singular beauty'. Having been taught that falling into the hands of the enemy would certainly result in brutal treatment from a set of sailors 'who had not seen a woman for near a twelvemonth', the three women took steps to conceal themselves and it was only with the greatest difficulty that they were persuaded to present themselves to their English captors. Walter, keen as ever to show Mr Anson's humanity, noted the captain's order 'that the women should receive no kind of inquietude or molestation whatever' and he instructed the ship's pilot to stay with the women throughout the voyage, as 'their guardian and protector'.

In terms of booty, the area was proving lucrative for Anson's fleet. On 10 November *Centurion* was a few leagues south of the island of Lobos de la Mar where they were to rendezvous with *Gloucester*. A hapless Spanish ship strayed into Anson's net and after a brief struggle yielded to the brute force of the English ship. The prize was *Nuestra Señora del Carmin* laden with 'steel, iron, wax, pepper, cedar, plank, snuff, rosarios, European bale goods, powder-blue, cinnamon, Romish indulgencies', all of which were of little interest to Anson's men. Their possible disappointment at the meagreness of the haul was swiftly assuaged when the value was ascertained as amounting to 400,000 dollars.

Of more value to Anson was the intelligence brought by an Irishman 'and papist', John Williams, lately a visitor to Paita (in north-west Peru) who revealed that the town's treasury was concealed at the custom house. The town was defended by a fort equipped with cannon and run by a small garrison and a raid on Paita would neatly combine two Admiralty objectives, to secure treasure and inflict serious damage to an important Spanish port. Paita was a stopping-off point for ships from Acapulco, Sonsonnate, Realeijo and Panama to take on provisions, notably fresh water, before continuing their passage to Callao. The town's inhabitants, numbering some 200 families, were principally Indians and a small black population.

Unaware that the town treasury had been moved to a secure hide-out, Anson decided to launch a night attack with fifty-eight well-armed men. The 'English dogs' were quickly spotted and the hue and cry raised. Anson's men stormed the town, making as much noise as possible to give the impression that the raiders were several hundred strong. The ruse succeeded and in fifteen minutes it was all over. The governor, fearing for his life, had leapt out of bed half-naked and fled into the hills, leaving his hapless seventeen-year-old bride, whom he had married three days before, to the tender mercies of the invaders, who 'carried [her] off in her shift'.

The crew went through the town, looting whatever they found. Lieutenant Brett was astonished to discover the men draping themselves in women's gowns and petticoats over their own greasy and worn clothing. They 'eagerly seized these glittering habits, and put them on over their own dirty trowsers'. The proceeds of the raid were prodigious despite the bulk of the town treasury having been spirited to safety; wrought plate, dollars and other coin amounted to £30,000 together with jewellery and trinkets whose value could not be calculated. It was the biggest haul of booty that the expedition was to make on that coast. The last act of the English pirates was to set ablaze the entire town, apart from the two churches, a gesture that was possibly a nod to Walter's sensibilities.

On leaving the bay of Paita, Anson's men seized six small Spanish vessels of which all but one, *Solidad*, were scuttled. The *Solidad* became the third prize to be incorporated in Anson's squadron, which now consisted of six ships: *Centurion*, *Tryal II*, *Carmelo*, *Teresa*, *Carmin* and *Solidad*. *Gloucester*, meanwhile, still on patrol off the coast of Valparaiso, had not been idle. She had captured two Spanish ships, one of which seemed to be of no monetary interest until the boarding party noticed that the ship's officers were dining off silver plate. The cargo, mostly cotton, was innocent enough but subsequent delving revealed that the innocent cotton package was hiding £12,000 in silver doubloons, causing the *Gloucester*'s crew to be 'agreeably surprized'.

Amply rewarded though they had been from the capture of Spanish merchant ships, Anson was steadfastly focused on the ultimate prize, the capture of the Manila *galeon*, which was expected to arrive in Acapulco from Manila sometime in January 1742. It was now November 1741 and Anson reasoned that he had more than enough time to intercept the Spanish *galeon*. He urgently needed water and food and on 5 December the fleet sailed north to the island of Quibo, situated at the mouth of the Bay of Panama.

Walter wasted no time in exploring the island. He was amazed by the prodigality of wildlife: huge flights of 'parrots, parroquets and mackaws'. Monkeys and guanos provided a plentiful supply of food. Turtles, weighing up to 200 lbs were stored alive on the ships and were 'generally esteemed … to be the most delicious of all eatables'. Turtle eggs, carefully excavated from the beaches, were an additional delicacy. The dense woodland also concealed a deadly flying snake that fell from the boughs onto its prey, killing it with its deadly poison. What especially fascinated Walter were pearl divers from Panama who stayed under water so long that blood issued from their ears and mouth.

Time was pressing and on 12 December *Gloucester* and her two prizes re-joined the squadron. In a council of war, Anson issued fresh instructions to his captains about the strategy for intercepting the Manila *galeon*. They were to station themselves to the north of Acapulco, patrolling the seas eight to ten leagues from the shore, until 14 February, a little over two months away. From there they were to rendezvous with Anson at the islands of the Tres Marias. Should *Centurion* not be at the appointed place, the rest of the fleet were to steer a course for Macao on the Chinese coast. Once again, the weather intervened. The trade winds, which they confidently expected would speed them to Acapulco, failed. Walter mournfully recorded 'we began at length

'Our Ideal Possession of the Peruvian Treasures'

to despair of succeeding in the great purpose we had in view, that of intercepting the Manila *galeon*'.

In an atmosphere of gloom and despondency, they reached the northern approaches of Acapulco on 26 January 1742, fearing that the great prize had already eluded them. A light was seen and the thought that this was the *galeon* raised spirits but it proved to be a false alarm, the light being a warning beacon on the shore. Even worse news followed. The Admiralty charts proved yet again to be at fault; Acapulco lay 150 miles to the north. Furious, Anson ordered a frantic change of course, fearful that they may literally have missed the boat. Upon finally arriving at Acapulco, they learned that the treasure ship had actually docked on 9 January and was being prepared for the crossing of the Pacific, with its departure set for 3 March. It soon became clear to Anson that the Spanish knew of his arrival and were in no hurry to release a ship full of treasure into the arms of a welcoming English pirate. The supposed day of departure of the Manila *galeon*, 3 March, came and went. Easter Week followed when no labour was permitted. By 15 March despondency was beginning to set in. Finally, news reached Anson that the Governor of the town had postponed the sailing of the treasure galleon until the following year.

Before Anson could change his strategy, he was forced to take on water and provisions at the port of Chequetan in Seguataneo Bay in Mexico. For Walter, it was an irresistible opportunity to put his feet on terra firma after four months at sea. Amongst the varied fauna, it was the torpedo fish that captured his attention. When touched, it imparted a numbness to the limbs. This anaesthetising effect even passed through the walking cane with which Walter prodded an expiring example of the fish.

Realising it was futile to remain off Acapulco, Anson ordered the fleet to steer a south-westerly course to catch the north-east trade winds that would take them across the Pacific to Macau, Canton and China, the route that the Spanish galleons would follow. It took Anson seven agonising weeks to find the usually reliable trade winds. Further disaster followed when *Gloucester*, having suffered irreparable damage to her mast, had to be scuttled and set ablaze. 'Thus perished his Majesty's ship the *Gloucester*', is Walter's laconic journal entry. More distressing still, scurvy reappeared, despite the best efforts of the surgeons and a much-improved diet of fish and fruit. So serious was the situation that recourse was had to 'Mr. Ward's pill and drop', the most notorious quack medicine of the eighteenth century. Mr Ward's 'remedy' proved ineffective; a dozen men were dying of the disease every day.

The fleet's intended destination was the island of Tinian. On 27 August, despite being buffeted by strong winds, they reached the island. The major discovery the indefatigable Walter made on the island of Tinian was bread-fruit or rhymay as it was called by the Indians. When baked it had the taste of bread and potato and it proved popular with the crew. There was also plentiful beef, hogs and poultry. Anson was wracked by scurvy and took to a tent on the island to recover. Their pleasant stay was rudely interrupted by a new drama when a violent storm on 18 September drove *Centurion*, with only a skeleton crew, out to sea, feared lost. After nineteen days of acute despair, *Centurion* managed to struggle back to its anchorage.

It was 21 October before Anson and *Centurion* were able to set sail for Macao. On 3 November the island of Formosa came into view. Two days later, they were within sight of the coast of China and on 9 November, a Chinese pilot offered, for 30 dollars, to guide them into the Portuguese colony of Macao where they anchored on 12 November. Although nominally independent, Macao relied on the goodwill of the Chinese to survive. At first the Chinese authorities were reluctant to accede to Anson's request for provisions. However, the threat of *Centurion*'s array of cannon persuaded the Chinese to alter their stance.

'Our Ideal Possession of the Peruvian Treasures'

Macao was a significant destination for Richard Walter, for it was here that he elected to return to England on one of the ships belonging to the East India Company. He was not alone. Four other officers took the decision to head home. The memorial plaque in St Andrew's Church gives the erroneous impression that Walter circumnavigated the globe with Commodore Anson. He did not. Why he decided to leave when potentially the most thrilling part of the adventure was about to occur, he does not reveal but perhaps two years of tumultuous seas and ferocious storms may have taken its toll on his 'puny, weakly' frame.

On 10 March Anson learned that a large Spanish *galeon* accompanied by two other ships had been sighted off the Grand Ladrone, part of the Mariana group of islands east of the Philippines. The now repaired *Centurion* weighed anchor from Macao on 6 April 1743 with a plentiful supply of provisions and a healthy crew, strengthened by the recruitment of twenty-three lascars. To put inquisitive Spanish man o' wars off the scent, Anson announced at Macao that he was intending to head for Batavia outside the channel normally used by the Spanish treasure ships. So persuasive was Anson that his intention was believed. So when he announced to his assembled crew his plan to capture the large Spanish *galeon*, 'they expressed their approbation, according to naval custom, by three strenuous cheers'.

Anson's true destination was Cape Espiritu Santu where he proposed to lie in wait for the Manila *galeon*. He arrived there on 31 May and immediately ordered the topsails to be taken down to avoid the ships being seen by lookouts on the Cape. The *galeon* was expected in June and Anson's crew were in a state of feverish excitement, eagerly watching every day for the appearance of a Spanish flag that would bring them a fortune beyond their dreaming. The days passed. Anson ordered the men to practise loading and firing the cannons. He selected thirty of his best marksmen, directing them to take up their positions high up on the masts. On into June they waited. 11 June, an empty sea. 19

June, would the *galeon* ever appear? The Spanish themselves were aware of the possible danger and the Governor of Espiritu Santo ordered two gunships to be fitted out, one with thirty-two guns, the second with twenty, and two sloops equipped with ten guns each. This fleet was ordered to make a pre-emptive attack on *Centurion*, but the onset of a monsoon forced them to withdraw to port.

On 20 June, after three weeks of anxious expectation, a sail was sighted. As it drew nearer, eyes were strained to confirm whether it was the *galeon* and whether it had a protective shield of Spanish warships. *Centurion* moved in closer to identify the ship. It was the Manila *galeon* herself, *Nuestra Señora de Covadonga* (Walter calls her *Nostra Signora de Cabadonga*) and she wasted no time in loosing off a threatening salvo from its thirty-six guns. Anson's strategy was to edge closer to the Spanish ship until it was within range of pistol shot, keeping to leeward to prevent the Spanish ship from taking advantage of the wind direction to head for safety in the port of Jalapay, some seven leagues (twenty-five miles) distant.

Gradually Anson manoeuvred *Centurion* abreast of the *galeon*, where he could put the next stage of his strategy into operation. With insufficient crew to man all the guns, Anson organised gangs of ten or twelve men to continuously load the guns whilst two of the crew moved from gun to gun keeping up a constant fire, thus preventing the Spanish, whose tactic was to lie on deck when they saw a broadside being prepared, from resuming their gun positions and re-loading. Meanwhile, Anson's select band of snipers positioned high up on the masts picked off any Spanish officer unfortunate enough to find himself exposed on deck.

As it had done so often, the weather took a hand. A sudden squall of wind and rain just after noon obscured momentarily the *galeon*. When it cleared, *Centurion* had moved closer to the Spanish vessel and at 1 pm, the Spanish crew could be seen hurling overboard cattle and lumber, a task that a brisk fusillade from

'Our Ideal Possession of the Peruvian Treasures'

Centurion's cannons quickly interrupted. Anson manoeuvred *Centurion* to the bow of the Spanish ship, training her guns at the enemy's masts, at the same time preventing the Spanish ship from returning fire. Anson's snipers continued to pick off any remaining officers or crew on the deck of the Spanish vessel. More cannon shot followed from *Centurion*, setting the Spanish ship ablaze. The end was not long in coming. Commodore Anson, sensing that the Spanish were now routed, ordered his men to desist from firing and with that signal, the capture of the *Covadonga* (*Nuestra Señora de Covadonga*) captained by General Don Jeronimo de Montero, was complete.

33 HMS Centurion *captures* Nuestra Señora de Covadonga

It had taken less than two hours to secure a treasure that amounted to a million and a half dollars. Lieutenant Philip Saumerez and ten men were sent over to inspect the damage. It was considerable; they were met by the horrific sight of 'carcasses, entrails and dismembered limbs'. Sixty-seven Spanish sailors had been killed, eighty-four wounded. On HMS *Centurion*, there was one fatality, with two more dying later of their wounds and seventeen injured. When the Spanish prisoners saw the age of the sailors who had captured them, they were outraged to have been defeated by 'a handful of boys'.

On 11 July 1743, with the help of two Chinese pilots, *Centurion* and her prize, the *Nuestra Señora de Covadonga*, came to anchor off the city of Macao. During that long month, Anson had carefully assessed the treasure. It was a vast haul: 1,313,843 pieces of eight, 35,682 ounces of virgin silver, as well as some cochineal and various other unimportant trophies. According to Walter, the value of the haul was around £400,000. The crew of the Spanish ship had managed to destroy other valuables and merchandise with an estimated value of £600,000. When *Nuestra Señora de Covadonga* left the port of Acapulco, it was carrying a treasure valued at in excess of £1,000,000. To his chagrin, Captain Anson learned that there was a second treasure ship, which had left Acapulco much earlier than usual and had he not been delayed in Macao, he could have added further bounty to his already fabulous hoard.

Before he could set sail for England, Anson faced frustrating delays, bureaucratic problems and the machinations of the Chinese authorities who effectively controlled the port. It was not until 10 December 1743 that *Centurion* finally set sail for the last hazardous stage of a journey that had begun nearly four years previously. Two days later in Macao, *Nuestra Señora de Covadonga* was sold for a paltry 6,000 dollars.

HMS *Centurion* reached Cape Town on 11 January 1744, where she remained for three months. When she put to sea again on 3 April 1744, Anson learned that England was at war with France and French naval squadrons were patrolling the Channel. A fortuitous bank of fog allowed *Centurion* to give any inquisitive French ship the slip and thus after three years and nine months at sea, Captain Anson brought what remained of his fleet back into its home harbour, to tumultuous acclaim. The casualty list made grim reading: of the original crew of *Centurion*, *Gloucester*, *Tryal* and *Anna pink*, only 188 survived. Altogether, of the original 1,900 crew of all seven ships, a mere 500 lived to tell the tale to their descendants.

The treasure from the *Covadonga* was paraded through the streets of London, greeted by vast crowds. Anson became a national hero, in the mould of Sir Francis Drake. When the spoils of the voyage were finally distributed, after several acrimonious legal battles, Anson received £91,000. During the nearly four years that the circumnavigation took, Anson's wages amounted to £719. For the crew, the bounty was generous. They each received £300, twenty years' wages for an ordinary seaman. Anson's subsequent career was eventful. From 1751 to 1756, and then again from 1757 to his death in 1762, Anson was First Lord of the Admiralty. He undertook a wholesale reform of the navy, tightening discipline and insisting on uniforms for commissioned officers. It was he who began the process of making the Royal Navy the most powerful naval force in the world.

For Rev. Richard Walter life in England was a much more tranquil affair. In 1744 he obtained his MA and in March 1745 he was appointed Chaplain of Portsmouth Dockyard, a post he held until his death in 1783. On 5 May 1748 he married Jane Sabbarton of St Margaret's, Lothbury, in Gray's Inn chapel and the couple had four children. The plaque in St Andrew's Church records that Richard Walter died on 10 March 1783 at the age of sixty-seven and was buried in this church, the manor at that time belonging to his family. In the same grave rests his wife Jane, who died in December 1813 aged ninety.

Walter's reputation received a severe dent in 1761, when he was seriously ill. It was claimed that *The Voyage Around the World* was actually the work of one Benjamin Robins (1707–1751), a gifted mathematician and scientist and an acknowledged authority on military ballistics. The case for Robins hinges on the inclusion in the narrative of detailed geographical co-ordinates and the lengthy discourse on inconsistencies in world temperature values, scientific skills which were beyond Rev. Walter's competence. Six years after the death of her husband, Jane Walter issued a fierce rebuttal to the claims of Robins: 'During the time of Mr Walter's writing that voyage, he visited me almost daily previous to our marriage and I have frequently heard him say how closely he had been engaged in writing for some hours … as his lordship overlooked every sheet that was written … and I have frequently seen Mr Walter correct the proof-sheets for the printer.' There is one indisputable fact about the *Voyage*: Walter was there, Robins was not.

Richard Walter MA, Chaplain of HMS *Centurion*, gave his own verdict on his stirring voyage: 'That though prudence, intrepidity, and perseverance united are not exempted from the blows of adverse fortune, yet in a long series of transactions they usually rise superior to its power, and in the end rarely fail of proving successful.'

15

The Handasyds, Father and Son

From their impressive memorial tablet in the Gaynes Chapel of St Andrew's Church, it would be tempting to think that the Handasyds, father and son, must have played a prominent role in local history if not on the national stage. However, this would be misleading. The military careers of both Handasyds were dutiful and diligent if scarcely brilliant but the memorial erected to them in the Gaynes Chapel, for which a Perpendicular window in the east wall had to be removed, had the effect of greatly magnifying their posthumous reputations and to the present day, it is one of the largest memorials in the church.

Thomas Handasyd was born c. 1645 in Elsdon, Northumberland. At a time when England did not have a standing army, it was customary for soldiers to hone their battlefield skills in the service of foreign sovereigns. Thomas Handasyd's baptism of fire came during the Franco-Dutch wars of 1672 to 1678, where he served with the Dutch army. He remained in Holland for the next decade; two of his five children were born there between 1687 and 1689.

Handasyd is next heard of following the 'Glorious Revolution' of 1688 when he served in William of Orange's army at the Battle of the Boyne in 1690.

History next hears of Handasyd in March 1694 when he was appointed Major in the 28th (North Gloucestershire) Regiment of Foot raised by Colonel John Gibson. The regiment was ordered to Newfoundland to recapture the fort of St John's, in Canada, taken by the French in June 1696. The fort was of strategic importance as it was close to the cod fishing areas of the Grand

Banks. The regiment arrived at the fort in 1697 to discover that it had been completely abandoned and destroyed by the French. So complete was the destruction that neither food nor provisions were left. Gibson ordered his men to set to work rebuilding and strengthening the fort but without provisions it was impossible to maintain a garrison of several hundred soldiers. Handasyd, 'a good, worthy man, of courage and conduct, who has served the King 24 years' according to a contemporary, successfully accomplished his mission to rebuild the fort, but 'worthy man' though he might have been, he did have to report, on his return to England in 1698, that in the course of the work no fewer than 214 of his men out of a total of 300 had succumbed to illness and malnutrition.

The experience seemed to have done Handasyd's reputation no lasting harm. On 20 June 1702, he was commissioned Colonel of the 22nd Regiment of Foot. The regiment was posted to Jamaica a strategic stronghold and provisioning point for the Navy. Hardly had the regiment arrived on the island when the commanding officer, Colonel William Selwyn, died and Handasyd took over command, and as a function of his rank, he also became de facto Governor of the island. Handasyd was described by the Earl of Peterborough as 'one of the best infantry officers we have'.

Handasyd's reputation continued to grow; in December 1705, he rose to the rank of Brigadier-General, but a fraught relationship with the sugar planters in 1710 led to him requesting to be relieved of his position. In 1711, now promoted to the rank of Major General, he returned to England and purchased the Gaynes Hall estate. In the same year, he passed the colonelcy of the regiment to his son Roger. He died at Gaynes Hall on 29 March 1729 at the age of eighty-five and is buried in the churchyard of St Andrew's Church.

Thomas's son Roger, born in 1689, is said to have been one of the longest-serving officers in the British army. Commissioned at the age of five in 1694, he remained in military service until his death in 1763. Despite this long service Roger Handasyd saw very little battlefield action.

The first decade of the eighteenth century was dominated by 'Queen Anne's Wars', a struggle between Britain and France for the control of the American colonies. In the war, Roger Handasyd served 'with reputation', and his reward was promotion to Lieutenant Colonel of the regiment in 1709 and Colonel in 1712, succeeding his father. Roger Handasyd was appointed Lieutenant-Governor of Fort St Philip, Minorca, a position he occupied for the best part of a decade.

In 1730, he was transferred to the 16th Regiment of Foot and on 9 July, was appointed to the rank of Colonel of the regiment by King George II. Further promotions followed; Brigadier-General in 1735, Major General in 1739, Lieutenant General in 1743. Roger Handasyd saw action in the Jacobite uprising of 1745 when an army under Bonnie Prince Charlie routed the forces of Sir John Cope at the battle of Prestonpans in September of that year. Handasyd, as Commander-in-Chief of English forces in Scotland, led a force that successfully occupied Edinburgh where he assumed the office of Governor. Handasyd's military prowess was not, however, regarded as impressive; he was described as 'a blundering commander'.

Taking time off from his undemanding military service, Handasyd embarked on a political career. It began on 10 May 1722, in the reign of George I, when, at the instigation of Lord Hinchingbrooke, he was elected unopposed as Member of Parliament for Huntingdon. In the reign of George II, he was twice re-elected as member for Huntingdon in 1727 and 1734, but he lost his seat in the general election of 1741. In 1747, thanks to the influence of Lord Carlisle, he managed to persuade the electors of Scarborough that he was their ideal candidate.

In 1751, King George II issued a warrant to Lieutenant General Roger Handasyd's regiment specifying the style and colours of the uniform to be observed henceforth by every regiment in the army, an injunction that would be profitably exploited by a soon-to-be resident of Great Staughton, James Duberly.

Roger Handasyd died at Gaynes Hall, Great Staughton, on 4 January 1763 at the age of seventy-four.

The Handasyds, Father and Son

34 Monument to Thomas and Roger Handasyd in the Gaynes Chapel

16

Mr Duberly Acquires an Estate in Great Staughton

The exact origins of the Duberly name are lost to history. In the court records of Edward I (1272–1307) there is a reference to a Henry de Dubele. The name, spelt variously as Dubarle or Dubberly, suggests a German origin but more likely is that the Duberlys are of Flemish or Wallooon stock. By the early eighteenth century the Duberlys, now settled in Monmouthshire, had established a business supplying army uniforms. The business prospered and the Duberly family became prominent citizens of the town. George Duberly was appointed High Sheriff of Monmouth in 1769. When James Duberly, born in 1758, took over the business, his financial acumen, together with the social status conferred on him as the grandson of a former High Sheriff of the county, brought him influence beyond the borders of Monmouthshire.

The Howards of Hampstead
In 1766, six years into the reign of George III, Gerrard Howard of Hampstead and his second wife, Ann (née Mawhood), announced the birth of their only daughter, Rebecca Elizabeth, born on 5 March 1766. Gerrard Howard was a prosperous landowner, Justice of the Peace and Deputy Lord-Lieutenant of Middlesex. By the time of Gerrard Howard's death in 1781, the family fortune was almost spent.

It was fortunate that James Duberly was smitten when he

35 Sir James Duberly

first encountered Rebecca Howard socially. Her mother, however, did not share this enthusiasm for the Monmouth 'army Taylor' despite the handsome dowry Duberly would bestow upon the union. Nonetheless, in 1787, the engagement was announced between the twenty-nine-year-old James Duberly of Monmouth and the twenty-two-year-old Rebecca Howard of Hampstead. Charlotte Papendiek, in her gossipy memoirs, *Court and Private life in the time of Queen Charlotte*, wrote: 'Mr Papendiek told me of D's intended marriage with a daughter of the late general in the army ... None of his family approved of the match, but he nevertheless proceeded with it and married.' Mrs Papendiek recorded an ugly moment when the snobbish Ann Howard bluntly informed Mr Duberly that 'those friends to whom you introduced her, as well as your own family, move in a very different society from what she has been accustomed to, and she was not happy' to which James Duberly responded phlegmatically: 'My family are worthy, friendly people, and my wealth that you looked after for your daughter has been appropriated to her advantage, both present and future.'

On 15 November 1787, James Duberly, 'in the prime and vigour of life' (to quote the later court documents) married Rebecca Elizabeth Howard at St Anne's Church, Soho, and the couple moved into James Duberly's newly acquired mansion at 35 Soho Square. Mr Duberly also had a country cottage in East Sheen, to which the couple were to repair at weekends and during the summer. Two children were born of the union: son and heir James in 1788 and a daughter, Ann, in 1789.

James Duberly, now a member of London fashionable society, wasted no time in demonstrating his fitness to be worthy of his new social status. He rented a large room in Brewer Street, Golden Square, where he instituted a series of subscription concerts and dances. Mrs Papendiek, whose musician husband was a vital contributor to the success of these soirées, attended many of the concerts. She recalled: 'The first of Duberly's was a dance beginning at eight and ending at twelve o'clock and it went off very well. I danced with Duberly and Salomon.' The Salomon mentioned by Mrs Papendiek was the celebrated impresario Johann Peter Salomon. Although the marriage was blessed with the two children, all was not well in the Duberly household, as Mrs Papendiek was to discover: 'I went to London once more to attend a musical night of these pleasant subscription meetings. … Mr Duberly was there, but not his lady, who seemed to be no longer inquired after … her desire appeared to be to show that she did not wish for their society.'

36 Rebecca Duberly née Howard

The relationship between the Duberlys and the Papendieks did not confine itself to mere friendship and a love of music. Charlotte Papendiek: 'I knew that Duberly, the army clothier, had already asked Mr Papendiek to get orders for him from regiments.' James Duberly's business, supplying uniforms to army regiments, continued to prosper. Despite the outward success of the union, the attractive 22-year-old Rebecca Elizabeth Duberly, if not actually unhappy with her married status and the financial security it brought her, may well have welcomed a little more excitement in her life. It was not long in coming.

It was almost certainly due to the influence of Christopher Papendiek that in 1788 James Duberly secured a lucrative contract to supply uniforms to the 65th Regiment of Foot, commanded by John Gunning, who recorded the moment: 'When I obtained the command of the 65th Foot in the beginning of the year 1788, I first became acquainted with Mr D[uberly] of Soho Square, who undertook to clothe it [i.e. the regiment] for me upon much more liberal terms than any other person in his line of business.' Gunning also foresaw that Mr Duberly's purse 'might prove very serviceable to me in case of necessity'. Contracts for the supply of army uniforms were a lucrative business. Until 1751, the style and design of army uniforms had been a haphazard affair. In July of that year, King George II issued a warrant to Lieutenant General Roger Handasyd's regiment specifying the style of the uniform and the colours to be borne not only by his soldiers, but that every regiment should observe a common standard in respect of their uniform.

John Gunning

The Gunnings' ancestral home was Castle Coote, County Roscommon, Ireland. Related through marriage to the 6th Viscount Mayo, John Gunning senior and his wife Bridget resided at the Manor House in Hemingford Grey, occupied later by Lucy Boston (L. M. Boston, author of *Children of Green Knowe*). The Gunning family lived in genteel poverty, but they did possess two remarkable assets, their daughters Maria (1732–1760) and Elizabeth (1733–1790), dubbed the 'Gunning Beauties', whose captivating beauty and fortunate marriages propelled the Gunning family into the highest ranks of Georgian society. For his part, John Gunning, born c. 1741, married into a less elevated rank in society. Whilst serving as Captain of the 49th Regiment of Foot in 1768, he married, at the age of twenty-seven, Susannah Minifie, daughter of James Minifie DD, a Somerset clergyman. It was not a match either to bring a substantial dowry, nor to ease the ambitious Gunning's entrée into London society.

Gunning's military career had taken him to Portugal during the Seven Years' War (1756–1763) and during the American War of Independence he saw service at the Battle of Bunker Hill, a 'sanguinary affair', according to the official history. Thereafter, John Gunning devoted himself to his preferred lifestyle of idleness and hedonism, easing himself into London's *beau monde* thanks to his well-connected sisters. In 1788, promoted to the rank of General, he was given command of the 65th Regiment of Foot, which brought him into contact with James Duberly.

Intrigue

General Gunning's smooth progress into the upper echelons of London society was brought to a dramatic halt in early 1791 in a grotesque affair of forged letters dubbed 'the Gunningiad' by Horace Walpole. The affair shredded Gunning's carefully cultivated relationships with the nobility. His debts mounted. Bailiffs came knocking at his door. Fortunately, a saviour was at hand, in the shape of James Duberly who not only paid off Gunning's £2,000 debts but invited him to the family home at 35 Soho Square.

It was not long before Gunning's eye was caught by the 'beauty, youth and sweetness of disposition' of the lady of the house, who must have found the solicitous company of this man of the world, telling tales of his military derring-do, a man with impressive connections to the royal circle, in startling contrast to her industrious and frequently absent husband.

Little did James Duberly realise the 'serpent he was fostering in his breast' as Gunning, now ensconced in close proximity to Rebecca Duberly, began to insinuate himself into her affections, 'with the grossest violations of beneficence and hospitality'. For two months in the autumn of 1791, Gunning lodged with the Duberlys in Soho Square, before moving to a new apartment in the then relatively new suburb of Somers Town. Gunning displayed a conduct 'most correct' and his behaviour was that of 'a polished gentleman'. As for Mrs Duberly, could there be any woman 'more correct in her extrinsic behaviour'? The flattering attention Gunning paid to his hostess finally broke down her defences and before long the couple were embroiled in a full-blown affair.

A Scandal

A routine was swiftly established. The Duberlys and Gunning spent the weekend in East Sheen, making it too difficult for Gunning and Rebecca to indulge their passion. It was James Duberly's custom to depart for London on the Monday morning, and on several occasions the adulterous couple were nearly undone. One day James Duberly returned unexpectedly early and could have caught the couple in flagrante but thanks to the quick thinking of Mrs Duberly's confidential maid, Gunning was quickly kitted out in a gown, ragged petticoat, apron and mob cap. Mr Duberly, 'little imagining a general officer of Great Britain could be disguised in the shape of an old woman, passed without the smallest suspicion'. Panic over, Gunning made his getaway via the back door and into his carriage, which usually awaited him there in case of just such an emergency.

The blissful liaison was to last until 25 September 1791, when Gunning learned to his dismay that the Duberlys were to spend two months out of town. He prevailed upon Mrs Duberly 'to indulge me with the possession of her person for one night previous to her departure'. The couple's plan was to pretend that she had business in Sheen, but in reality, she and Gunning would find accommodation in a Clapham tavern, 'indulge themselves' for the night, returning to London early the following morning. The lovers' carefully laid plan went wrong. John Gunning departed for town in his carriage in his usual dilatory fashion and was quickly overtaken by the energetic Mr Duberly, who was going to town to procure a horse for an intended journey to Bath. After an exchange of greetings, Gunning efficiently effected an about turn and rapidly returned to the arms of his inamorata. Meanwhile, Duberly, having secured the horse for his journey to Bath, commanded his servant to return to Sheen, with an instruction to Rebecca to look after the horse. The servant came back to the waiting Duberly with disquieting news. Rebecca Duberly was not at home. She had taken the coach to Mortlake that morning.

The Deceit

When Rebecca finally returned to the family home, the 'tortured, anxious' Mr Duberly demanded in no uncertain terms to know where she had been and with whom. To a friend, Mrs Gardner in Richmond, Rebecca replied, they were to go to the theatre that evening. Duberly, unconvinced by his wife's explanation, immediately set off to Mrs Gardner. In a panic, Rebecca rushed to Gunning's lodgings and poured out her tale of woe. Gunning then summoned his carriage and raced to Richmond, only to find Duberly had got there before him. With admirable presence of mind, Gunning wrote a short note to Mrs Gardner asking her to say that she (Rebecca) had spent the night with her. Mrs Gardner's response was to hand over Gunning's letter to Duberly. As the subsequent trial made clear, 'on the succeeding day the 26th of September, the defendant had criminal intercourse with the plaintiff's wife'.

The game was up. Rebecca and Gunning repaired to the Somers Town lodgings from where they both wrote tearful letters to Duberly begging for forgiveness. It was too late. Even Rebecca's heartfelt plea to her husband had no effect: 'that our Great Redeemer forgave the woman taken in adultery, oh be my redeemer and by the love you once bore, by the love you bear our tender babes, soften your heart'. Duberly did not even deign to open the letter. Rebecca Duberly was despatched back to her mother in Hampstead. James Duberly was not finished yet with John Gunning. He sent in the bailiffs to recover from Gunning a further loan of £130 he had given him. The debt was not repaid and Mr Duberly had no recourse other than to have Gunning confined to 'the magical compass of a spunging-house', a debtor's prison. They were not welcoming places. A description by a later unwilling resident tells the tale: 'what a place! I had an apartment … about the size of one of the beast receptacles at the Zoo. For this luxury, I had to pay two guineas a day. A bottle of sherry cost a guinea, a bottle of Bass half-a-crown.' Gunning was eventually rescued by two honest men who went bail for his debt.

Within two months James Duberly had sued for divorce on the grounds of his wife's adultery with John Gunning. In the legal terminology of the time, Rebecca Duberly was accused of crim.con, criminal conversation or in plain words, intercourse with a man not her husband.

The Trial
The trial between James Duberly Esq, plaintiff and Major General Gunning, defendant, for criminal conversation came up at Westminster on Wednesday 22 February 1792, the Right Honourable Lord Kenyon presiding, with a jury consisting of twelve specially chosen citizens. *The London Magazine or Gentleman's Monthly Intelligencer*, in volume 43 of the 1774 edition presciently summarised the essential facts of the case. 'Is it not a riddle that many of our ladies who are modest, sober women should admit into their company men of the vilest principles and worst of characters and should prefer the greatest rakes for husband to men of virtue and sobriety?' The trial itself caused a sensation and shortly afterwards, a summary of the proceedings appeared anonymously in print, with a preface that flatly though unconvincingly denied that its aim was to 'titillate the prurient

imagination of obscenity, or even to raise a blush on the cheek of the most modest female'. The pamphlet offered salacious titbits: 'Many curious Particulars; among others, an account of an extraordinary Game of Blindman's Buff; in which the Parties towzled each other Upon the Carpet, &c. &c.'

The TRIAL OF GENERAL GUNNING FOR CRIMINAL CONVERSATION WITH MRS DUBERLY, WIFE OF MR DUBERLY;

Before Lord KENYON, and a special Jury, in the Court of King's Bench, on Wednesday, Feb. 22, 1792

The plaintiff James Duberly was represented by Messrs Erskine, Shepherd and Wood. In Thomas Erskine, 1st Baron Erskine KT PC KC (1750–1823), James Duberly had secured the expensive services of one of the most celebrated lawyers in the country, later to become Lord Chancellor of the United Kingdom.

Lawyers for the defendant, Major General John Gunning, were Messrs Bearcroft, Mingay, Bower and Baldwyn.

The Case for the Plaintiff

In his opening statement, Mr Erskine emphasised the personal rectitude of Mr Duberly: '[he] is an eminent contractor of cloathing for the army; he is handsome in his person, and in the prime and vigour of life'. The marriage between Rebecca and James, he continued, 'was a union solely of inclination and affection'. Erskine went on to explain the business relationship between the eminently respectable Mr Duberly and John Gunning. Mr Erskine pulled no punches in contrasting the two men: 'the plaintiff was in the prime of life. The defendant was near sixty years.' In fact, Gunning was fifty-one years of age. James Duberly was 'presentable', whilst the defendant was a 'decaying edifice ... General Gunning's frame is infirm and disjointed – his hands are crippled – his feet lame'.

Mr Erskine briskly summarised the events of 25–26 September. He then read out Gunning's hastily scribbled note to Mrs Gardner, imploring her collusion in the deceit: 'My dearest Mrs. G[ardner]. Your dear friend R.E.D. [Rebecca Elizabeth Duberly] will be ruined if you do not tell D. that she slept last night with you.' The letter gave elaborate instructions to Mrs Gardner on what she should say to allay Mr Duberly's fears. The letter is signed 'John Gunning' with a note: 'Your servant has orders to give you this privately.' Gunning added a postscript: 'If you have already told Duberly that she was not with you, you can now say, that you only said so in order to prevent his being angry.' The indignant Mrs Gardner had immediately handed Gunning's letter over to James Duberly. As would become apparent, James Duberly and Mrs Gardner were friends of long standing. Mr Erskine made short work of this subterfuge, saying that Mr Duberly had spent two days in search of his wife, learning that 'she dined on one day at the Piazza Coffee-house and that she was then at Somers Town'.

The Witnesses

Mr Erskine called witnesses to testify to the deceit of Rebecca and Gunning. Jane Scott of *The Plough Inn* at Clapham, testified that 'a lady and a gentleman came there at about three o'clock, dined, supped and slept there ... The following morning, she went into the room and found the pair in bed together ...'

As the damning evidence against the defendant mounted up, Mr Erskine proceeded to demolish Gunning's attempt to explain away his conduct. Another letter from Gunning was read out to the jury. It was sent to Mr Duberly: 'Sir (it began) In consequence of the unhappy event of yesterday I received Mrs Duberly as a sacred deposit, until the tenderness of her family might be exerted to restore her to her former situation.' The self-serving letter continued, ending with a final exculpatory flourish: 'In regard to my future plan of life, your security with respect to pecuniary matters shall always hold the first place in my thoughts, I am, Sir, &c. John Gunning.' It was certainly true that 'pecuniary matters' would be uppermost in the thoughts of the ever-penniless John Gunning: there was the matter of the £2,000 James Duberly had lent him.

Gunning's letter arrived at the same time as a contrite explanation of her behaviour from Rebecca Duberly: 'Dear James, Although my heart bleeds for my conduct – though I have injured you in the most tender point, yet so great is my shame, that I cannot, dare not – see you …… Teach [their children] not to despise their mother.' At this point, Mr Erskine broke off theatrically from reading the remainder of the letter, saying that 'I have not nerves.' Concluding his opening address, he addressed the jury: 'Gentlemen of the jury … if such persons as the defendant are not punished, and if men's domestic comforts are thus to be invaded with impunity, the energy that unites the human race will be lost, and the welfare of the state at large endangered.'

Character witnesses for James Duberly were then called. Mr Rogers, clerk to Mr Duberly, whilst admitting that he was rarely in their company socially, recalled that the couple seemed perfectly happy together. Cross-examined by Mr Bearcroft, for the defendant, Mr Rogers denied knowing of Mr Duberly's connection with other women since his marriage, 'nor had he been employed in carrying letters between him and any other person'.

Another witness was George Duberly, James's brother, who was cross-examined by Mr Mingay, solicitor for the defendant, who demanded to know if he could recollect what had transpired at the Ranelagh club, where George and James Duberly had dined with General Gunning. No, he did not recollect any conversation between his brother and his wife concerning the party at

Ranelagh. And he most certainly did not let his brother James in at four o'clock in the morning.

The Case for the Defendant

It was now the turn of Gunning's lawyers to present their case. In his opening remarks to the jury, Mr Bearcroft sought to dispel the negative impressions of his client described by the plaintiff's counsel. However, Mr Bearcroft was at pains to point out that 'I am no advocate for the sort of trespass attributed to him [Gunning].' In other similar crim.con cases, he stated, damages as high as £10,000 had been awarded, but there were others 'though the plaintiff was a baronet and privy counsellor, the jury awarded him only five shillings'. Mr Bearcroft ridiculed the assertion made by the counsel for the plaintiff that 'such perfect happiness existed between the plaintiff and his wife', claiming that his learned colleague Mr Erskine had 'miserably fallen off in the proof of it'. He poured scorn on the witnesses called in Mr Duberly's favour. Why so few servants as he has so many? Why only call as witnesses occasional irregular visitors to the Duberly household? Why were not 'the mother, the brother, all the near relations' called if you 'desire to know how the parties lived together'? He then carried the fire to the plaintiff's counsel. 'There may be circumstances which may tempt a woman to infidelity even with an object not altogether desirable.' Such circumstances, Mr Bearcroft suggested, might be recrimination, revenge, inattention, neglect or inconstancy. And was it not true, he suggested, that 'Mr. Duberly was engaged in amours with other women … this injured man consoled himself with a lady whom he kept before his marriage. – He visited her at midnight and stayed late. I do not know if I can prove a criminal connection … for if he visited her at unseemly hours, the five shillings damages will be more than sufficient for him.'

'A Life of Extreme Gaiety'

Mr Bearcroft called witnesses to testify that the Duberlys led 'a life of extreme gaiety'. He began soberly. There was a *partie quarrée* at Mr Duberly's, consisting of Mr and Mrs Duberly, Mrs Gardner and John Gunning (a foursome with all that the term might imply). Mr Bearcroft outlined the lascivious goings-on that ensued. The candles at Mr Duberly's were often put out, and 'this old boy of sixty [Gunning was fifty-one] with the rest of the *partie quarrée*, began to play blind man's buff'. Unsurprisingly, John Gunning, 'the ancient rascal', with his infirmities, fell and the carpet 'was in a curious condition – rumpled and powdered'. What was learned counsel inferring?

Allegations Against Mr Duberly

Mr Bearcroft next called Ann Coleman, who lived in Bath and formerly lived with a Mrs Skipper of Goodge Street about five years previously. She stated that 'she was acquainted with the plaintiff, who kept her mistress when she first went to live with her, in the year 1787 ... the plaintiff continued to visit her subsequent to his marriage ... he visited her mistress in the evening and stayed generally till one or two in the morning.' Ann Coleman stated that she had observed 'several indecent familiarities between them'. This seemed to explain why Mr Duberly rushed to London to obtain a horse for a visit to Bath on 26 September.

In the face of this seemingly damning evidence of Mr Duberly's perfidy, Mr Erskine intervened. He put it to Miss Coleman that she was unaware that Mr Duberly was visiting Mrs Skipper with a view to settling an annuity on her, as Mr Duberly would cease to see her after his marriage to Rebecca. Nevertheless, Miss Coleman was sure that the plaintiff visited Mrs Skipper more than six times in a year.

The next witness was Elizabeth Hurst, a servant in the Duberly household for about three years. Her testimony reinforced the accounts of *parties quarrées* and gave details of some of what went on at such gatherings. She told the court that General Gunning was a frequent visitor to the house, and 'was often left alone with Mrs Duberly on evenings'. Mrs Gardner was also a constant presence in the household. One evening after the four of them returned from dining in Soho Square, they retired to the drawing room 'without candles'. Elizabeth Hurst went to the room to tidy up and was shocked to find the carpet and furniture in disarray. The green cloth on the floor was drawn up in heaps and covered in powder. On moving the sofa, she retrieved one of Mrs Gardner's earrings.

Then there were the letters. Elizabeth once saw a letter from Mrs Gardner to Mr Duberly and often saw General Gunning's boy bring two or three letters in a morning to Mrs Duberly. Cross-examined by Mr Erskine, Hurst admitted she had not seen Mrs Duberly or the General since leaving her employ. She agreed that the couple seemed to be fond of each other. She was unaware of any indecent familiarities taking place.

Erskine's Final Address to the Jury

The evidence was now concluded and in his closing address to the jury, Mr Erskine sought to dismantle Mr Bearcroft's assertion that Mrs Duberly's misconduct was born of a spirit of revenge at what she considered the inconstancy, the neglect, the breach of trust and alleged infidelity of her husband, which had caused her to descend 'from a celestial bed to prey on garbage'. Had my learned friend produced any evidence in support of his assertions? He had not. As for the witnesses, they have all attested to the warmth of the relationship between the Duberlys. The defendant clearly had a swaggering contempt for the court, for he admitted he is 'living in open and adulterous commerce and … Mrs Duberly is at this very moment pregnant by him'.

As for Mrs Skipper, it was only the day before that this affair had come to light and besides, since his marriage, Mr Duberly had

had no relationship with the lady. His visits to her were solely to arrange the payment of an annuity. He dismissed the testimony of the various servants called in Gunning's defence: 'God knows what a situation we would be in if the honour of families depended on them.'

Erskine now turned to the letter written by Gunning to Mrs Gardner: 'R.E.D. will be ruined if you do not say she was with you last night.' Why should she be ruined if Mr Duberly acquiesced in her behaviour? The letter concluded: 'you can now say that you only said so because he should not be angry'. Mr Erskine pressed the point: why would James Duberly be angry if he was unconcerned at his wife's behaviour? Could he have deemed it remotely possible that his wife would take up 'with such a mummy'? As for Gunning himself, Erskine tore into his character. He quoted a letter from Gunning to Mr Duberly: 'You have been a friend to me in distress, you have lent me money, I acknowledge your friendship, but you have a handsome wife, and my principles ... will not prevent me from endeavouring to debauch her.' And with that final flourish, the counsel for the plaintiff rested and he left to the jury his 'client's case with cheerfulness to your determination'.

The Summing-up and Verdict

In his summing up, the judge, Lord Kenyon, swiftly came to the key points of the case. Adultery had been proved. The plaintiff's conduct could not be ignored, but he always acted with propriety, which might justify large damages being awarded. There are, the judge observed, lights and shades in offences of this nature. It was clear that the judge was unconvinced by the case for the defence, but on the other hand: 'I confess I feel as much abomination as you can for this hoary, this shameful, this detestable lecher.' The jury then retired to consider the evidence; after a short deliberation, they gave their verdict, and the not inconsiderable sum of £5,000 in damages was awarded to James Duberly.

Aftermath

The question that remains after the judgement was delivered is a simple one: what could have attracted the beautiful Rebecca Elizabeth Howard to a 'hoary old lecher' twice her age? One answer was provided in a remarkable book published in 1792, mere months after the trial of General John Gunning. It was entitled, *Apology for the life of General Gunning*. The *Apology* followed the traditional template of libidinous memoirs: a few pages of maudlin self-pity and sham remorse followed by an inflated catalogue of the lothario's conquests. No author credit is given, but it was certainly written by someone with intimate knowledge of the old philanderer.

The *Apology* is an entertaining fiction but at the heart of this debauched, false and dissembling account, aspects of the real John Gunning may be lurking. Gunning, the silver-haired, silver-tongued rake was persistent, attentive, plausible and passionate and he successfully ensnared the apparently respectable wife of the wealthy and successful businessman James Duberly. Was Rebecca Duberly a willing participant? When she absented herself from her husband's musical soirées early in their marriage, as Mrs Papendiek recorded, how was Rebecca Duberly occupying her time? Was she perhaps at the theatre enjoying the stage debut of the 'clown prince' Joseph Grimaldi?

An amusing postscript to the *Apology* was added in the form of a letter dated 22 February allegedly written by a friend of Gunning immediately after the conclusion of the trial. 'Remember me to your dear little seducer ... A propos, I beg I may be looked upon as the sponsor of the sweet embryo ... As it will be the child of iniquity, where can you find so proper a god-father for it as an attorney?'

Flight

After the trial, Rebecca and Gunning fled abroad across revolutionary France, before settling in Naples, where, in the summer of 1794, Rebecca Duberly gave birth to a daughter, Ann, who was christened in that city on 15 August. On 2 September 1797 General John Gunning died of the dropsy at the age of fifty-six. In his will, he made provision for his natural daughter and for Rebecca. Following Gunning's death, Rebecca Duberly made the hazardous journey across Napoleonic France, taking only her baby daughter Ann and a manservant and returned to take up residence with her mother in Hampstead. Her remaining years were difficult financially and she died at the early age of thirty-seven in 1803. She was buried in Hampstead parish church in February 1804.

The Gaynes Hall Estate

In the year of Gunning's death, 1797, James Duberly, perhaps deciding that a country retreat might be a welcome relief after the scandal of the court case and divorce, purchased Gaynes Hall, the spacious mansion in Great Staughton. He immediately commissioned the noted landscape designer Humphry Repton (1752–1818) to undertake improvements and alterations to the gardens and Gaynes Hall became the seat of the Duberly family until the Second World War. The retreat from fashionable London society may also have been prompted by the production at the Haymarket theatre in London on 15 July 1797 of George Colman the Younger's play, *The Heir at Law*, which became one of the most popular plays of the day. The leading character, Dr Peter Pangloss (the naïve optimist in Voltaire's 1759 satire *Candide*), is a pompous teacher hired to tutor the merchant Daniel Dowlas, who has recently been elevated to the peerage under the title of Lord Duberly.

James Duberly was knighted by George III in 1803, on account, it was said, of the excellence of his horses. Following Rebecca's death, he married in 1805 Etheldreda St Barbe and the couple had four children. James Duberly quickly settled into the life of a country squire. The Enclosure Acts between 1804 and

Mr Duberly Acquires an Estate in Great Staughton

1812 extended James Duberly's existing landholding by a further 1074 acres. As a Justice of the Peace he presided over the numerous cases of illegitimacy which came before him. James Duberly died at the age of seventy-four at his residence of Gaynes Hall, Great Staughton and was buried in St Andrew's graveyard, where his imposing tomb can still be seen.

His son James, born in 1788, was the first of the Duberly family to distinguish himself in the service of Crown and Country. He served in the Peninsula War in 1811 and 1812 and was awarded a medal for gallantry. Three years later his regiment, the 11th Light Dragoons, confronted Napoleon's army at Quatre Bras and on 18 June 1815 was part of Wellington's army which finally put an end to the French Emperor's territorial ambitions. On the death of his father he inherited the Gaynes Hall estate. He married Emily Hannah Grey (of the tea dynasty) in 1837 and the couple had eight children. He died at Gaynes Hall in 1864.

James Duberly's second son, Henry, also served his country as paymaster in the 8th Hussars and saw action in the Crimea and India. In 1850, he married Frances Isabella Locke who was to achieve national fame when her *Journals* of the Crimean and Indian campaigns were published.

17

Unravelled: a 200-Year-Old Village Mystery

In 1971, Rev. David Fleming, vicar of St Andrew's Church, Great Staughton, deposited with the Huntingdon Records Office an impressive volume, measuring 13 inches by 8 inches and containing 566 pages of elegantly written script. It is bound in handsome cardboard covers and has a lightly decorated spine on which is inscribed, 'MISCELLANIES'. When the volume is opened, a loose slip of paper (undated) falls out, bearing the words: 'This book I found in the Sunday school cupboard much exposed to damp. I could ascertain nothing as to its history.' It is signed C. McN. (Collingwood McNeil) Rushforth, vicar of St Andrew's 1909–1917 and successor to Rev. Henry George Watson.

What is the book? When was it written? Who was the author? The first two questions can be speedily answered. On the final page stand the words: '*Finis* 20th December 1800'. The first page is equally revealing; it bears the title, *An Elegant Selection*. For the eighteenth-century reader, the title alone would almost certainly suggest that it was a commonplace book, a kind of home-made private encyclopaedia that could be a road map of an educational or intellectual journey, a source of religious or spiritual comfort, or simply an illustrated journey of a life. Mostly written by men, commonplace books combined the functions of an intellectual scrapbook, aide-memoir and diary. Not all commonplace books were compiled by private individuals. In 1803 for example, Oliver D. Cooke published *The Hive and Commonplace Book*, a volume of

216 pages whose subtitle explains the book's purpose: *A Collection of Thoughts on Civil, Moral, Sentimental and Religious Subjects: Selected from the Writings of Near One Hundred of the Best Authors ... Intended as a Repository of Sententious, Ingenious, and Pertinent Sayings, in Verse and Prose.*

To 'ascertain something of its history' and rescue the book from two centuries of damp obscurity, some detective work will be required but fortunately the book offers many clues to the ultimate identity of the Compiler.

An initial examination of the ten-page index of the Great Staughton Commonplace Book reveals a total of 436 separate items of which by far the largest category, with eighty-four items, is poetry. Of the selections, twenty-nine take Nature and Natural History as their theme. Other categories are difficult to classify but often take the form of homilies or meditations. Most of the selections carry a moral, religious or a more general spiritual message. To leaven the otherwise serious purpose of the book, the Compiler of the volume has interspersed the pages with thirty-nine anecdotes, some humorous, some with a more serious moral purpose.

To begin at the beginning: the first article in the book is entitled, *The Wisdom and Goodness of God Display'd in several curious Observations on Fishes and Birds*, which combines two themes: Nature and Providence. 'What abundance of Fish do the waters produce of every size'? it asks. The answer is immediately given: 'God has provided for it, by multiplying them in a prodigious manner, and making the weak race swifter in their course than the others.' The author of the piece aligns the behaviour of the fish with God's commanding purpose. Thus, shoals of fish that are enjoyed by humans congregate near the shore so that they may be easily netted by fishermen. On the other hand, fish which are useless for human nutrition live in remote seas. 'And what hand conducts them with so much care and goodness towards man'? It

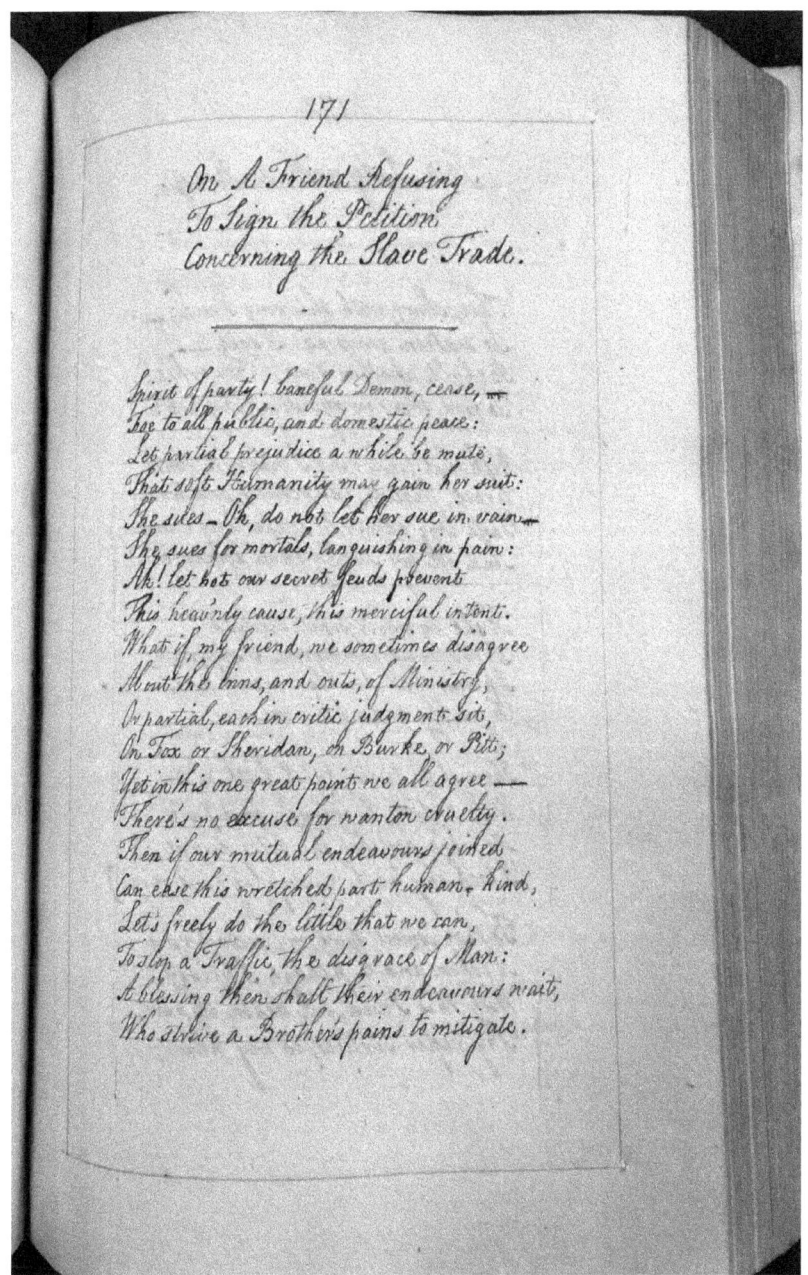

37 *Commonplace Book; an anti-slavery poem*

is the same for birds: 'What architect has taught them to build their elaborate nests'? The extract concludes: 'O Lord, how manifold are thy works, in wisdom hast thou made them all.'

This first extract was taken from a popular book published in 1797 and entitled *Interesting Anecdotes, Memoirs, Allegories, Essays, and Poetical Fragments: Tending to Amuse the Fancy, and Inculcate Morality*, Volume 2, by Mr Addison, author. Revealingly, the stated aims of Addison's collection were to *Amuse the Fancy, and Inculcate Morality*: education, edification and morality in a single volume. The Mr Addison referred to was the essayist, poet, playwright and politician Joseph Addison (1672–1719), co-founder with Richard Steele of the *Spectator* magazine in 1711.

A rapid review of the index reveals three further items referring directly or indirectly to Addison. The first reference is a quotation by him, the second is entitled *Tatlers and Spectators*, the celebrated political journal he and Steele founded, but it is the final reference that is much the most interesting: *Mr Addison's calm and tranquil Death*. The article purports to describe the essayist's final moments when he summons the wayward Lord Warwick, 'a young man of very irregular life and loose opinions', to his death bed. Lord Warwick asks Addison to 'signify your commands, and be assured I will execute them with religious fidelity'. Addison responds by saying 'observe with what tranquillity a Christian can die'. Once again, a religious theme emerges.

The source of this article is surprising, a book that exerted a powerful influence on European thought in the latter half of the eighteenth century. It was entitled *Über die Einsamkeit (On solitude)* and it was written between 1784 and 1786 by the German philosopher, physician and naturalist Johann Georg Zimmermann (1728–1795). An English edition of the book, published by Vernor and Hood, appeared in 1797, a useful pointer to the dating of our Commonplace Book. Forty-four items in the Great Staughton *Commonplace Book* are taken from Zimmermann's *On Solitude*, the most numerous by a considerable margin from a single author. The book clearly had a profound influence on the Compiler. *On Solitude* bears the subtitle, *Or the influence of occasional retirement upon the mind and heart.* The retirement the author speaks of is not the ascetic solitude of the hermit's cell or the seclusion of a monk's retreat. For Zimmermann and presumably the Compiler, the keys to happiness and contentment (a word that recurs constantly in *On Solitude*) are good health, friendship, the rejection of 'pomp, splendour and the triffles [*sic*] of life' and the cultivation of the pleasures of the mind. It is in solitude and especially the peace and tranquillity of rural life that 'the mind regenerates and acquires fresh force … it is there that creative genius frees itself from the thraldom of society … surrenders itself to the impetuous rays of an ardent imagination … and facilitates his search after true felicity.'

38 Johann Georg Zimmermann. Lithograph by P. R. Vignéron

The themes of Religion, Nature and Natural History recur constantly in the *Commonplace Book* and are nearly always associated with inner peace and contentment and the overriding design of Providence.

The second extract, *Reflections on the Death of an Amiable Young Lady*, is a spiritual meditation on the precariousness of life, inspired by the death of Miss B-----, a young woman. The conclusion of the piece includes a place and date: 'Whitchurch in Shropshire, S.S., dated 5th April 1798.'

The analysis of the first two extracts and a cursory examination of the index discloses the foundation stones on which the *Commonplace Book* is built. Thus, for example, religion features directly in fourteen extracts including *The Wisdom and Goodness of God, The blessings of divine revelation, A prayer,* and *A German Pulpit*.

The Compiler then introduces a group of four anecdotes on successive pages. The Compiler could have culled them from one of two sources. The first was a widely read humorous volume entitled, *Hutchin's improved: being an almanack and ephemeris ... for the year of our Lord 1776*. Another possible source was the popular *London Magazine, Or, Gentleman's Monthly Intelligencer*, 1774. Three of the anecdotes are mere harmless diversions but the fourth is more interesting. Entitled, *The Shy Quaker*, the anecdote comes from Addison's volume and relates the story of a bailiff seeking to deliver a writ on a Quaker. Presenting himself at the Quaker's house he is duly ushered in by the servant and told that 'Abimeleck shall see thee'. After an hour kicking his heels, the bailiff rings the bell and angrily demands to know why Abimeleck has not shown his face. The servant responds: 'Abimeleck has seen thee but he doth not like thee.' Quakers and other Nonconformists did not have an easy time of it in the eighteenth century. Denied entry to universities and forbidden by law from holding public office, could the Compiler be expressing sympathy for the Quaker?

Closer analysis of the index brings an entirely unexpected discovery: no fewer than forty-seven items (ten per cent of the entire *Commonplace Book*) are concerned with the role and condition of women across time, continents and cultures. Thus we find *Ceremony of the Jewish women, Hindustan women, Methods of Courtship at Constantinople, State of widows in primitive ages, Anecdote of an old woman and their present majesties*, to name but a few. A pointless sacrifice is described in *The custom of burning in India*, in which, on the death of her husband, his young widow is forced to sacrifice herself on the pyre in the ceremony of suttee. In a piece entitled, *Egyptian Women their Amusements*, the Compiler seems to nod approvingly at a scene depicting sportive diversions, which 'tend to invigorate the lady by unbending her mind', a sentiment that the Compiler may well have taken to heart. Many of these extracts are taken from *The History of Women from the earliest antiquity to the present time*, by William Alexander the Younger MD, of Edinburgh and published in 1782.

The most likely reason for the inclusion of so many references to women is the obvious one: the Compiler was a woman. The choice of five short poems must surely provide conclusive evidence of a women's hand behind the creation of the book: *A thought at waking*; *An exhortation, watch*; *The sceptic*; *A blush* and *The last day* were all taken from two sources: *The New Lady's Magazine, Or, Polite and Entertaining Companion for the Fair Sex*, Volume 2, for the year 1787, published by Rev. Mr Charles Stanhope and *The Lady's Magazine; Or, Entertaining Companion for the Fair Sex, Appropriated Solely to Their Use and Amusement* ..., Volume 29, G. Robinson, London 1798.

Is there any evidence in these items of the character and personality of the Compiler? The largest category by far in the book is poetry, with eighty-four items, drawn either from the collected works of the poets involved or from contemporary anthologies such as John Hinton's *The Universal Magazine of Knowledge and Pleasure*, or J. Murray's *The English Review, Or, An*

Abstract of English and Foreign Literature, Volume 15, both published in 1790. A year later came the publication of another collection of poetry: ELEGANT EXTRACTS: *Or Useful and Entertaining PIECES of POETRY, Selected for the IMPROVEMENT of YOUTH ... Being Similar in Design to* ELEGANT EXTRACTS IN PROSE.

No fewer than twenty-nine of the poems are drawn from the works of just two poets, James Thomson (1700–1748), whose *The Seasons* was one of the most popular and influential poetry collections of the eighteenth century. The poem, in blank verse, is a lengthy meditation on nature over the course of the four seasons and combines vivid depictions of natural phenomena with religious feelings of awe and wonder at the works of the Almighty. *The Seasons* was the inspiration for Joseph Haydn's secular oratorio of 1801.

The second poet was James Hurdis (1763–1801) whose *The Village Curate*, published in 1788 when he was twenty-five, brought him immense fame and popularity. Robert Burns, no less, requested a copy. *The Village Curate* is a pastoral idyll, an autobiographical meditation on rural life across the seasons, with its simple joys and pleasures as seen through the eyes and imagination of a rural pastor. The 'Autumn' section of Hurdis' poem conveys the rapturous mood of nature and the divine:

> In such a silent, cool, and wholesome hour,
> The Author of the world came down from Heav'n
> To walk in Paradise, well pleas'd to mark
> The harmless deeds of new-created man.
> And sure the silent, cool, and wholesome hour
> May still delight him, our atonement made.
> Who knows but as we walk he walks unseen.

The other extracts from Hurdis include: *A motive to contentment and thankfulness, Parnel, Lily of the vale,* and *The matchless maid.* All the poems are a natural complement to Zimmermann's *On Solitude*:

'There is scarcely any writer who has not celebrated the happiness of rural privacy', and who 'delights himself … with the melody of birds, the whisper of groves, and the murmurs of rivulets.'

Two writers bring a more overtly religious expression to the tone of the *Commonplace Book*. James Hervey (1714–1758), a Northamptonshire-born writer and poet, published in 1755 an influential three-volume work entitled, *Theron and Aspasio, or a series of Letters upon the most important and interesting Subjects.* Hervey supplies four extracts, including the longest in the book, entitled, *A walk through a picture gallery*, which runs to fifteen pages. It consists of a dialogue between Theron and Aspasio touching on art, nature and religion. The first painting they discuss depicts Hannibal's perilous crossing of the Alps and the shattered bodies of the soldiers who have fallen down the steep cliff face. Eventually, under 'the favour of Heaven', Hannibal's army successfully crosses the Alps and confronts the forces of Rome. In his text, Hervey marked the phrase 'the favour of Heaven' and appended a note in which he refers to the publication in 1748 of Richard Walter's account of Captain Anson's voyage around the world. Hervey notes regretfully that in his account, Richard Walter, himself a man of the cloth, had failed to acknowledge an 'interposing Providence in that masculine, nervous, noble narrative'. Hervey goes on to reveal his disappointment that the 'great commander (Anson) and his gallant officers did not express their gratitude for the power of Providence and Divine Goodness which 'passed unnoticed, unacknowledged and without any share of the Praise'.

Isaac Watts (1674–1748) is best known for his hymns, *Our God, Our Help in Ages Past*, and *When I Survey the Wondrous Cross*, both still sung today. It was in 1741, towards the end of his life, that Watts published *The Improvement of the Mind: Or, A Supplement to the Art of Logic and an addendum To which is Added, Discourse on the Education of Children and Youth.* Watts stressed the importance of education and learning especially for the young: 'The children of the present age are the hope of the age to come', is the motif of the work. The theme of education recurs several times.

There is another poet who features only briefly in the book but whose ghostly presence seems to permeate the whole work. Her name was Anna Letitia Barbauld, née Aikin, (1743 – 1825) one of the most remarkable women of the age, now all but forgotten: charismatic teacher, founder of schools, poet, essayist, polemicist and author of ground-breaking children's literature. Barbauld, born into a Nonconformist background, baptised at the Presbyterian Church in St Ives, Huntingdonshire, a mere twenty miles from Great Staughton, was one of the very few women to break through the male-dominated ranks of eighteenth-century intellectual society. It is tempting to speculate that the Compiler may have met this pioneering female intellectual. Barbauld's poetry was an influential precursor of English Romanticism although her reputation was subsequently eclipsed by the publication of William Wordsworth and Samuel Taylor Coleridge's *Lyrical Ballads* in 1798. Towards the end of the book, a piece entitled, *Immortality* depicts a philosopher, the pious and benevolent Hiero. Confronted with the prospect of the 'gloom of terrors of annihilation', in the darkness of his garden, he derives comfort 'aspiring hope may direct his views to immortality'. As sunrise vanquishes the enveloping gloom, he finds consolation in the tranquillity of nature. His thoughts move him to recite to himself the opening words of a poem, *A summer evening's meditation*, by Anna Letitia Barbauld.

> At this still hour the self-collected Soul
> Turns inwards, and beholds a stranger there
> Of high descent, and more than mortal rank;
> An embryo God, a spark of fire divine

Barbauld contributes a second poem in the Commonplace Book, an extract from *An Address to the Deity*, taken from her 1773 first collection of poems in which she reflects on the hope of eternal life.

> Teach me to quit this transitory scene
> With decent triumph and a look serene;
> Teach me to fix my ardent hopes on high,
> And having liv'd to thee, in thee to die.

This extract is chosen by the Compiler as an introduction to a series of four powerful poems denouncing the evils of the slave trade. Many of the anti-slavery campaigners, such as John Wesley and Samuel Wilberforce, shared a common background in Nonconformism; nine of the original twelve members of the Society for the Abolition of the Slave Trade were Quakers. Could this explain the inclusion of *The Shy Quaker* anecdote in the Commonplace Book? In 1791, Anna Letitia Barbauld had written a fierce polemic, *Epistle to William Wilberforce Esq. On the Rejection of the Bill for Abolishing the Slave Trade*, in support of the campaign in Parliament to abolish the trade.

The first poem in the anti-slavery sequence is entitled, *The negro's complaint*, by William Cowper and the Compiler may have come across it in the August 1793 edition of *The Gentleman's Magazine*, a publication that might well have been found in the Compiler's drawing room. The subject of the title laments his status as a slave 'men from England bought and sold me / Paid my price in paltry gold'.

> Forc'd from home and all its pleasures,
> Africa's waste I left forlorn
> To increase a stranger's treasure
> O'er the raging billows borne.

The poem ends with an impassioned plea for understanding:

> Slaves of gold, whose sordid dealings
> Tarnish all your boasted powers
> Prove that you have human feelings
> Ere you proudly question ours.

An even more savage indictment of the trade and a government that wilfully sanctioned it is *The Negro Boy and the Watch*. The poem originally appeared in *The Monthly Magazine: Or, British Register*, in the edition of 22 June 1796. It is signed '*Anti Doulos*' (Against Slavery). *The Monthly Magazine* carried a helpful note explaining the background to the poem. The African Prince who had lately arrived in England, being asked what he had given for his watch, replied; 'What I'll never give again – I gave a fine boy for it.' A white slave trader expresses remorse for the savagery with which he destroyed the family: 'His father's hope, his mother's pride / Though black, yet comely, to their view / I tore him helpless from their side'. 'He who walks upon the wind' will bring salvation to these people and the miseries that have been inflicted on them and:

> In his own time will soon destroy
> The oppressors of the Negro boy.

The final poem of the anti-slavery quartet is by one Mr Riley: *On a friend refusing to sign the petition concerning the slave trade*, because it was thought a party matter, an overtly political tirade urging the prominent politicians of the day – Fox, Sheridan, Burke, Pitt – to rise up in opposition to the disgrace of the slave trade. The source of this poem was *The British Poetical Miscellany*, published in 1798, whose motto read: 'To please the fancy and Improve the mind.'

> Yet in this one great point we all agree
> There's no excuse for wanton cruelty …
> Let's freely do the little that we can

To stop a Traffic, the disgrace of man.

The character and personality of the Compiler is now being revealed; a woman with a strong social conscience, possessing deep religious and moral convictions. There is also a prominent Nonconformist streak in her choice of contributors. James Hervey, greatly influenced by John Wesley and the Oxford Methodists; Isaac Watts, a pastor at a Congregational chapel in London. James Thomson's father was a pastor in the Church of Scotland. Anna Letitia Barbauld was brought up and baptised in a Nonconformist household.

The Great Staughton *Commonplace Book* ends, appropriately for a book so imbued with religion and Christian morality and teaching, with *A devotional reflection*, taken from *The Reader's Cabinet*, by John Kingston, published in London during the 1790s, and whose primary purpose was to *Instruct the Mind ... Reform the Morals ... and Amend the Heart*, an appropriate concluding sentiment for the sternly moral Commonplace Book.

> The follies of an early life I see
> Nor aught so shocking now appears to me
> Those actions never could from thought arise,
> Whose only fruits are penitence and sighs;
> O! may the Omniscient then, the whole impute,
> Not to the man, but to the incautious brute
> Sunk by corruption, and restor'd by grace
> The Gospel terms I gratefully embrace
> Since Reason and Religion both agree
> Comfort blest Saviour! Only flows from thee.

Under which appears, in large letters, written no doubt with a relieved flourish, the word '*Finis*' and the date, 20 December 1800.

Very often, a commonplace book occupied a whole lifetime of reflection and experience. Is there any indication of the length of the creative process in the case of the Great Staughton Book? Most of the extracts come from books mainly written in the last quarter of the eighteenth century, but there are a number of more ephemeral items, largely drawn from newspapers and journals of the day and dating from the two years between 1798 and 1799. Thus, *A Thunder Storm* gives a vivid account of 'a very extraordinary and powerful Tornado', which struck Ramsgate on 13 and 14 August 1799, causing much damage. *An Extraordinary Story* recounts the mysterious disappearance of a young lady who 'absented herself from her friends' in April 1798. *Phenomenon* records a remarkably hot day in Bourdeaux [*sic*] at the beginning of August 1798 when a violent 'burning gale' caused women and children to faint in the heat. Another newspaper report records that on 1 August 1799 the church of St Paul, Covent Garden, was consecrated by the Lord Bishop of London following decades of costly repairs and rebuilding.

The dates are compressed into a brief period mainly between 1798 and 1800. The elegant copperplate handwriting provides a further clue to the book, having been compiled in a relatively short space of time. Throughout its 566 pages, it betrays no trace of any deterioration that might have been caused by infirmity or old age. What can be stated with certainty is that the Commonplace Book was created in Great Staughton and subsequently deposited in St Andrew's Church, possibly after the death of its creator.

On 16 July 1796, Rev. James Pope was inducted into 'the real, actual and corporal possession of the vicarage of Stoughton Magna' in a ceremony performed by Rev. Edward Maltby, vicar of Buckden, Commissary, and Sir John Harding. James Pope, born in 1757, was the son of a prosperous landowner, William Pope, 'gent', of Hillingdon Middlesex. Like nearly all vicars of Great Staughton, he studied at St John's College Oxford, obtaining a BA degree in 1777; he became a Fellow of St John's

College and was awarded an MA in 1781. He obtained his Bachelor of Divinity degree in 1786. James Pope occupied the living of St Andrew's Church, Great Staughton, from 1796 until his death in 1822 at the age of sixty-five. He was buried in the graveyard of St Andrew's on 16 January 1822. A plaque in the chancel and a stained-glass window on the wall of the south aisle commemorate his ministry.

In the same year that James Pope took up his ministry, an entry appeared in the Church of England registers, recording the marriage, on 24 November 1796, of Rev. James Pope to the 26-year-old Miss Ann Havens of Donyland Hall, East Donyland, St Lawrence, Essex. Ann Havens was born on 1 May 1770, the daughter of Philip and Lucy Havens, into a devout Quaker family who occupied the substantial seventeenth-century moated manor of East Donyland Hall, near Colchester, Essex. By law, Nonconformists, such as Quakers, were not permitted to study at university and were barred from holding public office or entering the civil service.

The adult Ann Havens would have been expected to conform to the norms of society as an obedient wife to her husband and an attentive mother to her children. The law was the law and many Nonconformists, Philip and Lucy Havens amongst them, took the reluctant view that it was in the best interest of their children for them to undergo baptism in the Church of England. So it was that on 3 September 1775, Ann Havens was baptised at the church of St Giles-in-the-Fields in Holborn, London.

The newly married Popes settled in Great Staughton and Ann Havens took on the role of wife to the vicar of the parish. The union of James Pope and Ann Havens was fruitful. Between 1798 and 1813, James and Ann Pope had nine children: seven sons and two daughters, all baptised at the church of St Andrew, Great Staughton. Settled in the rectory in the rural seclusion of Huntingdonshire, perhaps Ann Havens thought of setting herself a challenge to assert her fervent Christian beliefs whilst also celebrating the virtues of her Nonconformist Quaker upbringing, expressing her sympathy for the poor and oppressed and acknowledging her admiration for women like Anna Letitia Barbauld. So in 1796, the year in which she and her new husband began their new lives at the vicarage in Great Staughton, Ann Havens embarked on her great project, compiling *An Elegant Selection*, her personal Commonplace Book. She may have set herself a target of completing the work in time to mark the dawn of a new century. In that, she succeeded, adding *Finis*, the final flourish to the Commonplace Book, on 20 December 1800.

After 200 years of damp obscurity, it is fitting that the Compiler of the book should now emerge into the daylight and receive this deserved and long overdue recognition. The *Commonplace Book* was conceived, created and compiled between 1796 and 1800 by Ann Havens, wife of Rev. James Pope, vicar of St Andrew's Church, Great Staughton.

There is one final item to be recorded. It appeared in volumes 182–3 of *The Gentleman's Magazine*, edited by F. Jefferies and dated 1847. It contains the following short obituary notice: 'Worcester 1 July 1847 at Mitton Parsonage Mrs [Ann] Pope, [née Havens], aged 77, relict of the late James Pope, Vicar of Great Staughton, Huntingdonshire.' Ann Pope spent her final years with Rev. Charles Wharton, his wife Anne and three servants at Lower Mitton parsonage in Worcestershire.

There is a modern postscript to this story. Sophia Ann Pope (1848–1920), granddaughter of James Pope, commissioned an impressive 20-foot-high cross from the noted Scottish architect Sir John Ninian Comper FSA (1864–1960) to be erected in Great Staughton burial ground in memory of her husband William Havens Pope (1840–1915). Of Rev. Pope's seven sons, James, born in 1801, went on to marry Anna Sophia Mills in London in 1843 and their daughter Sophia Ann Pope was born five years

Unravelled: a 200-Year-Old Village Mystery

39 The Pope Memorial

later, in 1848. Another of Rev. Pope's sons was William Havens Pope, born in 1808. He married Louisa Hogg in 1835 and five years later their son, also called William Havens Pope was born. In 1873, William Havens Pope married his first cousin Sophia Ann Pope in London.

18

The Unsung Heroine of the Crimea

The predominant image evoked by the Crimean War can be summarised in just five words: *Charge of the Light Brigade*, coupled with some half-forgotten lines of Tennyson. A moment's further reflection will almost certainly bring to mind the legendary exploits of the 'heroines of the Crimea', Florence Nightingale and Mary Seacole, whose popularity and renown continue to capture the public imagination to this day.

For more than a century and a half, these two formidable ladies have occupied a Pantheon all of their own but perhaps the time has now come for them to admit the third heroine of the Crimea, less well-known than the Lady with the Lamp or the proprietor of the *British Hotel* but who lived through and reported on the entire campaign. She was Frances Isabella Duberly and in her *Journal kept during the Russian War*, she gives a vivid account of the bloody battles at the Alma, Inkerman and Sebastopol and arguably did as much as William Howard Russell of *The Times* and the photographer Roger Fenton to bring the horrors and miseries of the war to the British breakfast table. Unlike her two more celebrated contemporaries (and the poet Tennyson), she was actually present as the Light Brigade thundered into the Valley of Death.

So who was Frances Isabella Duberly, and how did she manage to inveigle herself into the man's world of 'soldiering and death'? Frances Isabella Locke was born on 27 September 1829 to Wadham Locke and his wife Anna Maria Selina, née Powell, of Rowdeford House, Devizes, in Wiltshire. Wadham Locke was a banker and financial adviser to numerous local magnates and

Frances Isabella enjoyed a privileged childhood, attended by servants and surrounded by horses and ponies. Dispensing swiftly with her multisyllabic forenames, Miss Locke was soon transformed into Fanny Locke, expert horsewoman, gifted pianist, fluent in French and endowed with all the accomplishments of a young lady of her class. She was confident, spirited, self-assured and independent of mind. What could have induced this intelligent daughter of a wealthy, well-connected banker to swap Victorian domesticity for a life on the killing fields of the Crimea and India?

In 1850, at the age of 21, Fanny married Henry Duberly, the 28-year-old second son of Sir James Duberly of Gaynes Hall, Great Staughton. In 1847, Henry had been appointed Paymaster to the 8th Royal Irish Hussars, a position that seemed to have suited his quiet, unambitious temperament. As Paymaster, he occupied an influential seat in the army hierarchy (he was the money man), but he would not be required to exercise his not inconsiderable shooting prowess on the battlefield.

On the title page of her *Journal kept during the Russian War: from the departure of the army from England in April 1854 to the fall of Sebastopol*, the author signs herself 'Mrs Henry Duberly'. In the second edition of the book, published in 1857, the dedication reads, '*To the Soldiers and Sailors of the Crimean Expedition, this Journal is dedicated by an eye-witness of their chivalrous valour and their heroic fortitude*'. This time, the *Journal* was signed Frances Isabella Duberly.

Shorn of the complex web of treaties and alliances, the central strategy of the Crimean War was for the Allies, consisting of Britain, France and Turkey, to capture the Russian stronghold of Sebastopol, which would finally bring to an end the Russian empire's expansionist designs.

Fanny's *Journal* begins at the beginning, when she and Henry embarked at Plymouth on the *Shooting Star* on 25 April 1854, bound for the Bulgarian city of Varna, located strategically on the

Gulf of Varna and the principal naval base for the French and British fleets. The voyage out proved eventful: 'Although weakened almost to delirium by sea-sickness and awed by the tremendous force of wind and sea, I could not but exult in the magnificent sailing of our noble ship, which bounded over the huge waves like a wild hunter springing at his fences, and breasted her gallant way at the rate of sixteen knots an hour.' A day later she remarked sardonically: 'How unlike the quiet Sundays at home'!

The *Shooting Star* docked in Constantinople and the couple took the opportunity to explore 'the beautiful city ... embowered in trees ... a landscape such as I had never hoped to see save in a picture'. The beauty of nature, contrasting with the brutality of war, was a constant theme in the *Journal*.

Her mission might have been brought to an abrupt halt a month later on 25 May if the commander of the cavalry division, Lord Lucan, had had his way. 'Unless Mrs Duberly had an order sanctioning her doing so, she was not to re-embark on board the *Shooting Star*.' Henry, the soldier, looked upon it as an order. Fanny had a very different notion: 'I look upon it as a woman, and – laugh at it.' Lord Raglan, however, refused to intervene and Fanny, heavily disguised in a shawl, surreptitiously boarded the ship and settled herself and her horses down for the voyage to Varna. It was not her only lucky escape from the officious Lucan. A few weeks later she recorded: 'Lord Lucan ... scanned every woman, to find traces of a lady; but he searched in vain, and I, choking with laughter, hurried past his horse into the boat.'

Fanny's *Journal* is heavy with the name-dropping of the military hierarchy, not least Lord Cardigan himself whom Fanny treats at a respectful but largely amicable distance. She became particularly close to Captain Stephen Lushington, in command of the naval brigade at Sebastopol. There were many others whose dining tables and cabins were graced by the Duberlys: Major de Salis, Major General Sir George Cathcart, Lord George Paulet,

Colonel Poulett Somerset, Captain Edward Nolan and a Captain Chetwode, whom Fanny would meet again in India.

The realities of war were not long in making their presence felt. At a luncheon offered by Lord George Paulet, whose hospitality the Duberlys were to enjoy on numerous occasions, Fanny recorded laconically that 'Captain Wallace, 7th Fusiliers, killed yesterday by a fall from his pony, was buried to-day – the first-fruits of the sacrifice'! The consequences of being captured by the Russians were a concern. British soldiers would be treated as felons and sent to Siberia, prompting Fanny's waspish comment: 'if the Russians are as uncleanly, smell as strong, and eat as much garlic as the Turks, it will be the best thing that can happen to us under the circumstances'. The casual brutality of their allies, the Turks, was also the subject of after-dinner conversations: 'they will cut off three or four heads, string them together through lips and cheeks and carry them over their shoulders like a rope of onions'.

Fanny had serious concerns throughout the *Journal* for Henry's fragile health, for the well-being of the ordinary soldier and what she saw as the incompetence of the strategy deployed by the army commanders. Her overriding worry was Henry. 'I am his only comfort. He possesses the meekness of Moses, the patience of Job and the faith of Abraham.'

Fanny Duberly was well aware of her social rank and despite the privations of the Crimea, she was determined to maintain the standards befitting a country gentlewoman and the accommodation she was offered, a tent with few facilities, did not fit the bill. This problem was solved when, one after the other, officers of the High Command offered her comfortable, airy cabins on their ships, conveniently anchored to take advantage of refreshing sea breezes. Servants, or the lack and unreliability of same, was another regular refrain in the *Journal*. 'I induced Mrs. Williams ... to wash a few of the clothes which had accumulated.'

The Unsung Heroine of the Crimea

This, complained Fanny, was 'the first assistance she has ever thought fit to render me since I left England'.

The Allies' original strategy was to meet Russian forces somewhere near the Danube but by July the orders had changed; rumour had it that the troops were bound for Vienna. Finally on 16 August, orders came through that the Allies were actually to be despatched to the Crimea. After a twelve-day voyage, Fanny got her first sight of the Crimea on 16 September 1854.

The strategy of the allied commanders, Lord Raglan and Maréchal Jacques Leroy de Saint-Arnaud, to march on Sebastopol, thirty miles away, was rudely interrupted on 20 September when the Russian cavalry swept out of their impregnable fortress of Sebastopol and occupied the heights of Alma, from which strongpoint they bore down on the massed ranks of the Allied armies. Fanny, aboard the *Shooting Star*, could hear the roar of the guns and fretted for her husband's safety. Her first intimation of the slaughter was her maid – she had managed to find a suitable candidate – bursting into the Duberly cabin with the news that there had been a great battle; 500 English and 5,000 Russians had been killed. Fanny's immediate thought was to obtain hard and fast news of the battle from her military circle, but her enquiries were met with a non-committal shrugging of shoulders. It was not until three days later on 23 September that Fanny obtained any factual information. The *Journal* records her instinctive reaction: '2,090 English killed and wounded; the 7th and 23rd Fusiliers almost destroyed, and, thank God! the Cavalry not engaged. How can timorous, nervous women live through a time like this!' She imagines the terror of death, of lives 'extinguished in a moment; hands flung out in agony, faces calm and still in death; all our prayers unavailing now: no more speech, no more life, no more love'. Two days later came confirmation of the epic assault on the Russian forces. 'The charge of Highlanders was most magnificent ... they swept over the Russian entrenchments like a sea ... It is said that the whole garrison of

Sebastopol was engaged at the Alma – 50,000 Russians to about 45,000 English and French. I hear the English bore the brunt of the fight.' The Allies' overwhelming numbers ultimately gave them the advantage and the Russians were forced into a tactical withdrawal to their Sebastopol fortress.

It was one of the many peculiarities of the war that after some of the most ferocious fighting and bloody carnage, Fanny was able to take Bob, her beloved grey, cantering over a now deserted battlefield. A few days after the battle of Alma, on one such foray into the countryside, Fanny and Captain Brock (governor of Eupatoria) came across a deserted house in the dining room of which stood a grand piano. For Fanny it was like meeting 'a dear and long absent friend', and she enthusiastically demonstrated her musical skills with a rendition of *Rule Britannia* and Tennyson's *Break, break, break*. A week after her confrontation with the killing fields, Fanny Duberly celebrated her twenty-fifth birthday: 'Thus ends my birthday! – a day ever to be remembered, as on it I saw my first battle-field. How many more shall I see ere I am a year older? Shall I ever live to see another year?'

After the Battle of the Alma, the Allies' new strategy was to attack Sebastopol from the south where it was thought the Russians were more vulnerable and to this end, in late September 1854, British and French forces advanced on the town, to begin a siege that would last the best part of a year.

It was not until 4 October that the *Pride of the Ocean*, with Fanny and the 1st Royals on board, moored at the 'wonderful anchorage of Balaklava'. The pretty harbour met with Fanny's delight, but she was dismayed to learn of the deaths of several senior officers of her acquaintance. There were, however, some compensations on the social side. Invitations to church, luncheon and supper came thick and fast. At one such supper, Captain Portal offered to ride out with Fanny to view the Russian emplacements in Sebastopol. It was a risky undertaking, as the Russians were a mere 1,000 yards away, well within firing range.

They rode up to the Heights overlooking the city, the allied troops marshalled behind them and in front the enemy, spraying shots and shells in their direction. For Fanny, it was an intense moment: 'I could not but feel a high degree of excitement, and I think it was not unnatural. We were standing on the brow of a hill … the doomed city beneath our feet, and the pale moon above: it was indeed a moment worth a hundred years of every-day existence. I have often prayed that I might "wear out my life, and not rust it out," and it may be that my dreams and aspirations will be realised.'

A few days after this liberating moment, Fanny indulged her predilection for satire as Lord Cardigan's majestic private yacht entered the harbour, 'amidst all the rough work of war!' His yacht was 'as out of place as a "London belle" might be'. The mood shifted again within a few paragraphs, as Fanny criticised the lack of recognition towards soldiers committing acts of bravery (the Victoria Cross has its origins in the Crimean War). A rifleman, seeing a shell land near his trench, knocked out the fuse and for this act of bravery was mentioned in general orders. Fanny wondered why it was not possible to award such soldiers some form of decoration even 'a bit of red rag', to wear immediately as an honourable distinction 'instead of waiting for a medal he may never live to obtain, or may only obtain years hence, when it shall have lost half its value'.

It was not the only example of Fanny's compassionate concern for the trials of the ordinary soldier. She tells the touching story of a sergeant (whom she does not name), 'a steady and most respectable man', found dead by his own hand, near the stream. Could he, wondered Fanny, 'have had a foreboding of the lingering deaths of so many of his comrades, and so rashly have chosen his own time to appear before God?'

The following day she took her horse and rode off to survey the British encampment, where the Light Brigade and the 63rd and 68th regiments were preparing for the coming engagement with the Russians. Fanny made her return to camp through the French lines where she claimed to be flattered by the compliments showered upon her by soldiers who had seen few women and especially none as striking as 'the beautiful English Lady with the long flaxen curls'. Several days later Fanny had an unexpected visitor with whom she had a long and interesting conversation. Captain Edward Nolan, A.D.C. to General Airey, was a dashing cavalry officer whose theories on battlefield strategy had ruffled feathers amongst the obdurate high command of the army. Ten days later he was to play a controversial role in the most dramatic exploit of the war.

The bombardment of Sebastopol, a 'fearful rain of shot and shell', began in earnest on 17 October 1854, after three days of constant firing and shelling; the Round Tower in the city was shattered and the French and English fleets poured broadside after broadside at the Russian fortifications. The culmination of the bombardment occurred at ten minutes past three when the Mud Fort (Redan) exploded in a vast cloud of smoke and flame rising high in the air and falling gently to earth, a 'magnificent sight', according to Fanny and an event greeted with cheers and shouts from every throat. Fanny was 'half' swept away by enthusiasm, having seen and heard 'the magnificent din of war'.

Wednesday 25 October found Fanny feeling decidedly out of sorts. Peering out of her cabin at eight o'clock, she was surprised to discover her horse Bob on the beach, saddled and ready to ride. Moments later, she received a note. It was from Henry, telling her to dress with all speed and take to her horse. 'The battle of Balaklava has begun and promises to be a hot one.' Fanny was no stranger to the urgent summons to action. Mounting her horse, she rode as fast as she could through the narrow, crowded streets. Captain Howard told her that the Turks had abandoned their positions and the Russians were advancing with all haste. 'Lose no time', Fanny was told or 'you will not make it to the camp alive'. Thus began a hectic ride through the retreating Turks until the main road was reached where she was again confronted by a mass of Turks carrying booty from the chaos and confusion.

The Russians had seized three of the Turkish batteries. Ahead, Fanny saw the 93rd and the 42nd in position before Balaklava. The immediate danger was mounted Cossacks heading in their direction. Henry flung saddlebags onto Bob and urged Fanny to head for cover in a vineyard from where it would be safe to watch the action. Moments later Henry joined her, just in time to escape persistent Russian gunfire. In front of her she saw a line of Highlanders, standing in position, rifles raised, as the Cossack cavalry bore down on them. Sir Colin Campbell ordered his men to stand firm, in 'a thin red line'. The odds seemed impossible but the infantry waited until they could see the whites of the Russians' eyes before unleashing volley after volley that covered the hillside in dense acrid smoke. The ground was soon covered with the dead and the dying; a horse, badly wounded, staggered up to Bob and collapsed.

Reinforcements, French and British, were brought up and the cavalry awaited its orders to launch what became 'a matter of world history'. Events were moving almost too quickly for Fanny to take them in, even when recollected in tranquillity. Captain Nolan charged forward recklessly to the front of the Light Brigade, seemingly seizing the initiative from Cardigan. His bravery, or foolhardiness, had only painful death as consequence. Fanny could barely comprehend what was happening. Every bush and every stone seemed to conceal a deadly gun or rifle as fusillade after fusillade of Russian fire was poured upon the advancing cavalry, which charged faster and faster towards the Russian guns. The Light Brigade suddenly turned about and were lost to sight only to straggle back into formation moments later. 'What can those skirmishers be doing'? the *Journal* wondered before realisation swiftly dawned. 'Good God! It is the Light Brigade!'

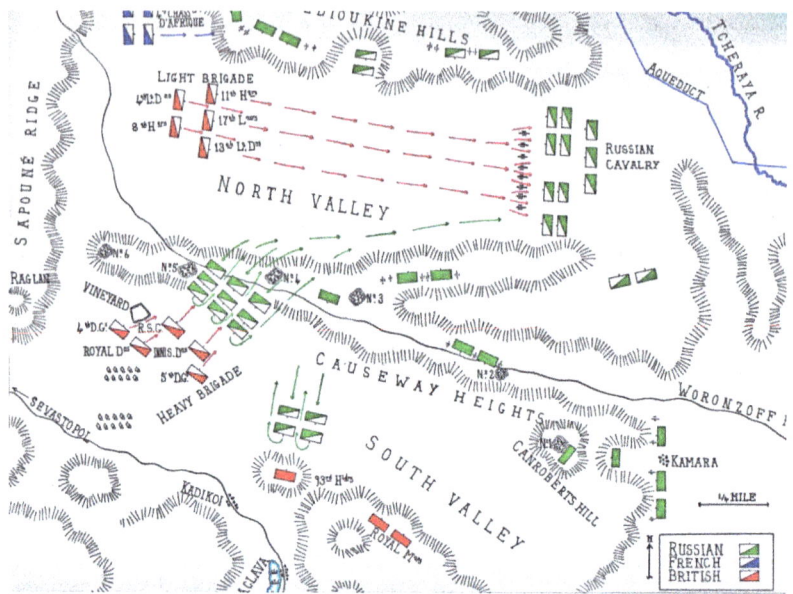

40 Battle of Balaklava

It was the late afternoon of the same day; the battle was over and Fanny and Henry returned to the scene to view the aftermath of the reckless, valorous charge. Fanny's nerves were shaking as she contemplated the desolation and destruction. 'Ah, what a catalogue!' her *Journal* recorded. Or as the French General Bosquet was famously to declare: 'C'est magnifique, mais ce n'est pas la guerre. C'est de la folie.' Madness indeed. As ever, horses were a significant concern for Fanny: 'one poor cream-colour, with a bullet through his flank, lay dying, so patiently!' Then there were the dead, from both sides: a Russian soldier, very still in death, the body of a Turkish soldier stretched out in a vineyard. Lord Cardigan, who had now become part of Fanny's increasingly influential circle, told her, several days later, the toll: 300 men, 24 officers and 354 horses. That night, Fanny struggled to sleep 'but even my closed eyelids were filled with the ruddy glare of blood'.

The Unsung Heroine of the Crimea

41 Balaklava as it is today

A curious epilogue to the disaster occurred a few days later on 1 November, when the effects of deceased officers were auctioned off. Fanny records that the prices obtained were 'fabulous'. An old pair of warm gloves fetched £1 7s 0d, a horse went for £12, whilst a common clasp knife achieved £1 10s 0d.

Barely ten days after the disaster of Balaklava, the Russians sought to increase their advantage, believing they had got the allied forces on the run. On the morning of 5 November, Fanny awoke to very heavy and continuous firing lasting all the morning, which heralded the start of the bloodiest battle of the war at Inkerman. She could discover nothing of what was going on until Henry appeared with news at midday. The day had begun with a blanket of fog shrouding the British positions, allowing a surprise attack by the Russians. In the confusion, it was impossible for the commanders to exercise any control of tactics; it was every man for himself, hand to hand fighting, a true 'soldier's war'.

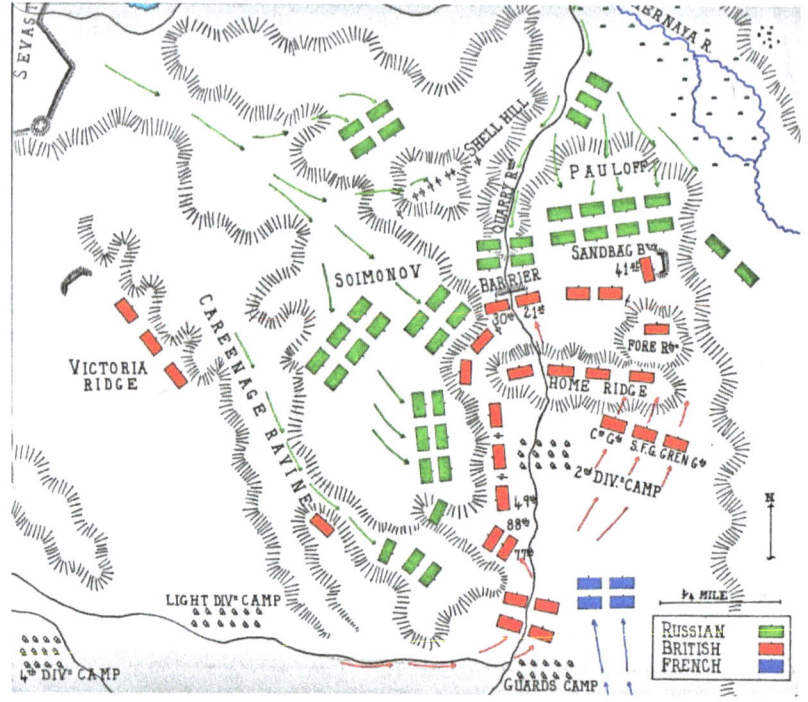

42 Battle of Inkerman

Fanny found it impossible to do justice to the 'horrors and glories of that day'. Overcoming all the hazards that nature had put in their way, 'from five am till three in the afternoon our troops fought with all the acharnement [savagery] of wild beasts'. Fanny, in her cabin aboard the *Star of the South*, begged Captain Buckley to accompany her on foot to the front. En route, they met the casualties of the day being borne on the makeshift ambulance carts. For Fanny there were personal losses: the gallant Sir George Cathcart had died a hero's death on the battlefield. His favourite vantage point would soon become his grave. 'Cathcart was a friend of mine and strange to say three days before he met his gallant death, he and I were talking within ten feet of the spot since chosen for his grave.' Next to him lay Major Wynne, 'whose head was taken off by a round shot... We lunched with him two days before', a laconic sentence that seemed to symbolise the bitter irony of the conflict, a handsome lunch followed by death.

The aftermath of the battle was horrific and it was to be two days before Fanny could pluck up the courage to conceive of visiting the battlefield and in the end her usual determination failed her: 'the thought of it made me shudder and turn sick'. She had to rely on Henry to learn of the full horror. 'The bodies of dead and wounded men and horses piled high, in a space no bigger than a square half mile. The field of Alma was child's play to this!' The detail is graphic: 'heaps upon heaps of slain, lying in every attitude, and congregated in masses – some on their sides, others with hands stiffening on the triggers of their muskets … a ghastly and horrible sight!' The total number of casualties amounted to 5,709 Russians killed, wounded or captured, 2,002 British and 560 French.

On 3 December 1854, after the disaster of Balaklava and the bloody battle of Inkerman, Fanny, on board the *Star of the South* reflected on the suffering endured by the wounded and sick and the daily death toll. In a page of Swiftian satire, Fanny described, with bitterness and anger dripping from her pen, the ingredients required to create a 'Model Balaklava' in England. 'Start', she wrote, 'with ruined filthy houses and hovels, add a generous portion of rain and dirt until the whole place resembles a swamp. Season with a thousand plague-ridden Turks and cram them into the hovels, ensuring that at least one hundred die every day. Cast them into shallow graves to rot. Next, collect all the animals, let them die of starvation and let the smell from their rotting bodies befoul the air. From the harbour pick up all the human and animal flotsam and jetsam and pile them all together in the water.' And to round off the little comedy, why not encourage a couple of sailors to enjoy a pipeful of tobacco whilst sitting on the barrels of gunpowder on the quay, 'which I myself saw two men doing to-day'. That, concluded Fanny, was the reality of Balaklava.

By the end of 1854, news of the horrific conditions endured by the troops was reaching Britain thanks to William Howard Russell and Roger Fenton and, not least, to the letters sent to the press anonymously by Fanny Duberly. The combined efforts of these three redoubtable characters prompted an urgent review of the situation by the government, the end result of which was that Florence Nightingale and thirty-eight nurses were to be despatched to Scutari to tend the sick and wounded. Fanny lamented that 'few people have any notion into what they send their sons and husbands. If it was all fighting and glory and crash and victory and excitement, it would be all very well, but it is months of misery, death of cold, starvation, sickness, long days and dreary nights, mud, rheumatism and lumbago.' The single positive note is that there had been no cases of insubordination or grumbling among the men, and that, she concluded was 'very fine'.

Throughout the *Journal*, Fanny reserved her most venomous criticism for the lamentable state of the army. By January 1855, a cholera epidemic had been raging for six months amongst the Allied forces. Medical care was inadequate, there was serious lack of ambulances and the men supposed to drive them were either dead or dead-drunk. Fanny watched in fury as the British soldiers were assisted by the more efficient, well-equipped and capable French forces. Even she could do better than this, she reflected. She ended her tirade with one of her most biting outbursts: 'Oh, England! England! blot out the lion and the unicorn: let the supporters of your arms henceforth be, Imbecility and Death!'

January 1855 turned out to be an interesting month for the Duberlys for an entirely different reason. Fanny was in her cabin with Henry, writing a letter. Her task was interrupted by the sudden entry of a sergeant who shouted, 'the ship's on fire', a circumstance greatly worsened by the fact that the ship had just taken on 1,000 tons of gunpowder and the fire was no more than six feet away. Fanny's maid was by turns screaming and praying to every saint in the calendar. For her part, Fanny saw it as some kind of personal *Götterdämmerung*. 'All felt that their last moment was come; and yet, a strange exultation possessed my heart in contemplating so magnificent a death – to die with hundreds in so stupendous an explosion.'

For some, the horrors of warfare presented an enticing opportunity to combine gruesome tourism and a healthy profit and the London firm of Inman was quick to identify this lucrative new market. For the princely sum of five pounds the company offered a two-week package tour to the Crimea, fully inclusive of all meals and accommodation with the added extras of visits to the delights of Constantinople and special excursions to the popular battlefields. It prompted the fashionable London elite to decamp to the Crimea for the macabre thrill of seeing their fellow countrymen being shot, shelled and blown up in vast numbers, complemented of course by fine champagne and lobster sandwiches, courtesy of Fortnum and Mason's newest and biggest emporium. 'Picnics were the order of the day', wrote Captain Portal, and the sight of crinoline-clad ladies enjoying the views of the sea from the cliffs became a familiar one.

Unseasonably warm spring weather in March 1855 was the stimulus for a series of horse races to be instigated, christened the 'First Spring Meeting', causing Fanny to remark that she should perhaps entitle her journal, *The Racing Calendar*. The first meeting took place on 5 March with a large turnout of riders and enthusiastic spectators. The day was a complete success with four races concluding with a dog hunt. Fanny rode with them some of the way but she 'could not countenance' the prospect of hunting a dog.

On the same day there was good news about the Duberly accommodation problem. Her great friend and admirer Captain Stephen Lushington had arranged for a hut to be built that would provide the Duberlys with accommodation appropriate to their status, enabling them to receive guests and host receptions. To celebrate the building of the hut, the Duberlys offered their first dinner party, consisting of an excellent soup, fish, hashed venison, roast chicken and a brace of woodcock.

The social merry-go-round continued ten days later, under a brilliant sky, when the Second Spring Race Meeting took place with an impressive list of personnel. Every regiment seemed to be represented, including a contingent of French horsemen. One of the latter, the boastful Comte Bertrand, amused Fanny with tales of his equestrian skills and descriptions of his mansion, which, he claimed, was fully equipped with ten English horses and there was even an English coachman, Johnson, on hand to attend to his stud. Comte Bertrand was also a dab hand at cards, particularly *écarté* (an old French casino game similar to whist) as he demonstrated at dinner aboard the *Star of the South*. One pleasing outcome of the race meeting was the welcome bonus of an invitation from Comte Bertrand to a splendid supper in which the Duberlys tucked into game pie and champagne.

And whilst all the racing was going on, the business of war continued. The Allies, besieging the Russian fortress, launched a spring offensive against Sebastopol, hundreds of guns bombarding the city but it was a desultory affair. The Russian position appeared impregnable and supplies and ammunition were still getting through to them from the north of the city.

A few days after the official opening of the Duberly hut, on Monday 8 April 1855, Roger Fenton arrived to take his famous series of photographs, one of which showed Fanny mounted on Bob, with Henry placidly looking on. Fanny ordered numerous reprints, which she was pleased to see often adorned the tents of both officers and men.

Fanny took advantage of the warm May weather to revisit the 'Valley of Death'. She found it richly carpeted with flowers, dwarf-roses, larkspur and forget-me-nots, 'warm and golden in the rays of the setting sun'. Remnants of the battle remained; carcasses of horses, canon shot, pieces of shell and bleached human bones. In

The Unsung Heroine of the Crimea

43 Fanny and Henry Duberly in the Crimea

memory of the fallen, whose bodies were once strewn over the battlefield, Henry and Fanny gathered a 'handsful' of flowers.

The arrival in the Crimea of Florence Nightingale and her team of nurses had gone some way to answering Fanny's trenchant criticism of the medical care offered to the wounded and dying. Fanny ventured to that 'stinkhole' Balaklava with the intention of calling on Miss Nightingale. Unfortunately, the heroine of the Crimea was ill with fever and unable to receive visitors. Thus what would have been one of the most memorable encounters of the entire war failed to take place.

The ferocious second bombardment of the Russian positions in Sebastopol began at dawn on 6 June. The crucial action would begin that afternoon, according to a tip-off Fanny received from the French High Command. 'Make sure you are here at 4 o'clock in the afternoon', she is told by General Bosquet's adjutant, 'and you will see the assault on the Mamelon by the massed French cavalry.' At three o'clock Fanny returned to see 25,000 French troops assembled to hear General Bosquet's rousing speech to his men, greeted with cheers, shouts and song. In an hour and a half, Bosquet confided to Fanny, indicating the advancing cavalry, 'ces braves seront morts'.

Fanny's position came under attack; a soldier nearby had his head taken off by a canon shot, forcing her to retreat to a more comfortable spot where her horse could graze and she was able to sit on the grass in relative comfort. She gives a thrilling account of the assault on the Mamelon; the Russian guns were silenced and the clatter of musket fire filled the air. The French seized the Mamelon and were now racing towards the second of the Russian batteries, the Malakoff. The British infantry began attacking from the other side of the Heights. Furious Russian fire poured from the Malakoff and as darkness descended, the sky was lit by rockets and gunfire.

The battle continued on the following day; the Malakoff, defended by a 20-foot-wide ditch, resisted the French forces and wholesale burials of the dead hindered the French advance. Thirty-three British officers were killed or wounded. The siege of Sebastopol resumed on 18 June, the anniversary of the Battle of Waterloo, but the outcome was not as positive. The French and British infantry were rebuffed; casualties were high including many of Fanny's acquaintances and Henry's comrades-in-arms. The most prominent death was that of Lord Raglan, commander-in-chief of British forces, who had succumbed to illness; news of his death reached Fanny a week later on 29 June.

Into July and the relentless bombardments on the Malakoff and infantry assaults were taking their toll on the Russian defences. The Russian heavy guns were silent and only the rattle of musketry made 'ghastly music in the ear of night'. The endgame was in sight. Despite ferocious assaults on the French and British lines, Russian resolve was weakening. On 8 September, as the siege of Sebastopol reached its climax, General Markham had some helpful advice for Fanny: 'Mrs Duberly, we shall have a fight tomorrow. You must be up here on Cathcart's Hill by twelve o'clock.' The Allies launched an assault on the Malakoff, the principal fortification of Sebastopol, which they successfully captured. Then followed the capture of the Great Redan on 8 September 1855. The following day the Russians retreated from Sebastopol. The siege, which had lasted eleven months, was broken and finally, on 11 September 1855, the signal went out that *Sebastopol est prise*. Sebastopol had fallen to the combined forces of France, Britain and Turkey. Henry and Fanny celebrated with a bottle of Crockford's champagne.

Two days later, on 13 September, Fanny found herself riding at last into the conquered city of Sebastopol. She and Henry looked down from the Great Redan at the half-filled trench below, the last resting place of hundreds of British soldiers. Henry tells Fanny that he was present as Mr Wright read the funeral service for 700 men. Sebastopol was a shattered, ruined city; bodies, many decomposing, 'a heap, a piled-up heap of human bodies in every stage of putrid decomposition, flung out into the street, and being carted away for burial'.

In the days that remained before the couple returned home, Fanny rode into Balaklava and was surprised to find it transformed from the filthy, abject squalor of two months previously. Now it was 'fresh, healthy and even pretty'. Fanny Duberly's *Journal* ends with a ringing summary of the campaign, praising the Press as 'our best general' and to it, she affirmed, the army owed an immense debt. It was the press that would carry a full and truthful picture of the war so that every man and woman in Britain will render thanks to the bravery and endurance of the British soldier. Fanny Duberly was being unnecessarily modest,

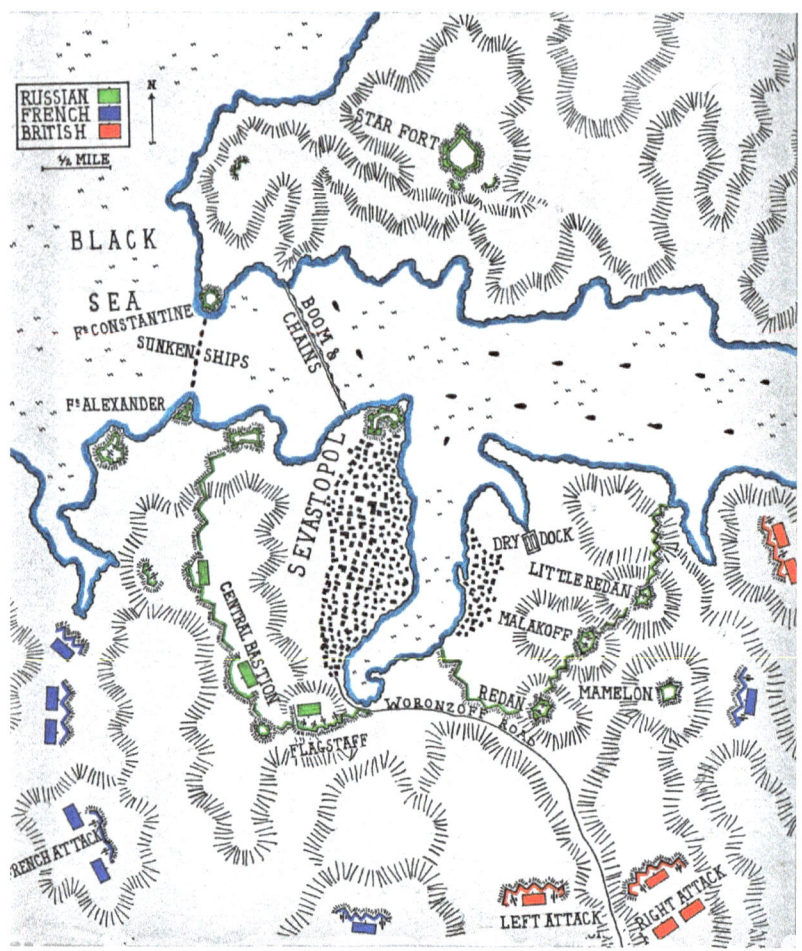

44 Siege of Sebastopol

she had made a significant contribution to 'this full and truthful picture'.

The day before his wife's birthday, Henry learned that he had been awarded the Crimea medal and three clasps, issued to those who had seen action in the major battles of the Crimean Campaign. Fanny was disappointed not to receive the same honour. On 27 September 1855 Fanny Duberly celebrated her twenty-sixth birthday with a long ride over the Crimean countryside to the Observatory and back, mounted on 'that prince of pretty Indian horses' as she called 'Café au lait' and with that pastoral interlude, Fanny Duberly takes her leave of the reader.

From the very start, Fanny was keen that her *Journal* should reach a wide public and was pleased when a London publisher offered £1,000 for the rights to publication. The Duberlys had left the Crimea, as did so many of the senior commanders, once Sebastopol had been taken. The war dragged on for another year before the Treaty of Paris, signed on 30 March 1856, officially brought an end to the conflict. By then, public interest had dwindled and Fanny rightly saw that her *Journal* would not have the same impact if publication were to be unduly delayed. Her *Journal* was first published in 1855 and went quickly into a second edition in the spring of the following year, testifying to its popular success.

The homeward journey of Fanny and Henry Duberly was broken at Portsmouth where they landed on 11 May 1856, to be welcomed and inspected by the Queen. The Queen and her retinue stepped from the royal yacht and went forward to the parade ground where the 8th Hussars were assembled. It was the fourteen-year-old Vicky (Victoria, Princess Royal), who excitedly pointed out Fanny Duberly 'heroine of the Crimea' to her mother. The Queen briefly inclined her head and passed on down the line. It was the only token of royal approval that Fanny received. Fanny Duberly had a more enduring memorial than a mere medal.

The 8th Hussars were posted to Dundalk in Ireland where they were to spend the next year and a half until the regiment was summoned to a very different theatre of war. The months spent in Ireland were given over to the traditional pursuits of their class: hunting, race meetings and lavish social gatherings. The Duberlys were to leave Ireland weighed down with a considerable burden of debt.

19

The Rajpootana Column

Dundalk must have been a dramatic and welcome change for the Duberlys from the roar of the canons and clatter of musketry in the Crimea, but the elegant social round they enjoyed was rudely interrupted seventeen months later when the regiment was summoned to a new military mission on the other side of the world. The Indian mutiny had broken out in May 1857 and although it had been quickly quelled, there were still outbreaks of popular discontent, in particular focused on the great Central territory of India, Rajpootana (Rajputan).

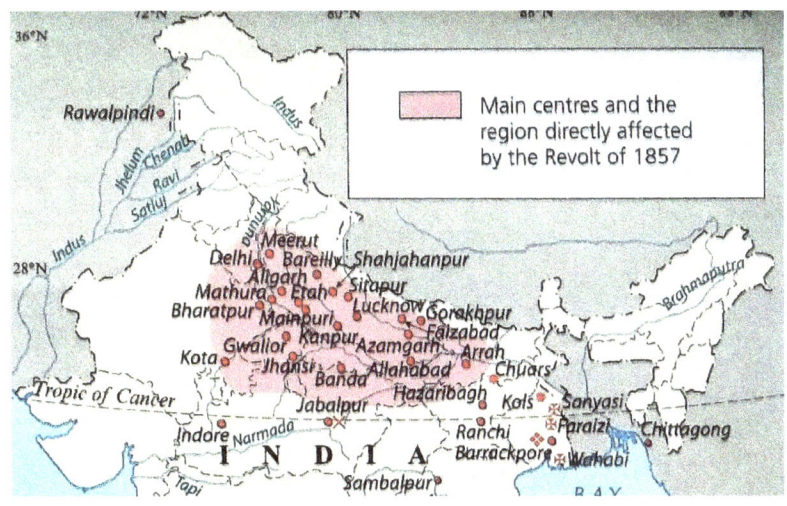

45 Indian Mutiny Map

So it was that on 8 October 1857, Fanny, Henry and his regiment, together with the 17th Lancers and the 56th Regiment stood on the quayside of Cork Harbour, preparing to board Isambard Kingdom Brunel's masterpiece, the SS *Great Britain*. It was the wonder of the age; 322 ft long, built of iron and equipped with a screw propeller with secondary masts for sail power, the ocean-going passenger liner was the longest and most advanced passenger ship of its time.

Angry weather bedevilled their first few days at sea until they reached Gibraltar when suddenly the seas became tranquil and 'the days were golden and the nights were of silver'. The ship put in at Cape Town to take on more coal, giving the Duberlys the opportunity to spend a few days on horseback exploring the South African countryside. Three months later, on 19 December 1857, the SS *Great Britain* steamed into Bombay harbour.

Fanny's journal of the Indian Mutiny, *Campaigning Experiences in Rajpootana and Central India during the Suppression of the Indian Mutiny 1857–1858*, was published in 1859. Alas for Fanny, it was not to prove as successful as her Crimean *Journal* and the reason is not hard to find. It lacks the colour, the vigour and the visceral immediacy of the bloody brutal war in the horrific conditions of the Crimea. Instead, Fanny found herself participating in a messy, inconclusive 2,000-mile route march ('wanderings' she dubbed them), the largely fruitless pursuit of an enemy who succeeded at every turn in eluding the ponderous British forces across Rajpootan, the bandit country of Central India. Here there was to be no Inkerman, no Balaklava, no Sebastopol. As with the Crimean *Journal*, Fanny made clear, early on in her account, where she believed her responsibilities lay as a writer, as an educated Englishwoman and a representative of a colonial power: 'if we desire to maintain our supremacy, it will not be enough to vindicate our mastership by force of arms. We must also prove our moral superiority and make that superiority an evident and incontrovertible fact.'

On arrival in Bombay, Fanny lost no time in conveying her initial impressions of the city. Making a foray into the busy heart of the city, she was appalled by the clamour, the unpaved streets crowded with merchants offering their wares, the huddle of rude wooden huts and the teeming bazaars with 'the funniest Parsee names, written in English characters'. This initial dismay rapidly gave way to a more generous opinion as she investigated the fashionable areas of the city around the fortifications. The tribulations of the Crimea became a distant memory as she and Henry inspected the luxurious accommodation they were offered in the city until the orders to mobilise were given. It was a very far cry from the Crimea. The Duberlys took residence in a large double-walled and double-roofed tent, 16 feet long by 14 wide, fully equipped with carpets, armchairs, tables, lamps and to Fanny's delight, there was even a piano. A second tent served as a bedroom and beyond them both was the bathroom.

The acme of Fanny's delight came when she discovered the phalanx of reliable servants that the couple were to have at their disposal. A butler was the first to be engaged and the recruitment process for the other servants took shape very quickly. Thus, there was a cook, a *mapaul* to clean the lamps and cutlery, a *bheestie*, or water-carrier, a *dhobie*, or washerwoman, a *dirsee*, or tailor 'to repair the ruthless damages done by the dhobie', a tent lascar, a *gariwallah* to drive the covered bullock cart (necessary for excursions in the sun) and finally, the wonderfully named *ghorawallah* to tend each horse. To complete the retinue, two horses were purchased in anticipation of the campaign to come: Pearl, 'my little nutmeg grey' for Fanny, and The Rajah, 'a very handsome mottled Arab four-year-old' for Henry.

The first three chapters of Fanny's narrative are expansive descriptions of her environment both geographical (the glories of nature) and social ('balls and dinner parties succeed each other rapidly').

The causes of the Indian Mutiny were many and varied but two principal reasons stand out: firstly, discontent amongst the native sepoy regiments of the British army and secondly a decree by Governor-General Dalhousie, known as the Doctrine of Lapse, which stripped the heir of a deceased ruler of his rights to inherit, often on the spurious grounds that the Governor considered the claims of the heir were without merit. The territory would therefore pass to the East India Company, 'with their usual grasping and illiberal spirit of covetousness', which thereby painlessly increased the territory, power, wealth and influence of the company. There were small indications of native unrest. Fanny reported that two suspected rebels had been 'blown away from guns', a picturesque phrase that disguised a brutal reality. Hapless insurgents were tied to the mouth of a canon that was then fired.

Brutality was not a monopoly of the British. A princely warrior called Nana Sahib, incensed by the injustice of the Doctrine of Lapse, mustered a huge force of rebels against British rule and in May 1857 stormed the garrison town of Cawnpore. Despite a promise to allow safe passage, he first slaughtered what was left of the garrison. His next act was destined to reinforce the hatred felt by British troops (and Fanny Duberly) for the mutineers. He ordered the women and children in the garrison to be summarily butchered and their remains thrown down a well. A matter of weeks later, Nana Sahib's forces captured the garrison town of Lucknow. In the six-month siege that followed, two relief attempts were mounted but it was not until November of 1857 that British forces finally managed to overcome the rebels. Savage reprisals were taken on the insurgents by British troops whose war cry, with memories of the recent massacre still fresh, was 'Remember Cawnpore'. Lifting the siege came at the heavy cost of 2,500 British casualties. Fanny read in the Calcutta papers news of the aftermath of the siege and had her own 'Remember Cawnpore' moment. 'When I think upon this terrible insurrection, and recollect how deeply the rebels have stained themselves with English blood, the blood of English women and of little helpless children, I can only look forward with awe to the day of vengeance, when our hands shall be dipped in the blood of our enemies and the tongues of our dogs shall be red through the same.'

46 Nana Sahib

Nana Sahib was one of three formidable opponents whose forces would harass the British during the campaign. His most accomplished general, the mastermind behind the guerrilla war that gave the Rajpootana Column the run-around for nearly a year, was Tatya Tope, a brilliant strategist who quickly understood that the way to undermine British morale was to ravage towns and villages and then swiftly withdraw before British troops could respond. Nana Sahib's second important ally was perhaps the most remarkable figure of all in the campaign. Not only was she a woman, albeit one who exercised at weightlifting, wrestling and steeple-chasing (all before breakfast) but she became an inspiration to her troops by her oratory and her courage. She was the Rani (queen) of Jhansi, or more correctly Rani Lakshmibai, who led her forces into battle dressed as a man. She too had fallen victim to the Doctrine of Lapse. On being dispossessed of what she considered her rightful inheritance, she declared 'I shall not surrender my Jhansi.' Fanny, also a woman in a man's world of soldiering, found it difficult to conceal her respect and admiration for this 'warrior queen' whose courage and brutality quickly earned her the nickname of 'the Jezebel of India'.

47 Tatya Tope

Not all of the Indian population took up arms against the British. Indeed, many, particularly the powerful Nawabs, Maharajahs and princelings of the provinces made a point of demonstrating their loyalty to the East India Company, de facto rulers of India. It was in the Central province of Rajpootan that intelligence reports of insurrection amongst the sepoys of the British army became so serious that the order to mobilise was issued.

The Rajpootana Column

On 29 January 1858, the 8th Royal Irish Hussars received orders to sail to the port of Mandavee (Mandvi) some thirty-five miles from Bhooj (Bhuj), the principal town of the Cutch (Kutch) district in Rajpootan. From here they were to march to Kotah (Kota), 500 miles east of Bhooj, where insurgents under Tatya Tope had already taken the town. On 31 January 1858, the troops, now to be christened the Rajpootana Column, were assembled at the fort town of Mandavee and at 2 am, after two days uncomfortably encamped on the beach, the Column began its long procession 'through very ugly country' to their first objective, Bhooj. Here they were joined by the 10th Native Infantry.

The daily routine of the campaign became a monotonous litany: reveille at 1 am or 2 am, departure at 4 am, five hours' march until breakfast at 9 am, a further five hours' route march until mess dinner at 2 pm. Throughout the twelve months and 2,000 miles of the campaign, the British forces battled intense heat and freezing cold, waded through mud, made a perilous crossing of the mountains, all in pursuit of a largely invisible enemy who refused to engage with them in the pitched battles to which Fanny had been accustomed in the Crimea. The Indian campaign was a mopping-up operation, a frustrating guerrilla campaign waged across the hostile 'bandit country' of Central India, between Delhi in the north and Lucknow and Cawnpore in the south. The rebels held the upper hand. Their 'attack and withdraw' tactics, avoiding pitched battles, forced the British into a demoralising route march, which took them repeatedly through towns and villages that would become wearisomely familiar over the long months: Mandavee, Bhooj, Kotah, Chuppra, Chandaree and the 'Delhi of the north', Gwalior.

For Fanny, there were compensations. The ten days at Bhooj were made more acceptable to the Duberlys by the offer from the Political Resident, Colonel Trevelyan, of a suite of rooms in the Residence. Such generous tokens of hospitality were to be repeated over the next twelve months.

Great Staughton and its People

48 Rani of Jhansi

Fanny eagerly accepted an invitation to visit the local Rani. Inside the opulent palace, she was taken aback by the amount of jewellery on show: 'I never saw such a profusion of jewellery in my life.' Every woman was adorned with a sumptuous array of jewels and gold, seemingly on every exposed part of the body, eyelid, nose, bosom, arm, ankle and glittering on dress and shawl. There were brooches, necklaces, bracelets, strings of pearls, a spectacular gold circlet and even the toes were embellished with gold. This was no mere fashion display: the Rani proved to have a shrewd grasp of the political situation in Europe and was well informed about Fanny's exploits in the Crimea.

The monotonous routine of the daily march was often enlivened by the senior officers' enthusiasm to get in some hunting practice. On several occasions throughout her narrative, Fanny mentions Major Chetwode who had made fleeting appearances in the pages of her Crimea *Journal* but in the Indian *Journal* he took a more prominent role as commander of the 8th Hussars. Wherever the Column halted, Major Chetwode could be relied upon to demonstrate his shooting prowess. Thus, on one occasion, he summoned a small army of beaters and disappeared into the undergrowth, returning several hours later bearing a substantial amount of the local wildlife, including a 'beautiful' antelope.

The most tiresome aspect of the entire campaign, apart from scarcely confronting the enemy, was the immense labour involved in striking camp. No fewer than seventy camels were required to transport the mess equipment alone and the native servants often took most of the night to load all the baggage. Once underway, the Column maintained a steady pace of between three and four miles per hour, too rapid for the *ghorawallahs* and the *gariwallahs* on foot to keep up. This was the routine that endured for the eleven months that the Rajpootana Column was pursuing the remnants of the Indian Mutiny.

Fourteen days and 200 miles of steady marching, without encountering the rebels, brought the Column to the 'English station' of Deesa, where they were joined by the Queen's 89th, the 10th and 17th Native Infantry, a native cavalry regiment and Captain Bolton's company of Royal Artillery. It was this formation, more or less (Fanny was herself never wholly clear on the composition of the Column), that was to pursue the rebels over the next twelve months.

At Deesa, the Column was informed, on the first of many occasions, of a change of plan, brought about by conflicting intelligence reports of rebel movements and the British forces' divided command structure. The Rajpootana Column was ordered to traverse the perilous eight-mile long Chutterbhooj ghaut (Chaturbhuj pass), a feat never before attempted by regular soldiers burdened with baggage carts and camels. The plan was to save sixty miles and join up with troops under General Roberts. After leaving Deesa, en route for the pass, the Column had its first frustrating engagement with the rebels at Rowa, a small village two days' march distant. A group of insurgents, some 200 strong, had taken the village. Fanny remarked on their tactics: 'they [the rebels] appear unexpectedly, descend like vultures, sack and pillage without mercy'. It set the pattern that would be repeated throughout the campaign.

At five o'clock in the morning of 16 March, the Column began their march along the rough and rocky path to Chutterbhooj pass, keeping up their average speed of four miles per hour. The crossing of the pass was fraught with danger; it was eight miles in length, impassable for carts, with no supplies of fresh water and ambush by rebels just one of the hazards. The path was narrow and treacherous underfoot with a sheer drop on one side and the possibility of insurgents concealed amongst the rocks on the other side picking off soldiers in the Column one by one. The many caves provided secure homes for another danger, bears. The Arab horses, usually careless on level roads, picked their way forward confidently, unconcerned at the peril around them. At four o'clock the next morning the Column began its slow and equally perilous descent down the rocky mountain path, eventually reaching the town of Chutterbhooj itself.

The Column had paused by a river and Major Chetwode, ever alert for shooting opportunities, spotted an alligator basking on the riverbank. When it saw a potential lunch approaching, the reptile slid forward towards the Major who quickly let off a couple of rounds into the beast which slithered, mortally wounded, into the river. None of the beaters was willing to risk their lives to bring out the wounded and no doubt angry reptile so the bold sportsman Chetwode immediately launched himself into the water and after a brief struggle landed the hapless eight-foot-long beast on the riverbank. In the absence of a visible human enemy, the alligator provided a modicum of excitement.

After two months and 570 miles of marching the most exciting action the Column had seen was Major Chetwode wrestling with an alligator but as they approached Kotah on 30 March 1858, hopes were high that there would be action against a rumoured 22,000 rebel forces. The Column was now two months into the campaign and had virtually nothing to show for it. Fanny recorded the bitter complaint of a Hussar from the 8th: 'I should like to see a live rebel … I begin to doubt if there are any at all.'

The assault on Kotah began at dawn with a heavy artillery bombardment. At 10 am, the massed ranks of the infantry stormed the town via the Rajah gate, overwhelming the insurgents and forcing them to flee through the East Gate. Meanwhile, the 1,500-strong cavalry, led by the 8th Hussars, had been despatched seven miles upriver to cover the open side of the town, the only escape route for the rebels. With little or no fire coming from the battlements, Fanny rode with Henry the mile and a quarter to a promontory overlooking the Rajah's Palace in Kotah to inspect the results of the preliminary bombardment. The insurgents had already fled to their safe haven, the 'Rebels' Village', where they were busy re-assembling their forces. 'Where was the cavalry'? Fanny asked in exasperation. Why hadn't they cut off the fleeing insurgents? As the cavalry was fording the river, with some difficulty, a keen-eyed soldier imagined he had spotted a sniper crouching on the opposite bank training his rifle on the approaching troops. The cavalry halted whilst the situation was assessed. It took some time before it emerged that the alleged sniper was in fact a harmless grazing water buffalo, but the incident had caused a serious delay. Having crossed the river, the cavalry halted on the riverbank and stood at ease, watching unconcerned as the rebels, ousted from the town by the infantry, fled across the plain, carrying their guns and ammunition and the town treasury. Eventually, after a confused series of orders and counter-orders, a squadron under Major Chetwode set off in belated pursuit of the rebels who were reported to be retreating deeper into Rajpootan.

When Fanny and Henry finally rode into the devastated city of Kotah to survey the damage, their horses had to pick their way amongst the bodies and streets strewn with plunder – garments, cushions, furniture and all manner of household utensils. Everywhere, bodies littered the streets and the ruined shells of buildings. Dogs and pigs were busy at their gruesome work.

The couple slowly made their way to the Residency where there was more bloody evidence of the rebels' handiwork. The walls of the building were still smeared with the blood of Major Burton, the Resident, and his two sons. He had apparently been betrayed by his clerk Lalla who, with a force of 1,500 men, had overcome the garrison until only Major Burton and his two sons remained. They had barricaded themselves in an upper room of the Residence and had fought a hopeless, last-ditch battle against 1,500 determined rebels. They managed to hold them off for a while but the ultimate outcome was never in doubt. The Major urged his sons, both excellent swimmers, to escape by the river, but they refused to abandon their father to his inevitable fate. They were overcome and their bodies hurled down to the waiting populace below.

Heroism was not confined solely to the plucky British. Whilst Fanny and Henry were contemplating the aftermath of the battle, she heard a story of what she termed 'antique heroism' by a leader of the rebels as British forces closed in on the city. The battle was going badly for them and to gain an overall view of the increasingly desperate situation, one of the rebel chiefs manoeuvred his horse with great difficulty to the rocky promontory at the top of the fortifications. From his vantage point he quickly realised that the position was lost. To fall into the hands of the British was an unpalatable and dishonourable option. For an honourable and brave warrior there was only one way out. He plunged his spurs savagely into the flanks of his horse, furiously urging the steed towards the walls of the fortifications. Without a moment's hesitation and without losing impetus man and horse cleared the parapet wall and plunged 120 feet onto the ground below, where their bodies lay crushed together in one tangled bloody mass, a prey to feral dogs and pigs.

The fleeing rebels of Kotah, whom the cavalry had shamefully ignored, now continued their murderous path towards Gwalior, the chief garrison town of Rajpootan, some 200 miles to the north-east. Nothing stood in their path as they ransacked village after village stealing horses, wagons and food and slaughtering anyone who stood in their path.

49 The magnificent fortress of Gwalior

It was April 1858 and the hot season was approaching and throughout the month and into May, the Column proceeded at a rate of ten miles per day. The temperature rose steadily, reaching 109° F and five degrees hotter inside the tent. The nights were equally oppressive; Fanny spent one hot night alternately bathing and fanning herself. Her servants were still several hours behind the main contingent and Fanny's hand-punkah was not available to waft cool air over her mistress.

There was some light relief when the Column reached Chuppra on 1 May. The Secretary of the Nawab of Tonk, accompanied by an escort of soldiers armed with swords, matchlocks and blunderbusses and arrayed like a medieval army, conducted the Column to their encampment. That evening, the

Secretary sent an elephant to Fanny so that she might make an appropriately impressive entry into town. Sadly, it was not to be; a ladder was required to mount the beast, lacking which the only recourse was for Fanny to make an undignified ascent via the animal's trunk, a gymnastic challenge she gracefully declined.

Four days later, on 5 May, the rightful commander of the Column, Brigadier Smith, joined them. Despite the oppressive heat, the Column maintained its ten miles per day, heading steadily towards Gwalior, the important stronghold that Tatya Tope had in his sights. The heat inflicted terrible damage on the Column. Fanny witnessed the horrific onset of heatstroke: the soldier falls, as if shot, his body is shaken with convulsions and his lips and face turn black. In moments, he is dead. One reason for the high death toll, as Fanny noted, was the heavy uniform the soldiers were obliged to wear, utterly inappropriate for the sweltering Indian climate. It cost £100 to equip and send a soldier to India, wrote Fanny in her narrative. Would it not make more sense, she mused, to have a uniform more suited to Indian conditions? A footnote in Fanny's narrative revealed that the 95th Regiment were subsequently kitted out with a lighter uniform.

In June, battered by debilitating temperatures of 114° F and the fruitless marching, Fanny, in extreme pain, was confined to a dooley (a stretcher borne on men's shoulders). She confided her situation to her *Journal*: 'It is sad to lie in pain and weakness amidst such stirring scenes; and to be so dependent, helpless, and exhausted, as to feel that the sleep of death would scarcely be sufficiently deep to afford relief.' 'True heroism', she wrote, 'is not to ride gallantly amid the braying of trumpets and all the pomp and circumstance of war, but to wrestle alone, in solitary fight, with darkness and the shadow of death.' Things were not going much better for Henry; he had sprained his ankle and complications set in, which had led to his leg becoming inflamed and swollen; he was confined to a *gharry*, a horse-drawn wagon. Fanny tells us frankly what she was up against – a husband who seemed to display little enthusiasm for his work, was frequently afflicted with a feeling of boredom and lacked the energy and dynamism that she, Fanny, had in spades.

The Column crossed the Antree (Antri) pass without incident and was soon encamped a mere fifteen miles from Gwalior, 'the Delhi of Central India', and the eagerly anticipated encounter with their principal foe Tatya Tope, whose forces now occupied the town. Fanny grasped Tope's tactics: 'We now begin to understand the object of Tatya Tope's erratic marches. He has evidently been endeavouring, by the rapidity of his transits from place to place, to draw away or separate the British forces, so that a passage might be left open for the Nana.' She gave grudging praise to this brilliant general. 'However we may abhor the crimes he has committed, we cannot refuse our respects to his good generalship and brilliant talents.'

Over the next few hours, the battle intensified and Fanny was in the thick of it as rebel shot screamed into the camp, bouncing dangerously around the tents and camels. Casualties, from wounds and heat stroke, poured into the makeshift hospital tents.

The fort of Gwalior occupied an almost impregnable position atop a vertical outcrop of rock but the infantry, crawling painfully up the hillside, managed to seize the enemy guns and turn the fire on the rebels. After the infantry had routed some of Tope's forces, confining them to a grove at the other end of the plain, the cavalry, led by the 8th Hussars, set off in hot pursuit of the enemy across the plain, thus atoning for the Kotah fiasco. Fanny, watching the action amidst a cloud of dust and the noise of the guns, could no longer resist the impulse to join the cavalry in a short, exhilarating gallop. 'I never, never shall forget the throbbing excitement of that short gallop, when the horse beneath one, raging in his fierce strength, and mad with excitement, scarcely touched the ground.' The battle won, the Maharajah of Gwalior could now safely resume his throne. Eager to show his gratitude, the Maharajah ordered vast quantities of champagne and beer to be distributed to the parched British forces.

The official news of the recapture of Gwalior was contained in a despatch from Sir Hugh Rose. After an engagement lasting five and a half hours, it read, Gwalior had been taken. There was a brief note added to the despatch: 'Ranee [*sic*] of Jhansi killed.' Various stories emerged on the fate of this charismatic woman warrior. It was said that a private of the 8th Hussars, having broken through the ranks of enemy forces, had run his sword through the body of a man dressed 'in a white turban and crimson tunic and trowsers'. It quickly emerged that this was the Rani of Jhansi, who led her troops into battle dressed in a soldier's uniform. Another story related that she had suffered two gunshot wounds. Mortally wounded, she had been carried from the battlefield and taken back to her palace. Close to death, she had commanded a pyre to be built on which she was solemnly placed. In the traditional ceremony of suttee, she then ordered the pyre to be lit and thus this most charismatic of leaders went to her death. Rani's sacrifice, concluded Fanny, in her epitaph to the fallen leader, was an 'instance of fierce and desperate courage that I can only listen to with wonder … on 17th June, her restless and intriguing spirit passed away: a subject of regret perhaps to those who admired her energy and courage'.

There was a curious conclusion to the Duberlys' sojourn in Gwalior. The Maharajah, 'a good-looking man' made an appearance and solemnly informed Fanny that he had designed a decoration to be given to all the troops who took part in the relief of Gwalior and he intended to ensure that she was also a recipient of the honour. Fanny, still bristling with disappointment at not receiving the Crimea medal, consoled herself with the thought that 'an Indian prince knows how to appreciate a woman's fortitude'.

From the luxury of Gwalior, Fanny found herself back on the road on 3 July. The Column pursued a zigzag course, heading for the town of Sepree where they had encamped a month before. The monsoon season had arrived and the progress of the Rajpootana Column was painfully slow, and that, together with the unremitting rain, thunder, wind and lightning, cast Fanny into depressive isolation. As the Column marched, casualties were high; horses and camels slipped up to their necks in the mud and many were lost. Rations were short, boots were disintegrating and the men were in abject misery. Unreliable communications (telegraph cables were cut) and contradictory orders given by inexperienced commanders, coupled with the ferocity of the monsoon, added to the horrors of the march. The result of these conflicting orders was that the Rajpootana Column found itself marching back and forth at the whim of senior commanders who were unable to give any strategic direction. 'Sir Robert Napier would have us march due north, General Roberts ... almost due west, and General Michel urgently required us south-east!' Fanny wrote in dismay. It was little consolation to her that on 27 September 1858, Fanny Duberly celebrated her 29th birthday.

Fanny's dejection was compounded in October by learning of the peaceful death of Bob, her steadfast companion of the Crimea campaign. 'I have to tell you of what I fear will give you pain, poor Bob's sudden death not by bullet, but in the common course of nature.' Fanny's favourite horse died peacefully after taking his morning feed. Her mind was taken off the tragedy by a natural phenomenon: Comet Donati, one of the two most brilliant comets of the nineteenth century, first seen by Fanny on 29 September, began to pass out of sight by October. The camp followers enquired whether the comet portended good or evil, but for Fanny, 'I cling to the hope that it will prove the herald of peace.'

Ominous news reached them in early October that Tatya Tope had entrenched himself strongly in Chandaree with a force of 12,000 men. Brigadier Smith proposed a bold plan to defeat the enemy. The town was located on the bend of the Betwa river, which was swollen at that time of year and unfordable. Lieutenant Colonel Robertson would cover the western approaches to the town, whilst the Central and North-Western roads would be blocked by Brigadier Smith. General Michel's cavalry would secure the southern approach and the river Betwa would close the final escape route. It could have put a decisive end to the insurrection. The weak point was the alleged rumbling stomachs of Michel's men. In a late communication to his fellow commanders, General Michel declared that he was unable to move his troops for nine days as his Europeans were out of groceries and could not march until they arrived. In nine days, the river would be fordable and the rebels would be able to make their escape. With heavy sarcasm Fanny offered her opinion on General Michel: 'Without inspecting the invoice we could not tell what condiments might be considered necessary to enable this luxurious force to move.'

A further thorn emerged in the side of British forces when a malcontent insurgent named Maun Sing was reported to have collected a sizeable force of 3,000 rebels and ejected the garrison at Fort of Powree, a stronghold of the Maharajah of Gwalior. It was to be the last battle action witnessed by Fanny Duberly in the Indian campaign. At 3 am on 20 November, a surprise night attack was launched against the sleeping insurgents. Fanny was unable to resist the thrill of the chase. She rode with her husband amongst the advance guard as the bullets flew all around them.

The Hussars and Lancers set off in hot pursuit of the fleeing rebels with Fanny Duberly in the midst of the swirling horses; bullets and gun smoke filled the air but the cavalry, undeterred and probably relishing the all too infrequent action, continued their charge, killing several hundred rebels. In the panic and confusion women and children were abandoned to their fate. A little girl, no more than twelve, wept by the body of her father. A small dog and a six-month-old baby were found lying on a bed and were rescued from the fray. Fanny adopted the dog. Maun

Sing took to his famous cream-coloured horse and galloped for his life, fleeing the carnage. His ultimate fate is unknown. Fanny speculated that he would withdraw to some holy place, change his name and dress and live the rest of his days in obscurity.

Whilst Fanny was savouring the last scent of battle, that most implacable enemy of the British, the resourceful and daring General Tatya Tope was fighting his last battle at Sikar on 16 November 1858 where he and his forces were soundly defeated. Surprisingly, Fanny gives no account of the defeat of Tatya Tope. He was brought to trial and executed on 18 April 1859.

Between October and Christmas Day 1858, the Rajpootana Column marched over 200 miles on a zigzag route that took them back to Seronge, a town that they had passed through twice during the previous months. Fanny's narrative finishes abruptly on 11 January 1859, some three months before the Mutiny was finally put down and almost a year since the untidy and frustrating Odyssey began and virtually in the same place. That day they found themselves within twenty miles of Kotah and it is here that Fanny ended her account. Her verdict on the campaign: 'It seems to me that all this Indian warfare is unsatisfactory work … there have been cases of ruthless slaughter, of which perhaps the less said the better.'

She concluded her narrative with the proud statistics of her journey: 'I close the record of our first year's Field Service in India, wherein that part of the Brigade, which was accompanied by my husband and myself, passed only one European station, Deesa, and marched in spite of Indian sun and Indian rain, and in the toilsome pursuit of an ever-flying foe, a distance of 2,028 miles, more than 1,800 of which I have myself accomplished on horseback.' After eleven gruelling months, Fanny's judgement of English rule in India may still resonate today: 'the Englishmen in India are not all evil, if they are not all good; and we must hope that the new administration will encourage and strengthen all that is good, and set its face against the evil'.

The Duberlys were to spend a further five years in India. Henry retired from the army in 1881 with the rank of Lieutenant Colonel and the couple moved to rural Wiltshire, a popular retreat for retired army offices and close to Fanny's family. Henry Duberly died in 1890 and a tablet to his memory was erected by his wife in St Andrew's Church. Fanny outlived her husband by a further twelve years, dying in Cheltenham in 1902 at the age of seventy-three. She is buried in St Peter's Church in Leckhampton. During the long years in rural seclusion, she was reluctant to talk about the campaigns she described so vigorously in her journals. It was only after a century of neglect that the exploits of this remarkable woman finally received the recognition they deserved, and the *Journals* of her experiences in the Crimea and India regained their rightful place as important historical testimonies to British power and global influence. In her eulogy for the Rani of Jhansi, Fanny recognised the qualities that drove this remarkable female warrior: 'a restless and intriguing spirit ... her energy and courage', an epitaph that might well apply to Frances Isabella Duberly.

20

Rev. Wilson and John Henry Newman: the Church Divided

A mere four years into the reign of Queen Victoria, a hugely influential document, entitled, *Tract 90*, was published and it threatened to tear asunder the Church of England. Two decades later, in 1860, another best-selling and controversial pamphlet caused uproar and brought the wrath of the church establishment upon the head of its author.

Two very different events, separated by a period of twenty years and yet both were connected in the perhaps unlikely shape of a former Professor of Anglo-Saxon at the University of Oxford. His name was Henry Bristow Wilson and from 1850 until his death in 1888, he was the vicar of St Andrew's Church in the parish of Great Staughton.

Henry Bristow Wilson (1803–1888) was educated at Merchant Taylors School, where his father Harry Bristow Wilson had been headmaster. Henry, a brilliant scholar, moved effortlessly to St John's College Oxford in 1821, graduating with a BA in 1825. He was appointed Fellow of the college at the comparatively early age of twenty-two, an honour he retained until his appointment as vicar of St Andrew's in 1850. He obtained his MA in 1829 and finally, in 1834, a Bachelor of Divinity degree. From 1839 to 1844, Wilson was Rawlinsonian Professor of Anglo-Saxon at the University of Oxford. Fellows were obliged to remain celibate and a convenient way for the College to 'retire' them to make way for younger men was to offer them a living when they did eventually marry. Thus, on his marriage, Henry Bristow Wilson became Great Staughton's parish priest.

In 1841, John Henry Newman, priest, theologian and poet, published *Tract 90*, subtitled *Remarks on Certain Passages in the Thirty-Nine Articles*. It was one of a series of pamphlets called *Tracts for the Times* in which a group of senior churchmen, principally based in Oxford (hence the 'Oxford Movement'), began to question whether the Church of England, founded by Henry VIII, had really divested itself of its European Catholic heritage. These tracts, which went on sale for mere pennies, attracted a wide readership, testifying to the importance and influence of the Church in the religious, social and educational fabric of the country.

Tract 90 examined in exhaustive detail the text of the *Thirty-Nine Articles*. These were established in 1571 in the reign of Elizabeth I and enshrine the doctrine and practices of the Church of England, asserting the newly proclaimed Church's independence both from Catholic ritual and the excesses of Edward VI's Calvinistic Protestantism. Newman's *Tract* called into doubt the legitimacy of the Church of England as established by the Act of Supremacy of 1534.

In his pamphlet Newman argued that the Church of England still retained the trappings of the Roman church and, in his view, should therefore return to its pre-Reformation liturgy and ritual. He campaigned for the greater use of ritual, vestments and Catholic observances in the church. For Newman, the church was 'catholic', a congregation of all the faithful, which should not be confined to a particular place.

His pamphlet put Newman and his Oxford sympathisers on a collision course with the established Church. Newman concluded in this way: 'Man had done his worst to disfigure, to mutilate, the old Catholic Truth; but there it was, in spite of them, in the Articles still.' Had Newman succeeded in persuading the Church and the public of the rightness of his views, the Church of England would again become, as it was before Henry's break with Rome, part of the European Catholic tradition.

The riposte to Newman's *Tract 90* was not long in coming. On 26 March 1841, Rev. Henry Bristow Wilson issued a thirty-page rebuttal to Newman in a pamphlet entitled, *A letter to the Rev. T.T. Churton M.A. Fellow of Brasenose College concerning no. 90 of the Tracts for the Times*, by J.H. Newman. In his response, Wilson appealed early on to the general reader, who might swallow Newman's argument whole, that it (*Tract 90*) 'should be repudiated or avowed'.

Wilson went through Newman's text paragraph by paragraph, concluding with a quotation from the *Books of Homilies* (1547, 1562 and 1571), when the Bible was still in Latin and priests were too ill-educated to compose sermons. The longest of the *Homilies* concerned the *Perils of Idolatry* and Wilson used a quotation to point out that the setting up of images in a church (which Newman was keen to re-establish, in accordance with Catholic liturgy) could soon lead to the worshipping of them and thus 'it will come to pass that eventually the whole world will fall into idolatrous ways'.

Wilson's arguments prevailed. The arguments in *Tract 90* were overwhelmingly rejected and Newman had no choice but to renounce his position in the Church of England: 'I would not hold office in a Church which would not allow my sense of the Articles' and in 1845 he was duly received into the Catholic church.

In 1879 John Henry Newman was made a cardinal and was canonised as a saint in 2019. Music lovers have a particular reason for showing their gratitude to him. He was the author of *The Dream of Gerontius*, set to music by Edward Elgar, and widely considered to be one of the English composer's greatest achievements. Perhaps Henry Bristow Wilson can be given a modest credit for his indirect contribution to the work.

Wilson's next appearance on the public stage took place in 1860, twenty years after his encounter with Newman. In that year a volume was published with the seemingly innocuous title of *Essays and Reviews*. It was the brainchild of Henry Bristow Wilson and it was he, as editor and contributor, who brought together the six senior clergymen and scholars of the Church of England, including Frederick Temple, later Archbishop of Canterbury. The book became a bestseller, going through thirteen editions in five years and selling 20,000 copies. Several hundred articles and books appeared, vigorously attacking or defending the views of its seven authors who were quickly dubbed '*Septem contra Christum*' (Seven against Christ) by enraged fellow clergymen. Eminent theologians and clerics hurled invective at each other from the pulpit, in scholarly journals and in the public arena. Even the government found itself being called upon to intervene in an attempt to resolve the conflict between the opposing parties. Wilson himself was brought before the highest ecclesiastical court in the land, the Court of Arches, and charged with heresy for his article, *Séances historiques de Genève. The National Church*. What did he write that proved so controversial to the church?

Wilson's essay began on a positive note. He was advocating a 'broad church', liberal in outlook, inclusive rather than exclusive, respecting those, particularly scientists, who held different but equally sincere views. If, said Wilson, people (he probably had scientists particularly in mind) expressed their doubts in an honest and sincere way, and reacted against church doctrine, the threat of eternal damnation would hold no fears for them. If the church persisted in its traditional view, concerned only for the faithful, it might simply decline into a fossilised sect.

The church, he argued, has survived numerous assaults in its 2,000-year history 'through Saxon rudeness, Norman rapine, baronial oppression and bloodshed' and now, in the present day, there can be no political or ecclesiastical changes so great that the church cannot again overcome them. The time has come, he argued, 'for raising fresh structures; a time for repairing the ancient paths, and a time for filling the valleys and lowering the hills in the constructing of new'.

In the present time, Wilson went on, how many of our fellow citizens are alienated from the Christian community and do not play any role in supporting the ministry? And were there not ancient civilisations that had stories of a virgin birth, a star in the east and the divine origin of earth and man? Surely the Emperor Constantine was right to use the power of the state to disseminate Christian teachings to the Roman Empire. This alliance between church and state, called 'unholy' by some, was the ideal foundation stone for a national church.

This National Church, as Wilson envisaged it, would include scientists, philosophers and the educated elite and its principal purpose was to produce good citizens. If this educated elite were to be excluded from consideration by the church, it would inevitably react by opposing the church's teaching. Indeed, said Wilson, Christianity readily accepted the influence of philosophers and scientists such as Plato and Newton. Why not also acknowledge the massive advances brought about by contemporary scientists? Darwin's *Origin of Species* of 1859 had appeared a few months before *Essays and Reviews*. Charles Lyell's *Principles of Geology* (1830–1833) had refuted biblical chronology. Henry Bristow Wilson made the heretical suggestion that Bible accounts were not necessarily to be taken literally and now scientists and some eminent theologians seemed to be endorsing Wilson's view.

From the start, reaction to the pamphlet from the Church of England establishment was hostile. A Christian journal described Wilson's argument as 'a *Tract 90* of the Broad Church trying to be Christian without the Bible'. A petition against it was signed by 11,000 clergymen, traditionalists who believed in the truth of the scriptures and eternal damnation. Protestants, Anglo-Catholics, Evangelicals found common cause in their opposition to the incendiary notions that they believed would shatter the moral authority of the church. Press, pamphleteers and government joined the howling mob. Those in the church wedded to the more traditional view of 'biblical inspiration and eternal torments' campaigned against the book. Demonstrating the ferocity of the debate, Samuel Wilberforce, Bishop of Oxford, obtained a 'synodical condemnation' of *Essays and Reviews*. If Wilson's liberal interpretation of scripture were to be permitted, it was argued, sin would be ubiquitous. The book was roundly condemned by both Houses of Parliament in July 1864.

Wilson, editor of *Essays and Reviews*, was duly brought before the Court of Arches in June 1862 where he was found guilty of three counts of heresy. Stephen Lushington, the Dean of Arches, presiding, pronounced sentence that Wilson should be suspended from his living for a period of one year. Wilson mounted an appeal against the verdict and on 19 and 20 June 1863, he appeared, not before the church authorities, but before the Privy Council, an instrument of government. It was said at the time that the Privy Council's decision to overturn the sentence had 'dismissed Hell with costs'. In many respects the Privy Council's judgement, that a priest who doubted eternal damnation could not be considered a threat to public morality, was a vindication of free speech.

Wilson's appeal was successful and Lushington's decision was quashed on 8 February 1864. Wilson duly returned to his pastoral duties as vicar of St Andrew's Church, Great Staughton. The reaction of his parishioners to his ordeal must have been heartening for Wilson. The *St Neots Chronicle* of 11 March 1862, when he was about to be arraigned before the Court of Arches, reported: 'We understand much sympathy has been expressed by the parishioners for Henry Bristow Wilson in his present position in the ecclesiastical courts, and confident hopes are entertained that he will be enabled successfully to resist his prosecutors.' In 1866, when urgent repairs were needed for the church, his student and friend Rev. Robert Bruce Kennard instigated a subscription in Wilson's name, not only to raise the necessary funds for the repairs but also to erect a memorial as a tribute to Wilson for his contribution to English theological thought. In his semi-retirement, Wilson continued to contribute articles on philosophy and scripture to the *Westminster Review*. One such article was a scathing attack on tithes, which benefited the clergy of populous parishes but did nothing for their sparsely populated rural equivalents.

Henry Bristow Wilson died on 10 August 1888 at the age of eighty-five and was laid to rest in the burial grounds of St Andrew's Church where his impressive tomb, inscribed with the words *Steadfast to the end*, can still be seen. His wife Jane (1820–1892) is buried alongside him. A eulogy to one of the intellectual giants of the Victorian church was delivered by his close friend Rev. R. B. Kennard on Sunday 19 August 1888 in the church of St Andrew, Great Staughton.

21

The South African Campaign 1899–1902

When the Second Boer War broke out on 11 October 1899, the reaction of the British public was an upsurge in patriotic fervour that saw no fewer than 100,000 responding to the call to arms. Great Staughton was no exception and in 1902, following the signing of the peace treaty, the church and parish magazine listed all the volunteers from the village who had served in the South African Campaign. A commemorative brass was erected in the church dedicated to three Staughton men who lost their lives as a result of the campaign: Private Edward Ernest Cowley, Private Arthur James Elmer and Private William Evans.

From the outset of the conflict, the Boers seized the initiative, besieging the important strategic towns of Mafeking, Kimberley and Ladysmith, inflicting heavy casualties on the mighty British Empire. Around 45,000 British troops were immediately despatched to South Africa to lift the sieges and restore British pride.

The relief of Kimberley proved to be a long, drawn-out affair, punctuated by four setbacks at Belmont, Graspan, Modder River and Magersfontein. One of the participants in the four battles was Grey William Duberly, born on 20 June 1875, one of seventeen Staughton volunteers who took part in the Campaign. Duberly was commissioned as a 2nd Lieutenant in the 3rd Battalion Grenadier Guards in May 1897 at the age of twenty-two. Two years later, his regiment was posted to Cape Colony to join Lord Methuen and his force of 9,000 men advancing to the relief of Kimberley.

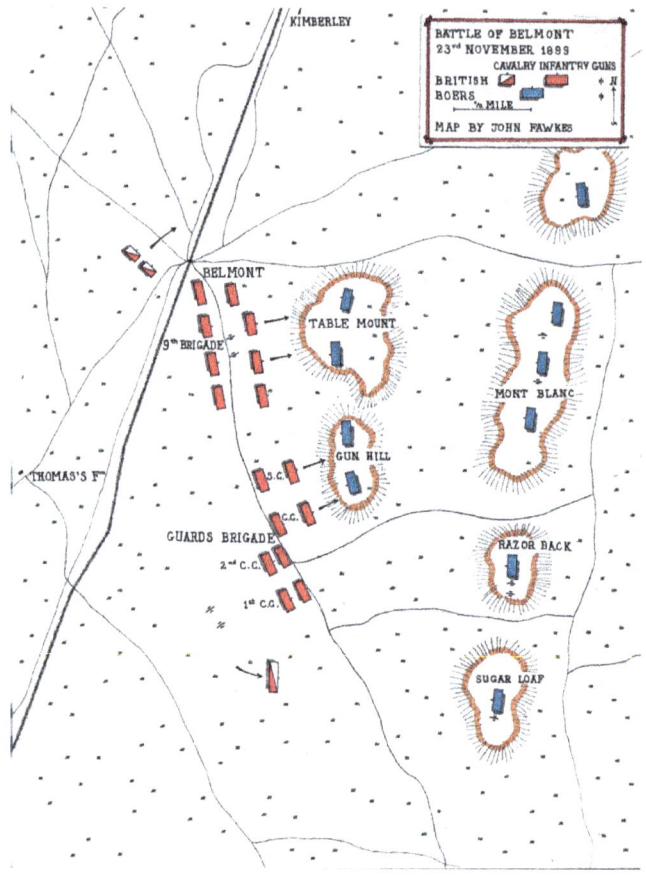

50 Battle of Belmont

On 22 November 1899, Methuen's forces reached Belmont and pitched camp on the open veldt. Behind them, to the west, was the railway line; ahead, ten miles to the east was a line of five kopjes (small hills) all running approximately north–south, parallel to the railway line. The two nearest kopjes, Table Mount and Gun Hill, were to be the scene of the battle the next day. A force of 2,500 Boer commandos under General Jacobus Prinsloo occupied the heights of the five kopjes. British default strategy was to bombard enemy positions with heavy artillery and then advance in formation, firing as they went, until they could affix bayonets and finish the job. It had proved successful when the enemy was armed with nothing more effective than machetes and spears; against long-range smokeless German Mausers, wielded by highly skilled and experienced Boer marksmen, the strategy was to prove disastrous. The Boer commandos proved to be a formidable enemy.

Methuen decided on a night march to outflank the enemy, sending the 9th Brigade to position themselves to the north of Table Mount, whilst Lieutenant Duberly's 3rd Battalion Grenadier Guards advanced under cover of darkness to the southern tip of Gun Hill. In a dawn attack the Boers would be caught in a pincer movement to the north and south whilst the bulk of Methuen's infantry would mount a frontal assault on the Boer positions at the top of the two kopjes.

The strategy might have worked if the maps had been accurate. As day dawned the Guards found themselves not on the Boer's left flank to the south of Gun Hill, as their maps had indicated, but on the open veldt in plain view of the deadly Mausers. British artillery ravaged the Boer emplacements at the top of the kopjes and the Grenadier Guards advanced. Facing a murderous fusillade, Lieutenant Duberly and his men were forced to lie flat and, for a torrid thirty minutes, return fire as best as they could. Casualties were high but sheer numerical strength eventually saw British forces move rapidly up the slopes of the kopje. As they were about to affix bayonets, the Boers abruptly left their positions, raced down the hill and leapt onto the horses they had previously tethered there, withdrawing quickly to the second range of hills, Mont Blanc, Razor Back and Sugarloaf, all occupied by their fellow Boer commandos. 'We just saw their heels', remarked one soldier of the debacle. British casualties of the battle of Belmont were seventy-five officers and soldiers killed and 223 wounded. Boer casualties were slightly higher, thus enabling the British to claim victory.

Two days later, Methuen was confronted by a considerable force of Boers occupying the top of the Graspan kopje. Adopting the same strategy of artillery bombardment followed by a frontal charge by the infantry, Methuen was met with the same result as at Belmont, the Boers withdrawing their forces before the numerically superior British troops could make use of their bayonets.

Methuen anticipated that the next encounter with the enemy would be at the crucial Modder River station, twenty miles further north. On 23 November Methuen reached the river to be confronted by a Boer force numbering 9,000 men under General Jacobus Herculaas de la Rey and General Piet Cronje. The Boers adopted a different strategy from Belmont and Graspan. Cronje and De la Rey reasoned that by firing from the top of a kopje downwards into the advancing British troops, the effective killing area of the Mausers was greatly weakened. De la Rey therefore ordered a five-mile trench to be dug stretching along the north banks of the Modder River and the river Riet on either side of the strategically important railway bridge. In front of the trench was open veldt offering no cover for advancing British troops.

The Guards, under General Henry Colvile, were ordered to advance to the junction of the two rivers on the right of the railway bridge where they were confronted by De la Rey's commandos. Lieutenant Duberly's detachment was in the centre of the frontline advancing cautiously towards the Boer trench. As they came within 1,200 yards of the river they were met with murderous fire from the Mausers. The Guards continued their advance into the relentless fusillade until they were brought to a halt, still 1,000 yards from the river. Strength of numbers eventually won the day and British forces were able to cross the river, compelling the Boers to withdraw. British casualties were seventy killed and 413 wounded, whilst the Boers lost an estimated 150 men. In an official despatch to the Queen, Methuen described the battle as 'the bloodiest of the century' and 'one of the hardest and most trying fights in the annals of the British army', in which his troops shelled the enemy 'out of their trenches and then charged'. The result, he concluded 'was terrible'.

After the battle, the Boers made another of their tactical withdrawals to Magersfontein Hill, which they began to strengthen, anticipating that this would be the site of the next confrontation. Methuen meanwhile waited for two weeks at the Modder River for reinforcements to arrive and on 10 December he was ready to give the order for his forces, now swelled to nearly 13,000 men, to advance to the Magersfontein kopje.

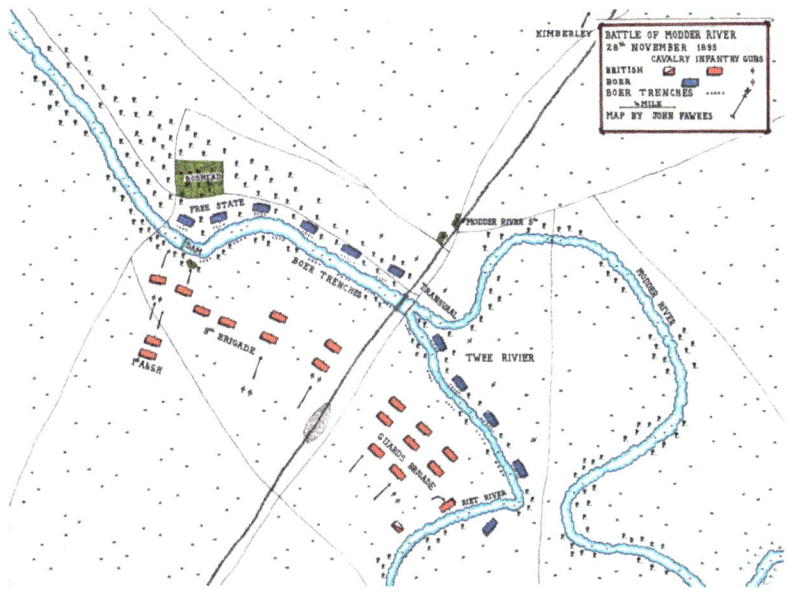

51 Battle of Modder River

The battle lasted the whole of 11 December 1899 and the result was even more disastrous than Modder River. Cronje's Boers and their smokeless Mausers efficiently cut down the British frontal assault, causing heavy casualties. The Grenadier Guards, in a support role, suffered only minor casualties. When the Boers opened artillery fire in late afternoon, British forces withdrew. It was a colossal defeat and brought to an end Methuen's command.

The misery was not yet over for the shattered British troops. They withdrew to the Modder River, exhausted and without food or water, to find the river littered with the corpses of men and horses, a fertile breeding ground for enteric fever against which the army had no defences. Hundreds of men died of the disease. Magersfontein was the second of three disastrous defeats suffered by the British army in the single week of 10–17 December 1899, the so-called 'Black Week'. The heavy defeat at Magersfontein led to a wholesale re-appraisal of British strategy. Methuen was removed and replaced by General Lord Roberts, who, with 25,000 reinforcements, took over command of the campaign. On 15 February 1900, three months after the defeat at Magersfontein, Kimberley was finally relieved by a cavalry division under Lieutenant General John French, after a siege lasting 124 days.

The siege of Ladysmith was finally lifted on 28 February 1900 after 118 days, by a relief column under Major Hubert Gough whose forces included the young Winston Churchill.

Lieutenant Duberly next saw action at Poplar Grove on 7 March 1900, at a critical stage of the war, when the demoralised Boers were decisively routed, allowing British forces to pursue the next stage of the campaign, to capture Bloemfontein, capital of the Orange Free State. We next hear of Lieutenant Duberly when the Grenadier Guards were posted to the Transvaal in May and June 1900 and saw action at the Battle of Diamond Hill, which took place on 11 and 12 June 1900. Fourteen thousand British troops were pitted against a Boer force of 4,000 and the result was never in doubt. Lieutenant Duberly's fellow Staughton volunteer Private John Wakefield was present to celebrate the victory.

After the Battle of Diamond Hill, the Boers' last desperate throw of the dice, Lieutenant Duberly ended his military service in the South African Campaign. He was mentioned in despatches

52 Lt Grey William Duberly (front, in bush ranger hat) at Modder River

for conspicuous service by Lord Roberts in the *London Gazette* in 1902 and was awarded the Queen's medal with six clasps, and later the King's medal with two clasps. A clasp designated the battles in which the recipient had served. Six of Lieutenant Duberly's eight were awarded in the reign of Queen Victoria and the remaining two in the reign of her successor, King Edward VII.

The *St Neots Advertiser* paid fulsome tribute to Lieutenant Duberly, reporting on the warm reception that he received upon his return from South Africa in August 1902. He was greeted at the station by a procession formed of brother officers and then borne by carriage to Great Staughton, which was appropriately decked out with bunting.

In May 1904 Lieutenant Duberly was appointed Captain and in July 1911, the year he resigned his commission, he was promoted to Major. Three years later, on 31 July 1914, he married Millicent Florence Eleanor, née Wilson, Countess Cowley, daughter of Lord Nunburnholme.

22

Rev. Watson's Talented Sons

This is an appropriate moment in the narrative to provide a little biographical information about the inspiration behind the present book, the man who was responsible for the first *History of Great Staughton*, Rev. Henry George Watson. He began the work after his retirement from the incumbency of St Andrew's Church in 1909 and the book was published in 1916. This first ever history of the village, was a considerable feat of scholarship undertaken in an era when research had to be conducted either by personal visits to the archive (not easy with relatively poor local transport) or by correspondence. It is a great tribute to Watson's industry

53 Rev. H.G. Watson with son Herbert and daughters c. 1901

that despite these formidable obstacles his work remains even now, a century later, an essential source of information.

Henry George Watson was born in London in 1838, the son of John Watson, a doctor. He attended St John's College Oxford where he was the Pusey and Ellerton Hebrew scholar. He obtained his Bachelor of Arts degree in 1860, followed two years later by an MA. He was a curate in Tring between 1861 and 1869. In 1863, at the age of twenty-five, he married the 24-year-old Lucy Eleanor Gillman. Between 1865 and 1880, the couple had ten children: seven sons and three daughters. Watson was appointed vicar of Long Maraton, Hertfordshire, where he served for two years from 1868. He then moved to St Leonards in Buckinghamshire where he was the incumbent until 1895, in which year he became vicar of St Andrew's Church in Great Staughton, a position he occupied until his retirement in 1909 at the age of seventy-one. He devoted the early years of his retirement to researching and writing his *History of the Parish of Great Staughton*. Henry George Watson died in 1929 at the age of ninety-one.

The second of H. G. Watson's seven sons, William Stephen, was born in Bloomsbury London in 1866. His life is celebrated in a stained-glass window in the south aisle of the church, and a modest memorial plaque in the church briefly commemorates his life. It reads:

> In loving memory of William Stephen Watson, dearly loved son of Rev. H. G. Watson, vicar of the parish. Born December 26 1865, died December 23 1900, at Mossel Bay, Cape Colony. In the hope of resurrection to eternal life through Jesus Christ.

The year of his death and the geographical location may suggest that William Stephen Watson was another casualty of the

South African Campaign, but this is not the case. He was a highly qualified, experienced and well-respected engineer in the water, gas and railway industries. After schooling at St Marks, Windsor and Merchant Taylors School, London (following in his father's footsteps in the latter), William Watson became a student at the Royal College of Science, subsequently being elected by open competition to a free studentship in the College. In 1886, at the age of twenty-one, Watson became an Associate Member of the College.

His first position was with a company that made brewing equipment. He remained with Gillman and Spencer for eighteen months until December 1887; his major responsibility in the company was to supervise the erection of brewing equipment at Gordon Wharf, Rotherhithe. His career then took an upward turn when he was articled to Jabez Church, whose reputation in the gas, hydraulic, and sanitary engineering sector would greatly enhance Watson's curriculum vitae and his reputation in engineering circles. After completing his articles in 1890, Watson was employed by Jabez Church as Resident Engineer on the construction of the Mid-Sussex Waterworks. A year later, on 1 December 1891, Watson was elected an Associate Member of the Royal College of Science.

His career continued to flourish. In 1892 Watson saw a better future for himself in the Cape Colony and for five years he worked with another reputed engineer, Thomas Stewart, on a number of varied projects. He undertook surveys for the Uitenhage and Bloemfontein Waterworks; he was involved in the Van Staaden River dam project; he worked on the Table Mountain storage-reservoir; and in particular, he designed a wire ropeway that brought materials and equipment for that project. He also worked on the reservoir at Kloof Nek. A more unusual project was the design and construction of a pier near Cape Town for landing fish. He further extended his expertise and experience in August 1897, when he was employed by the South African government to undertake a survey for the proposed railway connecting Cape Town and Port Elizabeth. He evidently impressed his employers because in 1898 the Cape Government appointed Watson as assistant engineer on the construction of the Oudtshoorn-Klippart Railway. The railway terminus was at Mossel Bay and in 1900, with the Boer War reaching a critical phase, Watson was duly transferred to that town to supervise the completion of the line. It was not however the battlefield that put an end to his life but enteric fever (typhoid), which Watson contracted in the winter of 1900 and on 23 December of that year, he succumbed to the condition.

William was not the only member of the Watson family to find himself in South Africa during the Boer War. The disastrous progress of the South African Campaign prompted his brother, Charles Gordon Watson, a surgeon, to volunteer. The fifth son of Rev. H. G. Watson and his wife Eleanor, Charles was born 18 April 1874 in St Leonard's Buckinghamshire.

54 Sir Charles Gordon Gordon-Watson

After studying at St Bartholomew's Hospital, Watson qualified in 1898 and was a house surgeon at the hospital. Charles went out to South Africa in 1899, serving in the Wynberg Hospital, Cape Town, before transferring to Kroonstad where he was on hand to deal with the great outbreak of typhoid during the spring and summer of 1900. He was described by fellow medics as 'an able surgeon, skilful with his hands, enthusiastic, and possessed of good judgment'. He was awarded the Queen's South Africa medal with three clasps as a tribute to his work.

Although he described himself as 'an incorrigible Tory', Watson was no stuffed shirt. In South Africa he enjoyed horse racing (as a follower and practitioner), polo, trekking, climbing (Table Mountain) and golf, along with the more sedate pastimes of bridge and whist.

After returning from medical service in the Boer War, Watson was anxious to establish his reputation, taking on posts in a number of London hospitals. He was Chief Assistant in the Orthopaedic Department of St Bartholomew's Hospital in the years 1904–1907. Watson is perhaps best known for his pioneering use of radium in the treatment of cancer of the rectum and he conducted his first operation with the new treatment in 1910.

Although a keen sportsman and man of the outdoors, he also enjoyed cerebral pursuits; he was an enthusiastic amateur actor and during the Edwardian era he was a regular theatregoer. Indulging his passion for daring exploits, he took part in motor-cycle races from London to Edinburgh and back, at a time when that mode of transport was notorious for its unreliability.

At the outbreak of the First World War, Watson was posted to a field hospital at No. 1 British Red Cross Hospital, Le Touquet. Watson was one of the first to recognise the syndrome of trench frostbite and to recommend an appropriate treatment for the condition. In March 1917, he arrived too late to save the life of his wounded brother Herbert whose story is told in Chapter

24. For his outstanding services to medicine, Watson was awarded the Order of St Michael and St George in 1916 and knighted in 1919. Watson was mentioned four times in despatches, one of which was signed by Winston Churchill. In 1920 he changed his surname by deed poll to Charles Gordon Gordon-Watson.

Major General Sir Charles Gordon Gordon-Watson, KBE, FRCS, died at his home in York on 19 December 1949 at the age of seventy-five. He was buried at Dorchester, Oxfordshire.

23

Staughton Manor Railway Station

John Edwards Presgrave Howey had a fortunate start in life. The family's history began in Goulburn, New South Wales, Australia, in 1838, when Henry Howey, a sheep farmer, travelled to Melbourne to purchase various parcels of farmland, which he subsequently sold on for a decent profit. He had also purchased for £128 three parcels of scrubland situated on the banks of the Yarra river. Clearing them for agriculture would have drained the Howey finances, so Henry could do little more than sit on his purchase and hope for an upturn in land values. The following year, he decided to move with his wife and six children to start a new life in Melbourne.

On 21 June 1838, Henry, his wife and their six children boarded the schooner *Sarah*. Neither they nor the schooner were ever seen again. The land he had purchased was passed down to various relatives. Then Fortune took a hand. The city of Melbourne was expanding rapidly and Howey's unenticing piece of scrubland became part of the business area of the city and was sold for a princely sum, thus making the Howey fortune. It was said that the scrub was the most valuable tract of land in Australia still in private hands. Howey Place, a fashionable shopping centre and the Presgrave Building still stand as memorials to the family. The land was bequeathed to various members of the Howey family in England until it was eventually inherited by John Howey, who attained his majority in 1907.

John Howey was born on 17 November 1886 and educated at Eton where he first became enthusiastic about trains and speed. On leaving school, he was keen to further his knowledge of engineering and joined Vickers as an apprentice, but the family's disapproval of John's choice of profession led to him reluctantly following in his father's footsteps by enlisting in the army. However, his enthusiasm for things mechanical and especially locomotives did not leave him and was further kindled when he visited the Rhyl Miniature Railway in Wales. He spent the day indulging his passion for speed by driving the locomotive, which came from the workshop of Bassett-Lowke, the celebrated Northampton-based engineering company that specialised in supplying miniature locomotives to enthusiastic wealthy amateurs. It was a day that would transform Howey's life. He began to conceive of building his own private miniature railway.

In 1907 Henry Howey's bad luck became John Howey's good fortune. In 1911 he set out on the search for a suitable residence with sufficient land to accommodate his ambitious plans for a narrow-gauge railway. He eventually settled on Staughton Manor, which he rented in that year from its owner, Harry Pickersgill-Cunliffe. The land on which the Manor stood was ideal for the construction of an ambitious ¾-mile line (which could be extended to 1½ miles; it never was). Howey wasted no time in purchasing a 9½-inch gauge locomotive from Bassett-Lowke. It did not long satisfy him. Having driven the 15-inch locomotive in Rhyl, he was unable to resist the temptation to follow suit.

Howey spared no expense in creating his railway. He was not alone in his enthusiasm for speed and miniature railways, which at the time were the fastest machines on land. The model railway pioneer, Sir Arthur Heywood, had created a three-mile line at Eaton Hall, near Chester, in 1896. Howey was fortunate in finding the ideal partner for his scheme – a brilliant engineer and enthusiast for miniature locomotives. His name was Henry Greenly and in 1901, Bassett-Lowke saw the potential in this 25-year-old engineer and hired him to design the company's range of model locomotives.

Staughton Manor Railway Station

55 John Howey and Staughton Manor Railway Station

By 1910 the company was an acknowledged leader in the design and manufacture of model railways, catering to an ever-growing market. Greenly's ambition matched Howey's own, and it was he, with Bassett-Lowke, who created the 15-inch gauge locomotive, named *Little Giant*, which powered the Rhyl railway. Howey promptly ordered a locomotive in the same class. It would cost him the not inconsiderable sum of £400. The work to lay the infrastructure for the railway occupied the winter of 1911. The design included an impressive 20-foot model of the Forth Railway Bridge and fully kitted-out station, which was quickly christened Staughton Manor Railway Station. Local builders Smith and Son were on hand to provide the timber and iron work involved in the construction of the line and by summer 1912, the locomotive, named *John Anthony*, was ready for its maiden journey.

Local legend has it that the railway was principally used for leisure purposes by Howey, in particular to fetch his vegetables from his kitchen garden in the grounds of the Manor. Another story has it that, if children were well-behaved and had regularly attended Sunday school, they might be rewarded with a ride on the railway, which could carry upwards of forty people, with room to spare for Howey's impressive collection of dogs.

Over the next year, Howey continued to enjoy the life of a member of the moneyed classes: shooting in Scotland, theatregoing in London and visits to his properties in Australia. The idyll was not to last, neither for Howey nor the country. At the insistence of his father, Howey had joined the Dorsetshire Yeomanry when war broke out, before transferring to the Bedfordshire Yeomanry, where he held a commission and it was with this regiment that Howey went to the front in 1914. The prospect of long years in the trenches cannot have been enticing for the young, speed-obsessed Howey and he soon enlisted in the fledgling Royal Flying Corps. The *John Anthony* was left at Eaton Hall, where it had been put through its paces on the three-mile line. Howey was not to see it in action again at Staughton Manor.

56 *John Edwards Presgrave Howey and* John Anthony *on the 15-inch gauge railway at Staughton Manor*

Despite his intense efforts, Howey did not qualify as a pilot and had to be content with the role of observer in the two-seater FE2 biplane. His squadron was based at Abeele in Belgium. An ambitious operation was proposed for 11 November 1915, in which aeroplanes from the 4th, 8th and 13th squadrons would take part in a mass raid on the important German aerodrome of Bellenglise.

The portents were not good. The plan was for the squadrons to assemble above the airfield and then proceed towards the target. Whilst the raid was in progress, cover would be given by 11 Squadron and their Vickers FB5s, which would patrol the St Quentin area warding off any German attempts to intercept the raiders. Lieutenant Howey and his pilot Claude Herschel Kelway-Bamber took off in their FE2c, flying with a half-load of bombs and duly arrived at the rendezvous with the other squadrons. Bad weather then took a hand; strong winds and heavy cloud caused many pilots to lose their way.

The plan fell apart. Kelway-Bamber's FE2c was attacked but his observer, Lieutenant Howey, with the machine gun, managed to shoot down the German fighter. The FE2c started to behave erratically and when Howey turned to Kelway-Bamber he noticed to his horror that a piece of shrapnel from the German fighter had inflicted a fatal wound on the pilot. There was only one thing for it and in an act that reads like something out of a *Boy's Own* adventure story, Howey clambered over the fuselage and took his place in the pilot's seat, squatting uncomfortably on the body of Kelway-Bamber.

He managed to bring the plane down safely, although wounded, and found himself behind enemy lines where he was quickly taken prisoner. Howey provided a remarkably phlegmatic account of what happened:

"Poor Bamber, I was sorry that he was killed. He was such a nice boy - and only 19. I had a fight with two German aeroplanes and then a shell burst very close to us and I heard a large piece whizz past my head. The aeroplane then started to come down head first, spinning all the time. We must have dropped about 5,000 feet in about 20 seconds. I looked around at once and saw poor Bamber with a terrible wound in his head, quite dead. I then realised that the only chance of saving my life was to step over into his seat and sit on his lap where I could reach the controls. I managed to get the machine out of that terrible death plunge – switched off the engine – and made a good landing on terra firma. We were at 10,000 feet when Bamber was killed and luckily it was this tremendous height that gave me time to think and act. I met one of the pilots of the German machines that attacked us. He could speak English quite well and shook hands after a most thrilling fight. I brought down his machine with my machine gun and he had to land quite close to where I had landed. He had a bullet through his radiator but neither he or his observer were touched."

In a letter home in January 1916, Howey wrote warmly of his captors:

"I met two German Officers there who knew several English people that I knew, and they were most awfully kind to me. They gave me a very good dinner of champagne, oysters, etc, and I was treated like an honoured guest. I then came by train the next day to Mainz, where I was confined in a room by myself for two days. I have now been moved into a general room with eight other English Officers where we sleep and eat. We are treated very well and play hockey and tennis in the prison yard. I shall never forget it as long as I live. The shock was so great that I could hardly remember a single thing in my former life for two days. Now I am getting better and my mind is practically normal again."

Howey's pilot, 2nd Lieutenant Claude Herschel Kelway-Bamber, is buried in the Harlebeke New British Cemetery II. A. 10, near Ypres, Belgium. His grave is inscribed: GREATER LOVE HATH NO MAN THAN THIS. Lieutenant Kelway-Bamber was the son of Herbert and Eliza Kelway-Bamber.

The Germans wasted no time in discovering Howey's back history. An English millionaire now in enemy hands was a considerable trophy for the German propaganda machine and they did not hesitate to exploit its potential to the full. Howey spent two humiliating years being paraded around various German prisoner of war camps before relief arrived in 1917, when he was declared unfit for active service and released on parole to the safe haven of Switzerland, bound to remain there until the end of the war. He was well cared for in the Swiss hospital, particularly by the wife of the doctor who had pronounced him unfit for duty. Gladys, Howey's wife, joined her husband shortly after his arrival and quickly appraising that the care he was receiving may have gone beyond normal nursing duties, allegedly lost no time in having the nurse transferred.

After the war, Howey was persuaded to sell the *John Anthony* to the Eskdale and Ravenglass Railway. The Staughton Manor railway fell victim to benign neglect. The track was torn up, the Forth Bridge dismantled and Staughton Manor Railway Station reputedly became a house for hens, a function that it maintained, according to local legend, for several decades.

Howey and his wife were now regulars on the London social scene, having bought a Mayfair residence. Meanwhile, like Mr Toad, Howey was consumed by a new passion, still involving speed and mechanical engineering. In 1923 he took delivery of a powerful 7-litre Leyland motor car. He took up motor racing, much more hazardous than the locomotive, but cheaper and faster. For two years he was a regular feature at Brooklands along with his friend Parry Thomas, who was later killed attempting the land speed record. In 1921 Howey found another speed and racing fanatic, a man who was even richer than he was, Count Louis Zborowski (1895 – 1924), whose family properties included much of Fifth Avenue and Manhattan. Zborowski's car was a 23-litre Mercedes, which covered the Brooklands course at an incredible (for that time) speed of 100 mph. His car achieved worldwide fame later, when its nickname, *Chitty-Chitty-Bang-Bang* was profitably appropriated by Ian Fleming and Hollywood. Zborowski achieved more lasting recognition as one of the founders of the Aston Martin Company. He and Howey struck up a close friendship in which locomotives and railways were a frequent topic of conversation. Before they could collaborate on any project, however, Zborowski was killed in the Italian Grand Prix at Monza, on 19 October 1924.

In 1925 Howey, still hankering for a really giant model railway, set in motion his plan for a completely new railway and commissioned Henry Greenly to come up with ideas for its location. The line would have to be at least seven miles long, thus eclipsing the Eskdale and Ravenglass, and it must be straight and level to allow the locomotives to achieve a decent speed. Laying such a track, even if a suitable location could be found, was not straightforward; local authority and planning permission needed to be sought. If, however, the line could be promoted as providing a public benefit, permission was much more likely to be granted. After various proposals came to nought, a line from Romney to Hythe presented itself as a likely candidate that would serve the public purpose whilst also bringing tourist income to an otherwise neglected area of England.

After two years' work, the Romney Hythe and Dymchurch 15-inch gauge railway was officially opened on 16th July 1927. The line ran originally for eight miles from the Port of Hythe, one of the original Cinque Ports, to the terminus at New Romney, but Howey quickly saw the potential for extending the line for a further five miles, and this new extension was completed in 1928. There are stops at Dymchurch, St Mary's Bay and New Romney.

The line proved enormously popular, attracting thousands of visitors during the season, as well as providing an efficient transport system for local people. The locomotive fleet comprised nine locomotives pulling luxurious coaches capable of carrying passengers in sixteen- and twenty-seat carriages.

For a decade the RH&D railway enjoyed popular success but political realities were already intruding in the late 1930s. The line was requisitioned by the War Office and during the war the locomotives pulled armoured carriages laden with equipment and materials for the construction of the Pipe Line under the Ocean (PLUTO) project. After the war, the RH&D was re-opened in 1946 at a lavish opening ceremony performed by the comedy duo Laurel and Hardy, an event that attracted thousands of visitors.

J. E. P. Howey died on 8 September 1963, at the age of seventy-six. He was survived by his wife, Gladys Mary née Hewitt, whom he had married in 1912, at the time he was living in the Manor at Great Staughton. There were two children of the marriage, Richard, killed in the Second World War and Gloria, who pre-deceased her parents. Howey's obituary appeared in *The Times* of Tuesday 10 September 1963. Appropriately, his ashes were buried in the station yard of New Romney. At the time of his death, the future of the railway looked uncertain. Happily, the RH&D railway, under new and dynamic management, has weathered the turbulent economic storms of the past fifty years and Howey would be gratified to learn that his dream continues to carry tens of thousands of visitors every year. Currently, the RH&D fleet consists of thirteen locomotives.

The Howey estate in Australia, which included Howey Court in the heart of the Melbourne Central Business District, was eventually liquidated and the value of the Australian holdings was put at £6m. Howey had not been as assiduous in managing the impact of death duties on his estate as he had on the well-being of his beloved locomotives and the proceeds of the estate eventually passed to the Australian and British governments.

There is a modern postscript to the Howey story. In 2014, lot 338 came up for auction at the Bonham auction house. It was a 1924 Hispano-Suiza H6C 8.0-Litre Short Chassis Sports, chassis no. 11024, engine no. 320098. The auction house's description: 'offered with restoration invoices, the 11024 represents a rare opportunity to acquire a legendary model from one of the world's most prestigious makes, fully restored and possessing the additional cachet of in-period Brooklands history'. It was thought that the car had originally belonged to John Howey but further investigation revealed that it was purchased by another member of the Howey family. John Howey did purchase, for £400, a similar vehicle and he drove the car in a West Kent MC meeting at Brooklands on 11th July 1925, winning the race. This was not his only racing venture. He took the car to Australia to attempt the Sydney to Melbourne record. The venture did not prove successful; a series of punctures impeded his progress, but the final straw was to be stopped by the police and informed that if he had continued, he would be prosecuted. Howey later sold the car for £800, thus making a decent profit on the deal.

24

The Sacrifice

At 11 pm on Tuesday 4 August, Great Britain declared war on Germany for violating Belgian neutrality. On Friday 4 September 1914, exactly one month later, the following notice appeared in the *Huntingdonshire Post*:

> BRAVO GREAT STAUGHTON!
> Eleven recruits, J. Bull, F. Hackett, E. Butty, H. Bosworth, C. Reeve, J. Waller, A. Bruce, F. Holyoak, J. Bruce, A. Hackett, and W. Hackett left on Wednesday for Bedford to join Lord Kitchener's Army. Great Staughton is further represented in the King's Force by Mr Howey in the Yeomanry, two reservists, H. Newman and J. Stratton, and three, E. Day, F. Cox and P. Stratton in the Regular Army. If we include H. Taylor, who has joined a London Battalion the total is raised to eighteen. Not a bad show from a small village!

One of the first men from Great Staughton to volunteer was John Reynolds Pickersgill-Cunliffe, who enlisted in the Grenadier Guards as soon as war was declared on 4 August 1914. He was born in 1895, the son of Harry and Arlette Pickersgill-Cunliffe of Staughton Manor. He underwent initial training at the Wellington Barracks in London where the battalion was the recipient of an unexpected honour. Returning to barracks after the day's training exercises, they marched past Buckingham Palace and were surprised to see the king and queen standing by the gates of the palace to watch the battalion pass by. It was soon to be a distant memory. The Grenadier Guards received their mobilisation orders on 12 August and embarked for France. On arrival, the 2nd Battalion was grateful to be billeted in the village of St Mard, in the valley of the River Aisne, where they were fed and watered by the inhabitants.

A month later saw the inauspicious beginning, under a cold, rainy sky, of the battle of the Aisne. The battalion spent the wet and rainy night of 13 September in the village as they were briefed on the strategy for the following day. They were first to advance to the hamlet of Soupir. Once this first objective was secured, the battalion was to advance a mile further on to take the farm and chateau of La Cour du Soupir.

At first light on 14 September 1914, with the valley shrouded in mist and cloud, the battalion stealthily crossed the river and moved towards the hamlet of Soupir. To the surprise and alarm of the senior British officers, German artillery left them alone even as the Grenadiers were at their most vulnerable crossing the bridge. Had the enemy not seen them? Lieutenant Cunliffe was leading one of the three detachments advancing towards Soupir. The men met no opposition as they entered the village and emboldened by the ease of their advance and the lack of enemy fire, Lieutenant Cunliffe cautiously ordered his men forward towards La Cour du Soupir. Too late, he realised he had lost communication with the other two detachments and suddenly the squad found themselves confronted by a German unit many times their number. Without any support from their comrades, the squad was quickly captured and in a brief exchange of fire Lieutenant Cunliffe was badly wounded.

Events then moved very quickly. Almost immediately, No. 1 Company emerged from the mist and rushed forward in support of Lieutenant Cunliffe and his men. The Germans now found themselves at the wrong end of British firepower. Outnumbered

The Sacrifice

by superior British forces and faced with death or prison camp, the Germans wisely performed a tactical retreat. Doing so meant leaving the prisoners to their fate. As the regimental history of the Grenadier Guards acidly noted: 'there was one thing at any rate that a German officer, remembering the teachings of his Fatherland, still could do' and with that, the senior German officer walked up to the wounded Lieutenant Cunliffe, calmly pulled out his revolver and shot him dead.

The German officer's subsequent fate is unclear. According to one account he was taken prisoner. Another claimed that a Captain Bentinck happened upon the incident with a Company of the Coldstream Guards; his men, outraged at what they had seen, promptly bayoneted the German. Neither version is credible, however satisfying the accounts must have been to Lieutenant Cunliffe's appalled comrades.

Second Lieutenant John Reynolds Pickersgill-Cunliffe, 2nd Battalion Grenadier Guards, killed in action on 14 September 1914, aged nineteen. He is buried in the Soupir Communal Cemetery alongside sixteen of his comrades.

The death of their son was not the only loss suffered by Harry and Arlette Pickersgill-Cunliffe in the war. In 1910, their daughter, Enid Saffron, married Arthur Bertram Randolph in Hanover Square, London. Arthur Randolph was born in 1882 in New York to a wealthy family, the son of a British father and American mother. After the wedding, the couple made their home in Norfolk. In 1912, Saffron gave birth to a son Patrick, a keen aviator.

At the outbreak of war, Arthur Bertram Randolph joined the British army under the name of Julien Randolph, using this false name as he feared he might be prosecuted by US authorities for swearing allegiance to the British Crown. He was killed on 27 September 1915, along with most of his battalion, in a futile

57 Lt John Pickersgill-Cunliffe

attempt to take Hill 70 during the battle of Loos, and he is commemorated as J[ulien] Randolph on the Loos Memorial.

Their son Patrick Randolph was killed, aged twenty-five, when the Percival Gull he was piloting crashed in Jaipur, India, in October 1937.

The Sacrifice

In 1917, Enid Saffron married Captain Evelyn Hugh James Duberly and in 1925 their son William Michael Cunliffe Duberly was born.

*****

Private Horace Holyoak born in 1899 of the 2nd Battalion London Regiment (Royal Fusiliers) died on 24 April 1918, aged nineteen, in an encounter that killed 104 of his comrades. On 2 May 1918, his mother received a letter from 2nd Lieutenant H. Howard:

> "It is with much regret that I have to write to tell you the sad news that your son, Private Holyoak, was killed in action a few days ago. You will of course hear further information from the War Office in due course. His death is also a great loss to all officers and men of the Battalion, for he was a splendid fellow and an excellent soldier, and was respected by all who knew him. May the consolation of knowing that his death was instantaneous be some comfort to you in your grief for I know it is hard to part with the ones we love so well. Please accept the sympathy of all officers and men in this Battalion in your sad loss".

Another letter, addressed, 'Dear Madam' was sent on 10 May, three weeks after Private Holyoak's death:

> "I know you will be rather surprised to receive these few lines from a stranger, but as your son was my pal, I thought I would send you these few lines, which I am sorry to say contain very bad news. I do not know if you have heard from the War Office but he got killed on 24 April. A shell dropped in the trench and killed all the gun team of which he was a member. He did not suffer, for it was instant death. I should

have liked to have sent some of his belongings, but I was unable to do so, as I have been wounded myself, so I hope you will excuse me for not writing before. I think I will bring my letter to a close". It was signed, "Yours sincerely, Private W Hobbs."

*****

The war memorial tablet in the church and the 1919 edition of Rev. Watson's *History of Great Staughton* both contain the name of Herbert C. Watson. Born in 1880 in St Leonard's, where his father was the vicar, Herbert Coleridge Watson was the youngest son of the Rev. H. G. Watson and Lucy Eleanor Watson (née Gillman), of 'The Wilderness', Aspley Heath, Woburn Sands, Bedfordshire.

58 Herbert Coleridge Watson

Herbert was educated at Nottingham High School where he was considered 'much above the average, both in ability and attainments'. He began his journalistic career at the *Nottingham Guardian* before joining the *Daily Telegraph*, where he was to spend eight years as a literary critic. Watson was also a barrister (non-practising) at the Inner Temple. He was initially rejected for the army on account of 'defective vision' but when physical tests became less stringent, he was able to join the 7th Battalion of the King's Royal Rifle Corps as a Private and was quickly promoted to Lance Corporal. He left England with a draft on 17 December 1916. During his service in France, he made many applications for a commission, requesting his brother Gordon (a doctor in the Le Touquet field hospital) and his mother to expedite matters. Army regulations of the time stipulated that men over thirty-five years of age (Watson was thirty-six at the time) had to serve in the ranks before obtaining a commission.

Between January and March 1917, he wrote numerous letters from the front to his mother, brothers Frederick and Gordon and sister Eleanor. One such letter to Eleanor mentions in passing the first edition of his father's *History of Great Staughton*, published a year earlier in 1916 and in particular a photograph in the book of the river Kym by the church. Herbert wrote that he was 'glad you liked the photo in Father's book … it was taken at 6 pm on an August evening'.

He refused to be downhearted by conditions in the trenches and by his unsuccessful attempts to secure a commission. On the contrary, he took every opportunity to continue writing the essays which after the war his family would collect in a volume as a tribute to his life and service. In his few spare moments in the two months leading up to his death in early March 1917, he produced 'Tents', a poignant essay on life in the army bell tents:

> The canvas roofs spring up like mushrooms in a land that is at war. … But with all its fearful discomforts, life in a tent always allures the adventurous. 'This is soldiering at last', says the ex-civilian, when he takes off his pack for the first time

within a bell tent … Never in our lives will those of us who have known it forget being one of fourteen soldiers cleaning their rifles and putting on their equipment by the light of a candle, in a bell tent in the Great War … But at night when we are all in and snugly laid, then we turn this experience to infinite jest. We impose penalties for any complaints of lack of room. We talk of taking lodgers. We pass round chocolate and cough lozenges. We sing. We are nice to each other … almost all of us have fallen fast asleep before 'lights out', and come snow, or rain, or howling tempest, we sleep sound.

In his last field card, Lance Corporal Watson wrote that he and his company had been ordered to join the advance on Grandcourt. After a 'terrible journey' in the dark, 'dragging bags of bombs, as well as the heavy kit' and repeatedly falling in the thick mud, they came under heavy fire and hurled themselves into a shallow trench but they did not go low enough and a bomb fell amongst them, killing six of the men and leaving Watson seriously wounded.

For five days he lay where he had fallen in the freezing cold, desperately pleading to be taken back to safety, but even in these desperate circumstances he managed to summon the strength of will to record his thoughts as the shells and gunfire continued around him. 'I was hit a sharp blow on my head but not serious, and then I felt a tremendous blow on my right side … I groaned for some time unable to move … Gradually I discovered the men around me were all dead.' Finally, two officers came to his aid and took him to No. 26 Hospital, Etaples. His brother Gordon was immediately summoned and rushed to his bedside.

For several days it was touch and go but Herbert then seemed to be responding well to treatment; he was awake and able to appreciate the anemones sent by his sister. On the Sunday, he received Holy Communion and listened as his mother's and sister's letters were read to him. His last words were to send a message of love to his family; in the early hours of the morning of Monday, 5 March 1917, Lance Corporal Watson died in his sleep. A fellow soldier recorded his last days: 'No murmur of complaint of hardship borne, as crippled on the shell-swept ground he lay for days and nights, untended and forgot, while hopes of help and home, each day, each night, more distant grew. His only thought, his only hope, how soon for home, and mother, father, sisters, brothers, friends! One longing wish for peace and rest.'

Lance Corporal Herbert Coleridge Watson, 1st Battalion King's Royal Rifle Corps, died 5 March 1917, aged thirty-seven. He is buried at Etaples Military Cemetery. His gravestone is engraved: I WILL GIVE THEE A CROWN OF LIFE.

After the war, Herbert's parents published his collected essays and reviews from the *Telegraph*, as well as his letters from the front, in a book entitled, *SELECTED ESSAYS AND REVIEWS: also his last letters from the front.*

*****

Lance Sergeant Frederick Elmer of the 6th Battalion Royal Berkshire Regiment was killed at the third battle of Ypres on 31 July 1917 aged twenty-three. The 1911 census records that the eighteen-year-old Frederick was serving as a houseboy in the household of HRH Princess Mary of Tieck and HRH Prince Rupert of Tieck in the Henry III Tower of Windsor Castle.

After Frederick's death, the following letter was sent to Percy Elmer:

> "I deeply regret to inform you that one of the King's men has heard from his son who was in the same company that Fred was shot through the head, therefore death was instantaneous. I need not mention to you, as I think you already know, that your brother was a great favourite of us

all, from the Princess downwards, consequently we all feel his death very much and I can assure that everyone in the house who knows him are [*sic*] weeping bitterly this morning, but we all feel glad that it was an instant death, and he has died a noble death fighting for his country. He did not wait to be called up but placed his services at his country as soon as war was declared and went through all the rough of it in the early days and rose to be a sergeant. It is indeed hard for him to be taken away now after having been wounded three times. He was indeed an example to us all by his upright and steadfast manner and I am sure he has died the death he would have wished for. I will now conclude with my deepest sympathy to all your family." The letter, dated 17 August 1917, was signed by A. Kennedy, House Steward, Henry III Tower, Windsor Castle.

*****

When in 1914, Major Grey William Duberly re-enlisted in the 1st Battalion the Grenadier Guards, he was thirty-nine years of age and had recently married. As a battle-hardened veteran of the South African Campaign, Major Duberly was appointed Second-in-Command to Lieutenant Colonel G.D. White to begin the process of transforming a bunch of raw recruits into the semblance of a disciplined fighting force. The official history of the Guards records that between them White and Duberly created a well-drilled body of men 'with N.C.O.s shouting out their drill as if they had never been away'. War was days away and 'the Army was no longer a profession, where a man could reduce to a science the practice of Reserve doing the least possible amount of work without getting into trouble. It was now a matter of life and death.'

The 1st Battalion Grenadier Guards was posted to France in early 1915 and were quick to see action in the disastrous battle of Neuve Chapelle, which lasted from 10 to 14 March 1915. The battle was typical of the many fought in the First World War – brutal, bloody and unsuccessful. Chaos and confusion reigned in the trenches and amongst the high command. Bungled communications meant that by the time that orders reached the trenches, they were often irrelevant, the situation having changed since the orders were first issued and officers were left to act on their own initiative.

After a fierce bombardment of enemy lines on 10 March, the Guards advanced. Major Duberly was joined by his younger brother, Lieutenant Evelyn Hugh James Duberly, the company's machine-gunner. Territory was gained then quickly lost as the Germans brought in reinforcements. The worsening weather played havoc with communications between the widely separated trenches. Major Duberly, commanding No. 8 Company, was ordered to advance along with the 1st Battalion. The battalion was caught in a ferocious German enfilade, which resulted in many casualties. Nonetheless, they continued their advance, under withering German fire; the slaughter was horrific, the wounded were left to their fate in no-man's land and no ground was gained. With many of his fellow officers dead, Major Duberly found himself in charge of the sector.

The order came through for the 1st Battalion, under Major Duberly, to attack an old mill, held by the Germans, which, it was hoped, would take the pressure off the beleaguered Royal Scots. It meant clambering in and out of old trenches, negotiating barbed wire, all under the threat of the watchful German machine-gunners and snipers. When the battalion finally reached the Royal Scots, they were dismayed to discover that they had not been able to launch their planned attack. To add salt to the wound, the trenches were so shallow that they offered no cover from enemy snipers and machine guns, which would pick them off at first light. The beleaguered 1st Battalion was in a desperate situation and certain death seemed the only outcome. For Major Grey

William Duberly, commanding No. 8 Company, time was running out.

The regimental history gives a graphic description of events: 'Major Duberly did all he could. Absolutely regardless of danger, he went about shouting to the men to dig themselves in where they were, and endeavouring to establish communication between the groups of men who were making themselves some sort of shelter. Soon after daybreak the firing became intense, and the whole ground was ploughed up with shells and furrowed with machine-gun bullets. Major Duberly was killed early in the day.' His remaining comrades were sitting ducks in the shallow trenches.

The casualties in the battalion at Neuve Chapelle were sixteen officers and 325 NCOs and men. Lieutenant E. H. J. Duberly, Grey William's brother, was one of three officers to survive the onslaught. The total British losses during three days' fighting amounted to 2,500 officers and men killed, 8,500 wounded and 1,800 missing believed killed. The king wrote a consolatory letter to the battalion commander: 'The King … is much distressed to hear how terribly the 1st Battalion suffered. It is indeed heart-breaking to see a good Battalion like this decimated in a few hours. His Majesty has heard from the Prince of Wales, who has seen the remnants of the Battalion, and he told His Majesty how splendidly they had taken their losses.'

Major Grey William Duberly is commemorated on the Le Touret Memorial, Panel 2. He was forty-one years of age. Major Duberly was the son of William Grey Duberly (1841–1888) and the Hon. Rosa Sandys and husband of Millicent Florence Eleanor, née Wilson, formerly Countess Cowley, whom he married in 1914. She was the daughter of Charles Henry Wellesley Wilson, 2nd Baron Nunburnholme, a shipping magnate. Millicent Duberly learned of her husband's death in two letters from the War Office, the first informing her that her husband had been wounded, the second stating that he had been killed.

The Sacrifice

A sombre occasion was recorded by the *St Neots Advertiser* in a report on the commemorative tablet that was unveiled in the church of St Andrew to the memory of Major Grey William Duberly. The tablet was erected by the tenants of the Gaynes and Ranson Moor Estates as a mark of their esteem and respect. The inscription reads in part: 'Grey William Duberly … killed in action … at the battle of Neuve Chapelle … He gave his life for his country … No man could do more.' The newspaper report

59 Major Grey William Duberly

concluded with a brief account of the Duberly family history as 'intelligent and progressive landlords ... friendly to neighbours ... genial and indefatigable as sportsmen'.

Mrs Sophia Ann Pope commissioned a Roll of Honour to be made commemorating all those who served during the war in the Navy, Army and Air Services. The names, 165 in all, are inscribed on vellum inserted into a Gothic frame. It was unveiled in 1919 when a Memorial Tablet and a new treble bell were dedicated in memory of the fallen of the Great War.

25

An Uneasy Calm

For two decades, the country went through a few years of post-war optimism, subsequently tempered by a general strike and the Great Depression before gradually sliding towards a second global conflict.

The period was marked by significant technological advances which were to radically alter the life in villages such as Great Staughton. Several of the more prosperous residents of the village were now proud possessors of a motor car and a telephone. A 'motor filling station' was quickly opened on the Highway. The local cycle dealer was able to offer the Motorped, 'ideal for ladies', a bicycle equipped with a petrol engine. In April 1925 a capacity audience in the village hall enjoyed a wireless concert provided by an enterprising local resident who had purchased one of the early valve radio sets with built-in loudspeaker. The British Broadcasting Company Ltd had begun offering this revolutionary entertainment just three years earlier but radios were a rare commodity so the audience must have felt that they were present at the start of a technological revolution.

For the less prosperous citizens of the village two innovations during the 1930s improved everyday life immeasurably: the provision of mains water (replacing the village pumps) and electricity. The 1940 edition of Kelly's announced that 'electricity is now available' in the village. Roads were also improved and the Number 9d bus service now offered villagers the possibility of an easy journey to the market and shops in St Neots.

Great Staughton and its People

On 1 September 1939, Germany invaded Poland. Two days later, the United Kingdom declared war on Germany.

By 1940, preparations for war, in particular to counter the threat of an imminent German invasion, were well advanced in Huntingdonshire. There were blackout exercises in every town and village and Great Staughton was no exception. The principal component of the country's domestic defences was the formation of Home Guard units which in Great Staughton was under the command of Captain E. H. J Duberly, a veteran of the Great War. The training that the squad underwent was thorough and often physically demanding and course were started in ammunition, weapons, camouflage, fieldcraft, signals, anti-gas and street fighting.

More dramatic changes to the rural landscape came in 1941 when substantial parts of the neighbouring village of Little Staughton were transformed into an airfield, which was occupied for a time by the B-26s of the USAF 17th bomb group. It was the 379th bomb group who made it their operational base from 1942 until the end of the war.

The evacuation of children from London and other cities in Operation Pied Piper began in September 1939 and over 2 million children were subsequently taken to safe havens over the course of the war. Great Staughton was to receive 120 children and twelve teachers and hosts were paid 10s 6d per week for their care.

26

Great Staughton in the Second World War

The Memorial Tablet in the church records that eight volunteers from Great Staughton lost their lives in the Second World War. One of the most notable contributions the village made to the war effort came not from men-at-arms but from a building – the long-established residence of the Duberly family, Gaynes Hall.

60 Gaynes Hall, Station 61

'Station 61'

In 1940, Gaynes Hall, occupied by the Duberly family since 1797, was requisitioned by the War Ministry. With its thirteen bedrooms, nine bathrooms, a ballroom with a grand piano and a well-stocked library, Gaynes Hall required a veritable army of servants and gardeners to keep it in good order and when many staff responded to the call to arms, Millicent Duberly (widow of Major G. W. Duberly) felt unable to cope with the demands of running this impressive mansion and the several hundred acres of its grounds.

And so it came to pass that the Inter-Services Research Bureau (ISRB) took over Gaynes Hall for its own special contribution to the war effort. The ISRB, based in Baker Street, quickly acquired the nickname of the 'Baker Street Irregulars' in a nod to Sherlock Holmes's band of spies.

The brainchild of Winston Churchill, it was better known under its official name, the Special Operations Executive (SOE). The SOE, sometimes referred to colloquially as the 'dirty tricks department', was set up to instigate undercover operations in enemy-held territory where SOE agents would organise resistance operations, sabotage German military installations and collect intelligence on German troop movements. Gaynes Hall was known by its codename 'Station 61' and became the headquarters for the Air Liaison Officers strategy, under the command of Wing Commander Thomas Odett. Before being parachuted into occupied territory, agents, usually natives of the country, went through a rigorous training programme to prepare them for the conditions they would meet on their mission. Agents destined for Norway, for example, spent several months undergoing winter training in the Scottish Highlands. Once training was complete, they would spend a few days in the luxurious surroundings of Gaynes Hall, where they would receive their final briefing. The signal that an agent was destined to depart that day was the serving of two eggs for breakfast (normal rations being one egg per week). From Station 61 the agents were then transported to Tempsford airfield, fifteen miles away, to board the Lysander or Hudson aircraft which would drop them behind enemy lines. Two of the

SOE's most celebrated agents, Odette Churchill (1912–1995), code name 'Lise' and Violette Szabo (1921–1945), code name 'Louise', spent their last few nights in Gaynes Hall before being dropped into enemy territory.

Station 61 made a vital contribution to the success or failure of the operations in enemy territory. Agents did not go empty-handed. They were equipped with a canister called a cell into which was packed all the equipment and vital supplies that the agent would require for their mission. The cell, a metal bin, consisted of an ingenious selection of weaponry and 'dirty tricks': explosives, incendiaries, silenced guns and other small arms, wireless sets, generators, itching powder and even, on occasion, miniature submersible crafts.

To residents of Great Staughton, the goings-on at Gaynes Hall behind high walls and barbed wire must have seemed mysterious, but they were also aware that whatever was happening was vital to the war effort. Farmers tending their crops suddenly found themselves being watched and accompanied around their fields by armed guards. If the field extended beyond the barbed wire, proof of identity would be demanded by the guards. Villagers enjoying a quiet drink in the local pubs might find themselves being gently pumped for information by soldiers from the Station keen to learn how much villagers knew about what was going on. In a letter to the present writer, the teenage Dennis Pell recalled attending the annual summer camp of the Home Guard, which took place in a field close to Gaynes Hall. He was given the job of cleaning their boots and making sure the brasses on the searchlights were well polished. A more pleasurable job for Master Pell was to go round the field next to the 'big house' catching rabbits, armed with a wooden mallet normally used for knocking in tent pegs. A share of the booty was his reward. Very often Master Pell would notice that his activities had an audience in the windows of the Hall. 'It wasn't until after the war', Dennis Pell wrote, that 'I found out that my audience must have been people being trained as secret agents, before being taken to Tempsford airfield to be dropped behind the lines.'

Gaynes Hall played its part in one of the most audacious exploits of the Second World War. In autumn 1942 a Minute circulated to the War Cabinet warned that the Germans had a stockpile of one and a half tons of heavy water, the vital component of an atomic bomb, at the Norsk Hydro plant in Norway. Three and half more tons of heavy water would enable the Germans to construct the deadly weapon. The plant had to be destroyed but its remote location, perched high on a sheer pinnacle of rock, made it impregnable to heavy bombing. It could only be destroyed from the inside. A special SOE unit was formed, code-named the 'Norwegian Independent Company No. 1', consisting of five highly trained Norwegian patriots led by Joachim Rønneberg.

After intensive training in the Scottish Highlands, the unit was sent to Gaynes Hall where it was given its own headquarters. Here the men were delighted to discover that they were to be sequestered with a group of 'fannies', more correctly the FANY (First Aid Nursing Yeomanry) who needed no second invitation to accompany the Norwegian warriors to the pubs and clubs of Cambridge. A noisy sing-song round the piano at Gaynes Hall in the wee small hours concluded many a night's entertainment. On 16 February 1943, the unit took off from Tempsford airfield with Norway the ultimate destination. After a perilous ascent up the rocky crag on which the fortress Norsk Hydro was built, the Norwegians entered the plant undetected, placed their explosives and made their escape without a shot being fired. The mission was a complete success. The vessels containing the heavy water were destroyed and the water drained away. The Germans never got their atomic bomb. The 1965 film, *Heroes of Telemark*, was loosely based on this heroic exploit.

The story of Gaynes Hall post-war is a sad history of decline. Its contribution to the war effort has been documented in numerous books and films, but this 'large and magnificent mansion', which must have seen numerous distinguished gatherings and lavish social entertainments for a century and a half, was now transformed into the administrative offices and governor's house of the Youth Correctional Centre (Borstal) that was established in the grounds. The Borstal was closed in 1983 and subsequently demolished. In its place Littlehey prison was established as a Category C facility for males. Gaynes Hall itself was leased to A.I.M. Technology the same year and they renovated and adapted the building to their needs. The company ceased trading in 1985 and five years later the Ministry of Defence sold off the building. It is now privately owned.

*****

In late 1943, Captain E. H. J. Duberly learned that his only son, William, a lieutenant in the Scots Guards, had been killed in action at the battle of Monte Camino on 8 December 1943, aged twenty. William Michael Cunliffe Duberly found himself thrown into the heat of battle in the brutal Italian campaign, which began in September 1943 and ended in April 1945. The bloody battle of Monte Cassino (17 January–18 May 1944) is probably the best known battle of the Italian campaign, but it was preceded by a less well-known but equally bloody encounter at Monte Camino from November to December 1943. William Duberly enlisted as a lieutenant in the Scots Guards, which was under the command of Major Richard Coke, later to be awarded the MC and the DSO.

Monte Camino, at 3,000 ft, is the highest point of a rugged massif that dominates the Liri valley and was the strategic gateway to Monte Cassino, ten miles to the north-east; ninety miles further on to the north-west lay Rome, the ultimate objective of allied forces. The Germans held the heights and from their seemingly impregnable position they had a clear view of any attempt to launch an offensive. The Grenadier Guards formed the vanguard, advancing down the valley before attempting to move up the barren rockface that separated them from the German guns. The German artillery soon found their range and the Scots Guards were subject to a massive attack with shells, mortars and deadly enfilades from the Spandau guns. To add to the difficulties, it rained, cloud covered the massif, and the nights were freezing. Lieutenant Duberly waited in the makeshift trenches huddled against the cold with his men. Twenty years of age, barely out of school, in charge of a group of older men whose only wish was for the battle to be over and done with as quickly as possible, it must have been a terrifying experience for the young man. The German artillery opened fire, mortars first, then the shells, a continuous bombardment of the exposed British positions. The stench of cordite, mingled with the odour of blood, filled the air; shattered bodies littered the bare landscape. The hideously wounded were borne down the mountain in makeshift stretchers to die in the valley below. Lieutenant Duberly would have been rallying his men and counting the wounded, the dying and the dead. In the early morning of 8 December 1943, Lieutenant Duberly, of the Scots Guards, fell in action. It may have been to a Spandau gun, to a sniper, or to a mortar shell. He was one of 3,992 casualties of the Battle of Monte Camino.

Lieutenant W. M. C. Duberly is buried in the Cassino War Cemetery. Underneath his name, service details and the date and location of his death is carved 'Bill'. William Michael Cunliffe Duberly, born 27 March 1923, was the son of Captain Evelyn Hugh James and Enid Saffron Duberly. On 19 October 1947, Captain Duberly submitted a petition to place a stained-glass window of antique glass coat of arms to the memory of his late son on the wall of the north aisle of the church, where it can still be seen.

Great Staughton in the Second World War

*****

Six months after Lieutenant Duberly's death in Italy, the Duberly family was to receive another shattering blow. A large military and civilian congregation was gathered for the 11 o'clock Sunday service in the Guards' Chapel of Wellington Barracks, near Buckingham Palace, on 18 June 1944, coincidentally the 129th anniversary of the battle of Waterloo. At 11.20, unheard by the congregation and high above their heads, a German V1 flying bomb cut its engines and dropped noiselessly towards the chapel. The V1 crashed through the roof of the historic building and exploded, destroying virtually the entire chapel and sending hundreds of tons of rubble falling onto the massed congregation. The bomb killed 121 soldiers and civilians, including the chaplain and many senior British army officers; 141 others were seriously injured. When the first aid teams attempted to reach the dead and injured, they were confronted with a scene of total devastation; huge mounds of debris made access almost impossible and it took forty-eight hours to bring out the injured and recover all the bodies.

Amongst the fatalities was James Arthur Grey Duberly, aged eighteen, whose remains were amongst the last to be recovered. James Duberly had enlisted in the Scots Guards on 9 August 1943 and served in the ranks until he was commissioned on 25 May 1943. In a tribute to him, it was said that 'his one idea was soldiering and to make it his career'.

James was the son of Major Montagu Richard William Duberly and his wife Lady Eileen, née Stopford, of the Red House, Buckden. He is buried in St Andrew's churchyard, Great Staughton, and is also commemorated on the War Memorial of St Mary's, Buckden, where his parents resided at the time of his death. A tablet of Hopton Wood stone, erected in St Andrew's Church, was subsequently dedicated to his memory. The Duberly prize is still awarded to the best soldier in the Junior Training Corps of Winchester College.

EPILOGUE

With the end of the war and the beginning of the great programme to rebuild the country, the moment has come to bring this story of 2,000 years of Great Staughton's people to a provisional conclusion. The story does not of course stop here; it will be picked up and renewed at some future date as new documents come to light and archaeology unearths new evidence of our ancestors, bringing a fresh perspective to the history of the people of Great Staughton. Despite the physical changes to the village and the astonishing advances in technology, John Leland, Valentine Walton, James Duberly and all the others celebrated in this book would almost certainly find themselves treading familiar paths should some magical Tardis bring them back from the pages of history.

The history of the village and its people goes on. The *London Gazette*, dated 13 June 2015, carried the following announcement:

CENTRAL CHANCERY OF THE ORDERS OF KNIGHTHOOD
St. James's Palace, London SW1
13 June 2015

THE QUEEN has been graciously pleased, on the occasion of the Celebration of Her Majesty's Birthday, to make the following promotions in, and appointments to, the Royal Victorian Order:

THE ROYAL VICTORIAN ORDER K.C.V.O.
To be Knights Commander:

Archibald Hugh DUBERLY, C.B.E., Lord-Lieutenant of Cambridgeshire, who now becomes Sir Hugh Duberly K.V.C.O., C.B.E., and his wife Lady Sally Duberly, former Deputy Lord-Lieutenant of Cambridgeshire.

What is certain that a hundred years from now, the future historian of Great Staughton will surely be recording other 'leaders of the people, the glory of their times' whose lives and deeds on the local and national stage will have begun in this modest English village in the little county of Huntingdonshire.

SELECT BIBLIOGRAPHY

In the course of researching this book I consulted with profit many hundreds of books by historians who have dedicated their careers to the study of particular aspects of English history. To include them all in the bibliography would be impracticable so I have listed only those books that were constantly by my side. My two inseparable literary companions were:

Page, William, Granville Proby, and S. Inskip Ladds (eds) (1932), *Great Staughton, A History of the County of Huntingdon*, Vol. 2, London: Victoria County History.
Watson, Rev. H.G. (1916, updated 1919), *A History of the Parish of Great Staughton, Huntingdonshire*, St Neots: Percy C. Tomson.

1 A Little Village in Huntingdonshire

Camden, William (trans. Philemon Holland 1610), *Britain, or, a Chorographicall Description of the most flourishing Kingdomes, England, Scotland, and Ireland*.
Leland, John (1549), *The Itinerary of John Leland in or About the Years 1535–1543*, London.

2 The Church of St Andrew

Hicks, Carola, (ed.) (1899), *Cambridgeshire Churches*, Stamford: Paul Watkins, 1997.
Owen, Rev. T.M.N. (1899), *The Church Bells of Huntingdonshire*, London: Jarrold & Sons.
Pevsner, Nikolaus (1975), *Bedfordshire and the County of Huntingdon and Peterborough (The Buildings of England)*, London: Yale University Press.

3   A Roman *Mansio*?

Bagshawe, Richard W. (1979), *Roman Roads*, Aylesbury: Shire Publications.

Greenfield, E., Poulsen, et al. (1985), *The Excavation of a Fourth-century AD Villa and Bath-House at Great Staughton, Cambridgeshire, 1958 and 1959* Cambridge Antiquarian Society, Vol. LXXX. Together with a note by Tebbutt C.F. (1973), *How I found a Roman Villa at Great Staughton* in Greenfield, et al.

Margary, Ivan D. (1973), *Roman Roads in Britain*, London: John Baker.

Zosimus, *Historia Nova*, Book VI.10.

4   Peoples From Across the Sea

Birch, W. de Gray (1884), 'Early Territorial Names in England', *Journal of the British Archaeological Association*, Vol. 40, No. 1, 28–46.

Gildas (c. 540), *De Excidio et Conquestu Britanniae (On the Ruin and Conquest of Britain)*.

Sandred, K.I. (1969), 'Beachampstead, a Complicated Place-Name in Huntingdonshire', *English Studies*, Vol. 50, 1–5.

5   The Will of Ælfhelm Polga, 31 October 989

Colgrave, B. and Mynors R.A.B. (trans.) (1969) Bede (AD 672/3–735), *Ecclesiastical History of the English People (Historia ecclesiastica gentis Anglorum)*, Oxford: Clarendon Press (*online version*)

'Ely Farming Memoranda', (2018) Breay, C. and Story, J., 'Anglo-Saxon Kingdoms' Exhibition 2018–2019, London, British Library.

Fairweather, Janet (trans.) (2005), *Liber Eliensis, A History of the Isle of Ely from the Seventh Century to the Twelfth Century*, Woodbridge: Boydell Press.

Gorham, G.C. (1820), *The History and Antiquities of Eynesbury and St Neots*, London: Harding, Mavor and Lepard.

Hart, C.R. (1966), *The Early Charters of Eastern England*, Leicester: Leicester University Press.

The Prosopography of Anglo-Saxon England (PASE), available online: https://pase.ac.uk. This is a website giving data on all the recorded inhabitants of Anglo-Saxon England from the late sixth to the late eleventh century. According to this account, Leofsige was Ælfhelm Polga's goldsmith.

Stenton, F.M. (1955), *Anglo-Saxon England*, Oxford: The Clarendon Press.

Victoria County History (1978), *A History of the County of Cambridge and the Isle of Ely:* Vol. 6, *The Parish of West Wratting*, London: Victoria County History, pp. 191–8.

Whitelock, D. (1930), *Anglo-Saxon Wills*, Cambridge.

Wood, Michael (trans.) (2005), *Foundations*, Part 3: *Anglo-Saxon Pedigrees Annotated*, Hereford: The Foundation for Medieval Genealogy, 1 (6): 445–57.

6   Tochestone, Huntedunscire

Morris, John (ed.) (1975), *Domesday Book, Huntingdonshire*, Bognor Regis: Phillimore Press.

Powell-Smith A. et al. *Open Domesday.*

7   Sir Adam de Creting, Knight of Edward I

Cokayne, G.E., *Complete Peerage of England Scotland Ireland Great Britain and the United Kingdom*, III:246 note (d). https://biblio.co.uk/book/complete-peerage-england-scotland-ireland-great/d/1465241244?aid=frg&gclid=Cj0KCQjw_viWBhD8ARIsAH1mCd60sGAUsIEmWXTckZ4JVXJXLhRrOPVAyyH6h_c7qb4kqnzEtzTWJK8aAmJKEALw_wcB

Kosminsky, E.A. (1956), *Studies in the Agrarian History of England in the Thirteenth Century*, Oxford: Blackwell.

Nicolas, Nicholas Harris (ed. and trans.) (1828), *The Siege of Caerlaverock*, London: J.B. Nichols and Son Available online at http://www.archive.Org/details/siegeofcarlavero00nicouoft

Rotuli Hundredorum (2 Vols, Record Commission, 1812–1818). The returns are in Vol. 2 (Huntingdon Records Office).

8 From Waweton to Walton: Birth of a Staughton Dynasty

MacDonagh, Michael (1914), *Speaker of the House*, London: Methuen & Co. Ltd.

Roskell, J.S. Clark, L. and Rawcliffe, C. (eds) (1993), *The History of Parliament: The House of Commons 1386–1421*, Stroud: Sutton Publishing.

9 'Pray For The Good Astate Of Olyver Leder'

Bindoff, S.T. (ed.) (1982), *The History of Parliament: The House of Commons 1509–1558*, London: Secker & Warburg for the History of Parliament Trust.

DeWindt A.R and DeWindt E.B. (2006), *Ramsey (Tax in Staughton in 1524)*, Washington DC: The Catholic University of America Press.

Turner, G.J. (ed.) (1913), *A Calendar of the Feet of Fines Relating to the County of Hunts 1194–1603*, Cambridgeshire. Antiquarian Society, Cambridge: Deighton Bell and Co.

10 '… that famous and most reverend judge …'

Foss, Edward, FSA, (1857), *Judges of England, with Sketches of their Lives*, Vol. 5, London: Longman, Brown, Green, and Longmans.

Pulling, Alexander (1975), *The Order of the Coif*, New York: W.S. Hein.

Wood, Anthony (1813), *Athenae Oxonienses:* Vol. 1, London: Rivington.

11 George Wauton's 'trayned band' and the Armada

Noble, Rev. W.M. (1896), *Huntingdonshire and the Spanish Armada*, London.

12   Valentine Walton: Curriculum Vitae of a Regicide

Bliss (ed.) (1891), *The Life and Times of Anthony Wood, Antiquity of Oxford (1632–1695)*.

Cooper, Charles Henry (1845), *Annals of Cambridge*, Vol. 3, Cambridge.

Dugdale, William, (1662) *History of Imbanking and Drayning of Divers Fenns and Marshes 1662*, London: Alice Warren.

Firth, C.H., (2004) *Oxford Dictionary of National Biography* (Online edition. Restricted access).

Noble, Rev. W.M , *Life of the English regicides*, (1798) Huntingdon Records Office. London: J Stockdale.

Noble, Rev. W.M., (1784) *Memoirs of the House of Cromwell*, Birmingham: Pearson and Rollason.

Waylen, James, (1897) *Memoirs of the House of Cromwell*, London: E. Stock.

13   John Gaule: 'Preacher of the Word at Great Staughton'

Garland, Anna (2003), *The Great Witch Hunt: The Persecution of Witches in England 1550–1660*, Auckland University Law Review, 9 Vol. 4, 1152–80.

Gash, Jonathan (1993), *The Lies of Fair Ladies*, London: Penguin (The Lovejoy series of novels).

Gaskill, Malcolm (2005), *Witchfinders, a Seventeenth-Century Tragedy*, London: John Murray.

Gaule, John (1646), *Select cases of conscience concerning witches and witchcrafts*, London.

Goodwin, Gordon, *Gaule, John*, entry in *Dictionary of National Biography*, Vol. 21, 1885–1900. (Online edition. Restricted access) ('He [John Gaule] was an unlearned and wearisome ranter.')

Oxford Journals (1866), *Notes and Queries*. Oxford: Oxford University Press, p.65.

14 'Our Ideal Possession of the Peruvian Treasures'

Baigent E., 'Richard Walter', *Dictionary of National Biography*, 1885–1900, Vol. 59. (Online edition. Restricted access).

Grann, David (2023), *The Wager*, London: Simon & Schuster. Only briefly mentioned in the present book, the fate of Anson's 'lost' warship, a tale of shipwreck, mutiny and murder and mayhem, is vividly told in this new book.

Walter, Richard (1748), *A Voyage Round the World in the Years 1740–4 by Lord Anson*, London and New York: J.M. Dent; E.P. Dutton.

Williams, Glyn (1999), *The Prize of All the Oceans*, London: Harper Collins Publishers.

15 The Handasyds, Father and Son

Black, C.V. (1975), *History of Jamaica*, London: Collins.

Cannon, Richard (1848), *Historical Record of the 22nd Cheshire Regiment of Foot*, London: Parker, Furnivall and Parker.

Cannon, Richard (1848), *Historical Record of the 16th Bedfordshire Regiment of Foot*, London: Parker, Furnivall and Parker.

Godfrey, Michael (1969–2022), 'Thomas Handasyd', *Dictionary of Canadian Biography*, Vol. II (1701–1740), (online edition) University of Toronto.

16 Mr Duberly Acquires an Estate in Great Staughton

Ackers, C. (1774), *London Magazine: Or, Gentleman's Monthly Intelligencer…* Vol. 43, London: C. Ackers.

Duberly family archives (by kind permission of Sir Hugh Duberly).

Duberly, James, *The Trial between James Duberly Esq. and Major-General John Gunning* (reprint of original), London: Ecco Print editions. (Reproduction from British Library. ISBN: 781170 404614.)

Gantz, Ida (1963), *The Pastel Portrait*, London The Cresset Press.

Gray, Gerrish (ed.) (2012), *Apology for the Life of Major-General John Gunning*, Richmond: Tiger of the Stripe. ISBN: 978-1-904799-46-7

17   Unravelled: a 200-Year-Old Village Mystery
The Commonplace Book is kept in the Huntingdonshire Records Office.

18   The Unsung Heroine of the Crimea
Duberly, Mrs Henry (1856), *Journal Kept During the Russian War*, London: Longman, Brown, Green, and Longmans.
Kelly, Christine (ed.) (2007), *Mrs Duberly's War: Journal and Letters from the Crimea*, Oxford: Oxford University Press.
Tisdall, E.E.P. (1963), *Mrs Duberly's Campaigns*, London: Jarrold.

19   The Rajpootana Column
Compton, Piers (1970), *Colonel's Lady and Camp Follower*, New York: St Martin's Press.
Duberly, Mrs Henry (1859), *Campaigning Experiences in Rajpootana and Central India During the Suppression of the Mutiny 1857–1858*, London: Smith Elder & Co.

20   Rev. Wilson and John Henry Newman: the Church Divided
Vidler, Alec R. (1961), *The Church in an Age of Revolution*, London: Pelican.

21   The South African Campaign 1899–1902
I am very grateful to John MacKenzie of www.britishbattles.com for permission to use the battle maps of Belmont and Modder River.

22   Rev. Watson's Talented Sons
Grace's Guide to British Industrial History, available online: gracesguide.co.uk.

23   Staughton Manor Railway Station
Derek Smith, Personal communication.

Snell, J.B. (1983), *One Man's Railway. JEP Howey and the Romney, Hythe, & Dymchurch Railway*, Newton Abbot: David and Charles.

Steel, E.A. and Steel, E.H. (1973), *The Miniature World of Henry Greenly*, Red Hill: Model and Allied Publications Ltd.

Photographs by kind permission of the Archivist, Romney, Hythe and Dymchurch Railway.

24   The Sacrifice

Bell, John (1998), *Huntingdonshire Heroes of the First World War (Original Letters To and From the Front)*, St Ives: Popular Publications.

Ponsonby, Lieut-Colonel, the Right Hon. Sir Frederick (1920), *The Grenadier Guards in the Great War of 1914–1918*, 3 Vols, London: Macmillan and Co.

Watson, Herbert Coleridge (1919), *Selected Essays and Reviews, Also His Last Letters From the Front*, Bedford: F.R. Hockliffe.

25   An Uneasy Calm

A chapter based principally on the Great Staughton Parish Magazines 1943–1968.

26   Great Staughton in the Second World War

Clifford, Caroline and Akeroyd, Alan (2007), *Huntingdonshire in the Second World War*, Stroud: The History Press Ltd (in HRO).

Freeman-Attwood, Warren (1943), *A Young Platoon Commander's Memories of his First Battle* (Monte Camino, Italy, November 1943).

Milton, Giles (2016), *Churchill's Ministry of Ungentlemanly Warfare*, London: John Murray.

Ruggiero, Anna Maria, (2010) *West End at War (the V1 Bombing of the Guards' Chapel, Wellington Barracks)*, London: Westminster City Archives. Available online http://www.westendatwar.org.uk

ACKNOWLEDGEMENTS

There are many people to thank for their help and support in bringing this book to fruition. Much of it was written in the Huntingdon Records Office and I am truly grateful to all the staff for their knowledge and expertise in locating relevant material from this vast storehouse of documents, books, manuscripts and references which are the foundations of this book.

Sir Hugh Duberly kindly loaned me the invaluable family archive compiled by Major M. W. R. Duberly; he also drew up an extended family tree of the family from 1797 which was to prove indispensable in tracing the Duberlys over a period of two centuries. James Duberly, the present resident of Place House, provided images of his ancestors James and Rebecca Duberly.

John MacKenzie, creator of the British Battles website very kindly allowed me to use his maps of the battles of The Crimea and the Boer War. (www.britishbattles.com).

Rev. Neville Brook, vicar of St Andrew's 1989–1996, drew my attention to the improbable connection of Rev. John Gaule with *The Lies of Fair Ladies*, by Jonathan Gash.

Michael Stephenson's careful transcription of the monuments and gravestones of St Andrew's Church was also extremely helpful.

Derek Smith provided valuable material about the Howey family in a series of personal emails to the author. I owe thanks to the archivist of the Romney Hythe and Dymchurch Railway who supplied rare photographs of Howey's railway in Great Staughton.

For research into the volunteers who fell in the two World Wars I am indebted to my friend and neighbour, Margaret Emeleus.

Mary Matthews took my manuscript by the scruff of the neck and transformed it into a wonderful book. Simon Emery drew the parish map and designed the cover. Amanda Kay proofread the entire book and offered many fruitful suggestions on how it could be improved.

Thanks to Kat Moir who diligently posted weekly episodes from the book onto the village website.

Finally, I am grateful to numerous residents of the village for their time and their memories.

BIOGRAPHY

Anthony Withers was born in Prestwich Manchester in 1945 and attended Stand Grammar School. He studied Modern Languages at Queen Mary, University of London and subsequently spent twenty years in the corporate world. In 1989 he founded Anglia Translations Ltd of Huntingdon. He retired in 2015.

Anthony Withers has a son and daughter and five grandchildren. He lives in Great Staughton. He can be contacted at aw.staughton@gmail.com

www.ingramcontent.com/pod-product-compliance
Lightning Source LLC
Chambersburg PA
CBHW042113100526
44587CB00025B/4032